W9-AEW-460

CULTS, CULTURE, AND THE LAW

ÆR

American Academy of Religion
Studies in Religion

Editors
Charley Hardwick
James O. Duke

Number 36
CULTS, CULTURE, AND THE LAW
Perspectives on New Religious Movements
Edited by
Thomas Robbins, William C. Shepherd,
and James McBride

CULTS, CULTURE, AND THE LAW
Perspectives on New Religious Movements

Edited by
Thomas Robbins, William C. Shepherd,
and James McBride

Scholars Press
Chico, California

CULTS, CULTURE, AND THE LAW
Perspectives on New Religious Movements

Edited by
Thomas Robbins, William C. Shepherd,
and James McBride

Library of Congress Cataloging in Publication Data
Main entry under title:

Cults, culture, and the law.

(AAR studies in religion ; no. 36)
Includes index.
1. United States—Religion—Addresses, essays,
lectures. 2. Cults—United States—Addresses, essays,
lectures. 3. Law—United States—Religious Aspects—
Addresses, essays, lectures. 4. Religion and state—United
States—Addresses, essays, lectures. 5. Religion and
Sociology—Addresses, essays, lectures. I. Robbins, Tom.
II. Shepherd, William C. III. McBride, James. IV. Series:
Studies in religion (American Academy of religion) ; no.
36.
BL2525.C85 1985   291.1′77′0973   85-10873

ISBN 0-89130-832-6 (alk. paper)
ISBN 0-89130-833-4 (pbk. : alk. paper)

Printed in the United States of America
on acid-free paper

CONTENTS

CHURCH, STATE, AND THE CHRISTIAN NEW RIGHT

"There is No Separation of God and State":
The Christian New Right Perspective on Religion
and the First Amendment

PREFACE

Thomas Robbins and James McBride

As an affiliate of the Graduate Theological Union in Berkeley, California, the Center for the Study of New Religious Movements has conducted research over the past seven years in order to promote the objective study and analysis of new religious movements and the controversies which surround them. During the academic year of 1981-1982, the Center sponsored a seminar, co-organized by Thomas Robbins and William Shepherd, which facilitated a dialogue between prominent scholars and professionals with differing perspectives on legal and civil liberties issues relating to controversial "cults." Attorneys, psychiatrists, sociologists, philosophers, and other scholars in the field of religious studies were invited by the Center to present and discuss papers on these issues with regular seminar participants from the University of California/Berkeley, Stanford University, and the Graduate Theological Union, including co-editor James McBride, Research Associate with the Center. The presentations made at the seminar provided the basis for the papers collected in this volume.

Several of the papers, including the contributions by Herbert Fingarette and Robert Jay Lifton, constitute edited versions of taped transcripts made from original presentations. Other papers have undergone significant alterations. The contributions by Richard Delgado and Robert Shapiro are abridged versions of articles originally published in the *Georgia Law Review* and the *Southern California Law Review* respectively. William Shepherd's short essay on the emergence of Section 1983–1985 litigation involving converts to new religious movements is reprinted with permission from *The Center Magazine*, a publication of the Robert Maynard Hutchins Center for the Study of Democratic Institutions, Santa Barbara, California. "The Tax-Exempt Status of Communitarian Religious Organizations: An Unnecessary Controversy" by Meade Emory and Lawrence Zelenak originally appeared in the *Fordham Law Review*. Originating in the discussions of seminar participants, the article by James McBride on the Christian New Right addresses certain legal issues which enjoy a heightened significance in light of the Supreme Court's decision in the Bob Jones University/Goldsboro Christian Schools case. In order to put this volume into perspective, the lead article by Thomas Robbins serves as an overview which places these papers into the context of current scholarly discussions on civil liberties and the new religious movements.

The editors wish to thank Jacob Needleman, Director of the Center for the Study of New Religious Movements, whose dedicated leadership made possible both the seminar and this volume, and Paul Schwartz, whose administrative prowess guaranteed the success of our endeavors. We also wish to express our appreciation to Carolyn Chapin and Amy Kurkjian for typing both the seminar transcripts and the final versions of the papers collected in this volume and to Robert Hopcke for preparing the word-processed text. Finally, the surviving editors deeply regret the untimely death of William Shepherd whose commitment to religious freedom inspired this project and to whose memory this book is dedicated.

This work was made possible through the assistance of research grants from the National Endowment for the Humanities, a federal agency.

EDITORS' INTRODUCTION

Thomas Robbins and James McBride

As a collection of scholarly articles on the phenomena of new religious movements, this volume hopefully will serve to infuse clarity into the controversies surrounding "cults" by careful analysis of competing legal and moral claims. In his paper "Religious Movements on the Frontier of Church and State," Thomas Robbins provides a general overview to these controversies, as perceived and discussed in academic and professional circles, and presents a conceptual framework within which readers can approach the conflicts surrounding the new religious movements.

Following Robbins's opening essay, the section entitled "New Religious Movements: Culture and Society" includes papers by sociologists Roland Robertson and Robert Wuthnow which outline these developments within the context of changing socio-cultural configurations in the modern world. In his discussion of "The Relativization of Societies, Modern Religions, and Globalization," Dr. Robertson argues that the rapid growth of new religious movements as well as religio-political fundamentalism, e.g., the Christian New Right, cannot be grasped adequately without taking into consideration the global nature of religious revival emerging in the face of worldwide technological revolution and the consequent "world civil religion" problem. This global development leads to an intensification of intra-societal strife, specifically in church-state and other religio-political conflicts. Dr. Wuthnow, on the other hand, stresses the continuity between key aspects of contemporary new religious movements and modern technocratic and scientistic values which all too frequently are looked upon as being antithetical to the religious values of these new social groups.

Shifting from global and sociological foci, "New Religious Movements and Coercive Persuasion" draws attention to the psychological and legal aspects of religious conversion to these groups. In "Cult Processes, Religious Totalism, and Civil Liberties," Robert Lifton discusses his model of ideological totalism, derived from his classic study of thought reform in the People's Republic of China, and its application to what many have termed the more authoritarian new religious movements. Stressing that each group ought to be judged individually, he suggests that legal intervention ought to be avoided except in clearly abusive cases, but nonetheless warns of the dangers that the new religious apocalypticism might hold for American society-at-large. Reversing the popular usage of Robert Lifton's "religious totalism" paradigm against "cults," Lee Coleman forcefully argues that this model of thought reform is more applicable to the coercive "deprogramming" of religious adherents than to the process of conversion initiated by recruiters for new religious movements which he feels have been unjustly maligned. Finally, Herbert Fingarette frames the discussion of "coercive persuasion" within the legal tradition of coercion and skillfully shows in what limited legal sense the term coercion may be used to describe religious conversion to new religious movements.

Deconversion by parents and professional deprogrammers and the resistance of new religious movements to what they see as an encroachment upon civil liberty has established the courtroom as the battleground on which the fate of the religious convert and the groups themselves is determined. In the section on legal intervention, four scholars have contributed their views of the legal developments and proposals on the issue of conversion and deconversion processes. William Shepherd's paper "Legal Protection for Freedom of Religion" discusses the evolution of a tenuous legal remedy for restitution to forcibly-abducted devotees who may sometimes be able to sue parents and deprogrammers for deprivation of civil rights. Cataloguing a range of initiatives aimed at "cults," Jeremiah Gutman offers a sharp critique in "The Legislative Assault on the New Religions" which upbraids both state and (to a lesser extent) federal governments for the harassment of new religious movements. Taking a diametrically opposed position, Richard Delgado argues in his important essay "Cults and Conversion: The Case for Informed Consent" that the methods of recruitment and indoctrination employed by these religious groups are so manipulative and so potentially harmful to converts that the state has a moral responsibility to ensure informed consent. Delgado suggests mandatory disclosure in the conversion setting of the identity and nature of the religious group which the recruiter represents. Hence, the convert who leaves the group either through deprogramming or by his/her own volition has legal recourse for compensatory and punitive damages if that conversion was effected by gross deception and mental coercion. In his paper "'Indoctrination,' Personhood, and Religious Beliefs," Robert Shapiro finds the arguments for legal intervention to be flawed since they assume personality change in itself is evidence of legally definable coercion. In a philosophical discussion of personhood, he contends that becoming a different person is not sufficient grounds for state intervention unless mental incompetence is established. Although anti-cult activists sometimes argue that converts have ceased to be persons and thus may be considered "robots," mental incompetence cannot be shown in this instance unless these individuals have lost their capacity to hold religio-philosophical views.

While these policy-oriented papers deal with entrance/exit legal issues arising from individual participation in the new religious movements, the last two sections review the impact of state regulation in the institutional development of groups which share in America's contemporary religious revival. In his article "The 'Deformation' of New Religions: Impacts of Societal and Organizational Factors," James Richardson discusses a model of evolutionary development in new religious groups which describes the changes in organizational and even doctrinal patterns caused by the reactions of governmental agencies and society-at-large. In particular, the actions of the Internal Revenue Service are pivotal in the organization's growth since its determinations on tax-exempt status frequently hold in the balance the fate of the organization. Attorneys Lawrence Zelenak and Meade Emory address this issue in "The Tax Exempt Status of Communitarian Religious Organizations: An Unnecessary Controversy." Zelenak and Emory argue that the IRS crackdown on religious communes represents in most cases a discriminatory policy against non-traditional and esoteric communitarian groups.

Finally, in his paper "'There is No Separation of God and State': The Christian New Right Perspective on the First Amendment," James McBride describes and analyzes the view of the Religious Right, typified by the Moral Majority and religiously oriented political action committees, which considers the Supreme Court's position on the separation of church and state to be a betrayal of the American Constitution. Arguing that the First Amendment proscribes only a state church and ought to permit the unrestrained religious activity of denominational pluralism (even under the auspices of the state), the Religious Right has become the most vocal political expression of America's religious revival which claims that the secular state has evinced a deep-seated animosity toward religious values.

NEW RELIGIOUS MOVEMENTS ON
THE FRONTIER OF CHURCH AND STATE

Thomas Robbins

Issues involving the relationship between church and state and the constitutional guarantee of "free exercise of religion" are likely to become increasingly salient in the 1980s. A significant aspect of contemporary discussions of church and state relations in America entails questions arising from controversies over stigmatized unconventional religious and therapeutic movements or "cults."/1/ There are controversies and allegations against cults in a variety of areas, including tax evasion, financial mismanagement, unauthorized practice of medicine, child abuse, exploitative employment policies, and commercial fraud. The most persistent allegations, however, concern the use by cults of techniques of "mind control" and "brainwashing" to enslave converts, break up their families, and imprison members in pathological mental states. These controversies raise a number of vital issues including the authority of the government to regulate spiritual movements and scrutinize individual consciousness. On one level these are *legal* issues; their full analysis, however, requires an understanding of the role of "new religions" in modern America, the needs to which these movements respond, the cultural and social conditions in which they are flourishing, and the psychological processes which operate within them.

In our view, controversies surrounding cults are closely related to an emerging *general crisis of church and state relations* as well as to significant currents of social transformation in the United States. However, this relation has been obscured by the way in which controversial discourse over cults has bee patterned. Primary attention has been directed toward the question of *how people become converts*, and, in particular, whether they are victims of "forced conversions," accomplished and sustained through "mind control." The most vigorous critics of "cults" have attempted to define the issues and conflicts surrounding cults as constituting primarily a *mental health problem*. Defenders of cults have argued that, in actuality, esoteric beliefs and rituals have been arbitrarily transvalued and interpreted as "coercive" and as pathological mind control./2/ As one civil liberties lawyer complains: "A religion becomes a cult; proselytization becomes brainwashing; persuasion becomes propaganda;

missionaries become subversive agents; retreats, monasteries, and convents become prisons; holy ritual becomes bizarre conduct; religious observance becomes aberrant behavior; devotion and meditation become psychopathic trances."/3/

The present essay is intended as an introduction to this volume and a brief overview of the cultural and social context in which the present conflicts over new religious movements arise. It is our view that the underlying situations which give rise to these conflicts have been distorted by the employment of a "medical model"—a way of perceiving new-age religions and their adherents that emphasizes physical and mental pathology. The attraction of this model lies in the way it articulates an "appropriate" attack on disfavored religions which disavows any intent to control beliefs. For reasons developed later in this chapter, we believe that this approach to cult issues has limited utility and, indeed, may seriously mislead./4/ It is our hope that ultimately the focus of controversy and projected remediation will shift away from questions pertaining to intrapsychic consciousness and mental coercion, and away from entry-exit questions (i.e., issues of brainwashing and deprogramming), and will be redirected toward a more direct confrontation with the underlying issues discussed in this essay.

CHURCH, STATE, AND CULT

The emerging crisis of church/state relations is partly a product of the increasingly comprehensive state regulation of society and organizations within society. The state increasingly regulates all manner of organizations in the United States, business and non-profit; however, religious organizations and specifically "churches" enjoy special exemptions. They stand apart from the state-regulated society as privileged enclaves. As the state more and more dominates society, the privileges and exemptions of churches become increasingly conspicuous and appear problematic and potentially controversial. At the same time, a variety of leaders and entrepreneurs become motivated to label their enterprises "religious" to take advantage of the privileges accorded to churches. It seems unlikely that certain movements such as Synanon or Scientology would have defined themselves as churches or even as "religious" movements were it not for the legal protections the Constitution affords such groups./5/

In effect a *regulatory gap* exists between secular and religious organizations. The "regulatory gap" is not intended as a normative concept; the gap may indeed be defensible in terms of guaranteeing religious freedom and church/state separation. Nevertheless, the concept is essential to an understanding of rising church/state tensions. However, it is not the regulatory gap by itself which underlies today's tensions. *The more the activities and functions of churches broaden and begin to resemble those of secular organizations, the more provocative are the exemptions and privileges of churches.* Conversely, the more "privatized" religion becomes and the more restricted its scope of authority and activities, the less probable becomes the potential conflict implicit in the regulatory gap. It is arguable that as a dimension of "secularization" in the twentieth century, churches have reduced the scope of their activities and authority and have become more "specialized." Yet presently there are signs of a reversal of this tendency. For example, a number of factors including the decline of public education, resistance to racial integration, and the desire to ensure that the right values are being transmitted to one's children has produced the current growth of new "Christian Schools."/6/ In general, religious movements are becoming more important as *mediating structures* which fill the gap left by the decline of other institutions such as extended families, homogeneous "folksy" neighborhoods, personalistic work setting, etc. Mediating structures "stand between the individual in his private life and the large institutions of modern society."/7/ Mediating structures provide participants with a sense of belonging and a basis for holistic self-definition, as well as a context for gratifying communal relations and adult "familial" milieux, and a support and transmission system for social values. They provide social services in a non-bureaucratic manner, with linkage to overarching social and spiritual values. As two anthropologists have noted, in contemporary America religion is now "the only place where social experimentation is possible." Today's proliferation of diversified religious movements represents "a folk answer to a system that is over-diplomaed, over-certified, too specialized, and too conscious of where one receives certification. It is the last voice for decentralization and the free enterprise system."/8/

Given the "regulatory gap" we have identified, any expansion and diversification of the activities and authority of religious organizations can easily lead to an increase in church/state tension and resentment directed against religious organizations. Groups such as the Unification Church or the Church of Scientology are situated at the cutting edge of church/state tension because they are highly diversified and multifunctional entities with their fingers in numerous pies. Although this is true of many other religious organizations, e.g., surging evangelical movements,/9/ various groups stigmatized as "cults" would appear to provide extreme examples. Indeed, it might be anticipated that today's diversified cults are, perhaps half-consciously, moving toward the "Japanese model" of diversified omnicompetent sectarian organizations embodying diffuse and paternalistic religious authority./10/

In short, cults are controversial in part because they are particularly *diversified and multifunctional* enclaves lying outside the web of regulation which increasingly enmeshed "secular" organizations. It may also be significant that, unlike evangelical groups, "cults" are unfamiliar and lack grassroots support and are thus particularly vulnerable to stigmatization and social control.

Yet the expansion and diversification of cults have serious consequences. In Richard Ofshe's terms, movements such as Synanon have consolidated "protected empires" consisting of myriad activities and enterprises which would be subject to substantially greater governmental scrutiny and regulation were they not carried out under "religious" auspices./11/ They are involved in commercial and financial enterprises (e.g., Sun Myung Moon's fishing fleet), education, communal and residential structures, child care institutions, nursing homes, political lobbying, healing, psychotherapy and other quasi-medical processes. Some groups can be said to have developed vast commercial and financial empires which are alleged to be undertaxed, underregulated, and underinvestigated.

The diversification and alleged underregulation of certain religious organizations produces resentment against the perceived "illicit gains" of unorthodox religious leaders. More generally, there is a feeling that the more authoritarian and "totalistic" of today's new religions fail utterly to "know their place" and acknowledge the separation of secular and religious realms which is normative in our "secular" culture. On the individual level, a person who is encapsulated in a single multifunctional communal movement appears to be lacking the *personal autonomy* and dignity which is expected of adult citizens in a modern, highly differentiated society. A cult convert appears not to manifest a "self" transcending multiple segmental roles and group ties./12/ The convert is thus perceived as being less than a "legitimate person" capable of competent decision-making and self-directed social action—hence the interpretation of cultists as inhumanely "programmed" and in need of forcible therapeutic intervention to restore personal responsibility. Yet it is precisely the presumptive personal autonomy of individuals which, as seen by civil libertarians, coercive therapeutic intervention and "deprogramming" violates. While critics of cults charge that totalistic movements undermine personal autonomy and that liberation of "cult slaves" is in order,/13/ some civil libertarians reply that personal autonomy is not merely a *desideratum* but also an assumptive factor or a priori philosophical premise underlying our legal system. If peer pressure exerted in a formally voluntary context is accepted as negating free will, then the assumption of personal autonomy is eroded and the legal system is transformed./14/ If autonomy is considered as norm or ideal, however, can it be *enforced* without being simultaneously destroyed, i.e., can someone be "free" if he is not free to surrender freedom? Can one be "forced to be free"?

Because cults are multifunctional, they address multiple needs and, therefore, encourage a strong dependency, not merely psychological but very tangible, on the part of participants. This dependency has implications for *exploitation*. Without appealing to notions such as mind control, it is nevertheless arguable there is an imbalance or inequality of power between the authoritarian leadership of some movements and the individual participants. The latter may surrender substantial resources to a communal movement in exchange for an implicit but non-enforceable understanding that the devotee will be cared for in perpetuity. The helplessness of participants may thus be structural rather than psychiatric. Ultimately these issues arise because of the multifunctional diversity of religious movements operating as privileged autonomous enclaves in an otherwise increasingly governmentally-regulated society.

CULTS AND CONFLICTS

In performing communal, therapeutic and other "mediating" functions in an innovative and relatively unregulated manner, religious movements necessarily come into conflict with more conventional mediating institutions and their members, e.g. families, conventional religious institutions and clergy, the certified therapeutic and counseling establishment, which ordinarily enjoy a monopoly of mediating and therapeutic functions.

Cults and Families. Modern society is characterized by a degree of structural differentiation: kinship roles are differentiated from occupational roles, and residential land is segregated from business land. Young persons are increasingly encapsulated in homogeneous peer contexts such as schools and colleges which are detached from parental supervision. This extreme "structural differentiation" underlies the increasing *isolation of the family*, an isolation which is exacerbated by the concurrent decline of traditional mediating structures such as extended family systems, folksy neighborhoods and conventional churches and synagogues which provide supports and services to nuclear families.

This isolation of the nuclear family produces a sharp discontinuity between the diffuse affectivity or "loving" quality of familial roles and the "impersonal" quality of adult roles in education and occupational milieux. This is the context for a search by many young persons for *surrogate families* in extrafamilial relationships. Today's new religions commonly conceptualize themselves as "families." They provide "alternative kinship systems promising unequivocal acceptance, warmth and structure. The unconditional welcome ('We love you,' 'God loves you,' 'Jesus loves you') made the order imposed by even the most disordered of minds seem appealing. More sophisticated or traditional-minded Americans have found surrogate fathers (seldom mothers) and siblings in therapies like *est* or evangelical religions. These are generally less demanding families than the ones developed by Jim Jones or Reverend Moon, but they provide structure, meaning, and a full schedule of family activities."/15/

Religious movements vary significantly in their orientation toward traditional familism. The traditional family concept has been alien to Hare Krishna practices. In contrast, the Unification Church confers a sacred significance on the institution of the family, defined as a "god-centered family" centered on "Father" Moon. Although the Unification community can, under certain conditions, provide a supportive context for family stability among devotees, it is also a surrogate family for devotees and it is therefore often involved in a sharp conflict with the putatively "non-God-centered" (i.e., non-Moon centered) original families of devotees. Converts to the Unification Church quite frequently sever relationships with parents and spouses when they join the movement. Bitter child custody disputes explode when one partner in marriage joins or leaves a communal cult such as the Unification Church.

In a recent report on conflicts arising between the Unification Church and parents of devotees, the authors wrote that the Rev. and Mrs. Moon "were designated as the devotee's true parents" (as opposed to biological parents). The general supercession of the biological family by the "true family" of the spiritual community represented one basic source of tension between devotees, relatives, and the church. When young converts "radically re-oriented their life-styles and values and concomitantly rejected those career/domestic aspirations which until then they had shared in common with their parents, the latter were predictably distraught."/16/ Two therapists, who work with families who have "lost" a member to an encapsulated communal sect, particularly a wealthy and diversified movement such as the Unification Church, report that the families feel as if they have been superseded "by a bigger, richer, more powerful alternative family."/17/

Cults and Clinicians. It appears that in general therapeutic and "helping" professionals such as psychiatrists, psychologists, and social workers are predisposed to be hostile to cults. Mental health professionals are naturally concerned with the negative consequences for mental health which have arisen in connection with some persons' participation in new religions. Although the frequency and intensity of mental injuries associated with "destructive cultism" are debatable,/18/ the reality of divided and traumatized families is palpable. In this connection, mental health professionals in the United States tend to define their clientele as *families* as well as individuals. They are naturally predisposed to view conflicts between cults and families from the standpoint of the concerned relatives and to perceive involvements with cults as similar to drug use and other "deviant behaviors" which destroy and alienate young persons and in the process undermine familial relationships, vocational prospects and general health. For their part, middle class families feel increasingly dependent upon health professionals for assistance and comfort and they are therefore drawn toward quasi-medical and social scientific metaphors such as mind control or coercive persuasion to account for the apparent desertion of their children. Families have ceded much of their authority to clinical and social welfare professionals; yet, they are still held "responsible" for their children's development. By accepting a medical-psychiatric mode of explanation, they hope to mobilize the support of those professionals on whom they feel dependent and to whom they have ceded their authority./19/

The conflict between mental health professionals and cult leaders is heightened by the hegemonic desires on the part of both groups. In a sense, gurus and spiritual masters have become *competitors* of licensed therapists; moreover, they are unregulated competitors who may appear to enjoy an "unfair advantage" over certified psychiatrists and psychologists. As competitors of conventional psychotherapists, gurus may benefit from the inadequacies of the standard medical model in coping with the routinization of psychotherapy as a conventional life experience for "normal" persons./20/ It is in this competitive context that established psychiatry must necessarily oppose "cults, quacks, and non-professional psychotherapies."/21/ The purported "scientific" nature of psychiatry enhances the salience of a sharp delineation of its boundaries. Psychiatry wants access to the institutional rewards and subsidies which accrue to other sciences, but desires that these rewards be limited to certified scientific and responsible practitioners—no gurus or scientologists need apply.

Finally, it is noteworthy that the intense concern over "destructive cultism" creates the basis for the elaboration of an *opportunity structure* whereby certified professional helpers can develop new and prestigious roles as counselors, rehabilitators, and even deprogrammers of "cult victims." Therapy and counseling have been urged for cultists, ex-cultists, and families traumatized by the association of a family member with a cult. To a large degree the legitimation of the expansion of therapeutic and counseling services for persons whose lives have been touched by cults presupposes the pathological quality of cultist attachments.

Cults and Churches. Certain church leaders have been active in attacks on cults. Other church spokesmen have been active in the defense of the rights of cults. The competitive relationship between conventional church and unorthodox religious movements is obvious. Many dynamic sects have succeeded in eliciting from devotees an intense and diffuse commitment which most conventional church organizations have not been able to match. On the other hand, many church leaders are sensitive to civil liberties issues and perceive a threat to the free exercise of religion and its correlate, *church autonomy*, in the prospect of governmental intervention against cults. Thus, there has emerged an interesting paradox: some clerics have been at the core of the agitation against cults and the emergence of the "anti-cult movement."/22/

Others have been among the staunchest and most effective defenders of beleaguered movements. In particular, the opposition of the National Council of Churches has been instrumental in building resistance to the legalization of deprogramming through conservatorship legislation in New York.

Liberal Protestant church leaders have been foremost in defending cults against repression; however, the attitude of conservative evangelicals may be crucial. Evangelicals often tend to interpret the rise of cults in demonic terms, and some evangelicals have displayed some concern over governmental scrutiny of (putatively irregular) church finances, an area where some evangelical groups may be vulnerable. The diversification of some evangelical movements renders them dependent upon broad interpretations of religious liberty and church autonomy. There are presently some indications that the professional opponents of cults, including deprogrammers, are increasingly turning their attention to independent Christian fellowships or even to established fundamentalist groups.

Finally, it is worth noting that Jewish leaders appear to be particularly conspicuous among anti-cult activists. Allegations have risen that Jewish youth are disproportionately represented among cult recruits, although this may represent merely a preponderance of urban intelligentsia or persons from secularist backgrounds, often nominally Jewish. Since "Jewishness" is an ethnic as well as religious property, the detachment of young persons from the fold through conversion to other faiths is particularly resented by many Jews. In general, Judaism does not proselytize and therefore Jewish leaders may be less inhibited in denigrating interfaith conversion as an insidious and harmful mind control process.

"The family that prays together stays together." This tendency is related to the practice of many churches and synagogues in organizing themselves in terms of family rather than individual involvement. The onset of a religious flux in which individuals join religious groups as individuals strikes at the basis of American denominationalism. Thus, clerics as well as doctors are likely to sympathize with parents aggrieved over the "defection" of a youthful cult recruit. On the other hand, professional students of religion are often supportive of cults, since the upsurge of new movements appears to enhance the importance of religion and provides interesting research opportunities. Divine Principle, the theology of Sun Myung Moon, has demonstrated some appeal among students of religion.

STRATEGY OF MEDICALIZATION

Of the groups antagonistic to cults, psychiatrists and psychologists have played a particularly vital role. In most cases in which the opponents of cults have scored important legal victories, "expert" testimony has been offered to the effect that cultist rituals and indoctrination processes are injurious to mental and physical health and tend to destroy participants' free will. On this basis, adult devotees have been removed from communal religious groups and placed in the legal custody of relatives. Parents and their agents who have seized and imprisoned devotees without obtaining custody orders have been spared legal penalties; cults have occasionally been forbidden to open spiritual retreats; and cults have been defeated in civil litigation.

Although some charges against cults center around concerns for the physical health of members, an important group of objections springs from notions of "mind control" and allied constructs which implicitly identify involvement in a cult as a *mental pathology* induced through planned trauma and conditioning, i.e., the pathological syndrome of "destructive cultism."/23/ Persistent involvement in a cult is thus viewed as essentially *involuntary*—an inexorable disease process from which helpless "cult victims" must be rescued and healed. On this basis an argument can be made for increasing the regulatory authority of mental health professionals (and of the state via *parens patriae*) over religious movements.

Although controversies over cults rage in other countries besides the United States, particularly in Western Europe,/24/ the situation in the United States is unique with respect to the degree to which the *medical model* is applied and the allegations against controversial movements are formulated in medical and psychiatric terms. This probably reflects in part the greater importance and prestige of psychiatry in the United States. However, lesser reliance on the medical model in anti-cult agitation in France and Germany may also reflect the weaker norms of religious tolerance in Europe where there is no stringent civil libertarian tradition requiring circumvention by the raising of the medical and mental health claims. In Europe, it is possible to attack cults directly because they are viewed as anti-social and subversive of dominant social values./25/

In the United States, however, in the context of the constitutionally-grounded guarantee of the "free exercise of religion," it is difficult for those who feel disturbed or threatened by cults to proceed effectively against them directly for being totalistic, authoritarian or multifunctional, or for competing with other institutions. The focus of the attack accordingly shifts to the allegation that the processes of indoctrination in cults in effect "brainwash" converts so that the latter are not really voluntary participants and their involvement does not entail a truly "free" exercise of religion. The "cult problem" thus becomes medicalized such that the inflicting of "involuntary harms" through traumatic and pathogenic processes of coercive persuasion is deemed by some legal authorities to constitute grounds for government intervention against cults which is compatible with general norms of religious freedom./26/

The application of a medical model to controversies over cults also serves the needs and interests of various groups which are antagonistic to cults: *mental health professionals*, whose role in the rehabilitation of "cult victims" is highlighted; *parents*, whose opposition to cults and willingness to use forcible methods to "rescue" cultist progeny is legitimated; *ex-converts*, who find it meaningful to reinterpret their prior involvement with highly stigmatized groups as passive and unmotivated (something done to them rather than something they did); and *clerics*, who are concerned to avoid appearing to persecute or harass competitors. A powerful anti-cult coalition of these groups depends upon medical and mental health issues being kept in the forefront. The medical model is thus utilized in a manner which allows the opponents of cults to disavow any intent to persecute minority beliefs and to stress the healing of involuntary pathological conditions.

The employment of a medical model has had another important consequence. It keeps in the forefront those controversies over cults which relate primarily to the social psychological processes through which individuals enter, become committed to and exit from new religious movements, i.e., controversies over "mind control." These sensational issues continue to overshadow more mundane issues concerning the tax breaks of diversified religious movements or the regulation of their commercial, political, financial, social service and employment policies, although legal outcomes pertaining to these latter areas may ultimately be more crucial to the continued viability of new organizations./27/ It is as if the public, including the critics of cults, agreed with the statement in Justice Jackson's famous dissent in the *Ballard* case that, "the chief wrong which false prophets do to their following is not financial . . . the real harm is on the mental and spiritual place . . . the mental and spiritual poison they get." There seems to be far less agreement, however, with Justice Jackson's conclusion that the "mental and spiritual poison" disseminated by false prophets "is precisely the thing the Constitution put beyond the reach of the prosecutor."/28/

THE LEGAL PICTURE

There is as yet little scientific consensus regarding the allegations that involvement in cults produces psychic injuries and impairs decision-making capacity. Should these allegations be valid, the legal effect to be given these findings is unclear. Although the picture is presently ambiguous with respect to the legal rights of religious movements and their participants and the available legal "remedies" for the putative abuses of cults, it is likely that important court opinions and possibly legislative enactments will surely emerge in the next few years./29/ In particular, the influence of the medical model and the resultant stress on "rescuing" and counterindoctrinating (deprogramming) "cult victims" has produced a heated controversy and a large number of court cases. Many civil libertarians have become alarmed at what they perceive as a serious threat to freedom of belief./30/ The Minnesota Supreme Court seems to have accepted some of the claims of supporters of deprogramming. Its opinion in *Peterson* v. *Sorlien* quoted Professor Richard Delgado, one of the more outspoken critics of cults, in finding that parents or their agents may restrict the movements of an adult child without civil liability for false imprisonment if two conditions are met: (1) the parents have reason to believe that the adult child's judgment has been impaired, and (2) the child at some point (but not necessarily at the outset) consents to what is being done./31/ In *Weiss* v. *Patrick* a somewhat similar decision was rendered by a federal court which acceded to a deprogrammer's defense of consent and dismissed a civil complaint./32/ It appears that a coerced deprogrammee who does not *continuously and strenuously resist* will be unable to establish "meaningful deprivation of liberty" or will be believed to have been rational only during an interlude of non-resistance to abductors. By contrast, several federal appellate courts have established new law by allowing deprogrammees to sue alleged conspirators who deprive them of liberty under the Civil Rights Acts, originally established to protect racial minorities. The significant innovation involves the acceptance of membership in a stigmatized minority church as a sufficient foundation for a "class-based animus."/33/

Deprogramming cases frequently produce civil litigation because officials frequently decline to prosecute abductions-for-deprogramming. When criminal prosecution is undertaken, it is frequently unsuccessful. The sympathies of the judges and juries are frequently engaged by defendants who employ a "defense of necessity" and allege an impairment of the deprogrammee's health and autonomy./34/

The above refers primarily to deprogramming and forcible confinement which is effected without the explicit prior sanction of a court custody order./35/ However, numerous deprogrammings involving physical constraint have occurred under the auspices of special guardianship and conservatorship orders which a superior court had granted over five members of the Unification Church (*Katz* v. *Superior Court*)./36/ The implication of the *Katz* decision is that existing general conservatorship and guardianship statutes may be inadequate for the purpose of forcibly confining religious converts who are not severely incapacitated and "gravely disabled." Nevertheless, legislation establishing special coercive custody arrangements for persons whose personalities and values are alleged to have been altered by "systematic coercive persuasion" and deception has been introduced in several state legislatures./37/ Other proposed legislation entails punishing deceptive proselytizing/38/ and regulating the hours of work within religious movements in which conditions of "slavery" may exist./39/ There is also some sentiment for allowing disillusioned ex-devotees to sue religious groups which require payments by participants and promise psychological benefits (which are allegedly not forthcoming)./40/ This proposal, like proposed sanctions against deceptive proselytizing, raises a key issue: can and should the government protect the "religious consumer"? The ambiguous boundary of religion and psychotherapy is also highlighted here.

Another important issue concerns the financial solicitation and general finances of new movements. The California Attorney General's action against the Worldwide Church of God, which was placed in temporary receivership, provoked acute controversy./41/ A subsequent statute enacted by the California legislature has since made a repetition of this action very difficult. Nevertheless, it is arguable that new movements with charismatic leadership are especially prone to financial mismanagement because they lack built-in bureaucratic devices for accountability./42/ There is, however, sharp division over the notion, advanced by the Attorney General of California, that the funds of a church constitute a *public trust*./43/

In 1981 the United States Supreme Court, in *Heffron v. The International Society for Krishna Consciousness*, upheld a Minnesota State Fair requirement limiting both religious solicitation and the free distribution of religious literature to assigned booths./44/ In *Valente v. Larsen* (1982),/45/ however, the Supreme Court, by a 5 to 4 decision, overturned a Minnesota statute requiring religious organizations which obtain less than half their funds from membership contributions to make a comprehensive financial disclosure. The case had been successfully pursued in federal courts by the Unification Church which had obtained a decision from the Eighth Circuit Court affirming that the regulation discriminated against smaller religious groups which lack a membership base sufficient for conventional financing and thus violated the establishment clause of the First Amendment. Although the Supreme Court's 5–4 decision favored the church, there were several dissents, including an opinion by Justice Rehnquist to the effect that the Court need not have decided the constitutional issues since it had not yet been clearly established that the Unification Church was a legitimate church./46/

At the present writing, Rev. Sun Myung Moon has been convicted of tax fraud; the case is under appeal. The appellate brief notes that the prosecution relied heavily on the assertion that Reverend Moon had expended funds for "personal" or "business" rather than for "religious" purposes and that this established that the funds really belonged to Reverend Moon and not to the Unification Church. The appellant's brief argues that the distinction between "the religious" and "the economic" (or "the personal") is "itself a constitutionally protected religious distinction" such that "the jury was bound to accept the Unification faith's *own* definition of what was religious. . . ." The judge is alleged to have erred in empowering the jury "to decide, on whatever basis it wished, whether various expenditures were 'religious.'"/47/ Likewise an *amicus* brief filed on the appellant's behalf by several mainline church groups complains that the Court's evidentiary rulings prevented the attorneys for the defendant from eliciting from witnesses testimony bearing on the relationship between the defendant's commercial enterprises and the financial needs of the church in order to pursue its religious mission. The *amicus* brief expressed "grave distress" at the alleged "breach of religious liberty."/48/ What seems clear is that *the question of who determines which economic involvements or financial allotments are for religious as opposed to non-religious purposes is of crucial importance to highly diversified movements with far-ranging operations and investments.* "Cults" are egregious but not unique in their diversification—hence the concern of other, non-stigmatized churches to support the claims of Reverend Moon.

The embattled Unification Church, however, has triumphed in the highest court of New York State which has held that the church must be considered "primarily religious" for legal and tax purposes./49/ An intermediate court had held that political and religious elements were so intermingled in the church's doctrine that it could not be classified primarily either religious or political. The Unification Church has also been declared "a bona fide religion" by the U.S. District Court of the District of Columbia which has ordered the Immigration and Naturalization Service (INS) to permit overseas Unification missionaries to enter the United States on the same basis as missionaries from other churches./50/ Despite the ruling, the INS has refused to grant permanent residence to Swami Bhagwan Sri Rajneesh on the grounds that his vow of silence will undermine the fulfillment of his declared purpose of leading his church for which he had sought permanent residence.

CONCLUSION

It is arguable that some additional regulation could and should be imposed on the far-flung involvements of diversified spiritual movements. Certainly the diversification of today's new movements is exacerbating the tension and accentuating the ambiguity along the present church/state "boundary." Yet some observers feel that unpopular new religions are being selectively targeted. Although some regulation and control may be necessary, "the danger is that such laws will be enacted and enforced as a way of continuing to persecute novel religious minorities."/51/ "As organizations whose purpose is essentially ideological, churches are more likely to be victimized by selective repression than businesses are. The free exercise clause necessitates a higher standard; the protection given to churches should more closely approximate that afforded to private individuals."/52/ Yet how is this dictum to be maintained when churches increasingly operate businesses? Critics look askance while "protected empires" are consolidated under the shield of the First Amendment and the presumed ideological vulnerability of religion.

The controversies over religious brainwashing and deprogramming have raised issues other than freedom of religion and separation of church and state. The assumption of personal responsibility, essential to American law and the conception of human rights, cannot withstand the notion that "thought control" without physical coercion can undermine free will. "The assumption that a person who is induced to join a high-demand sect is free to reject sect-imposed tenets ignores the rapidity with which individual identity can be destroyed," comments one writer./53/ Individuals are thus alleged to be helpless before the demiurge of mind control. But if this is the case, the rationale for constitutional democracy is at risk, i.e., dare we allow self-government and "rights" to such frail reeds?

In the twentieth century a "therapeutic state" has evolved which has generated a clientele "by developing categories of deviance which reflected an assumption of illness. Psychopath, alcoholic, and drug addict are categories applied to those whose sexual, drinking and drug behavior is thought to be beyond their control."/54/ What may presently be emerging is a special category identifying persons whose religious behavior is viewed as having gone beyond their control.

And religious liberty? "To the degree that 'thought control' abrogates individual autonomy and destroys the ability to generate ideas, it cannot be said that the new convert is effectively exercising religious freedom protected by the free exercise clause."/55/ Systematic indoctrination, evocations of sin and guilt, dichotomous and absolutistic thinking, repetitive chanting and "obsessive prayer" have all been alleged to vitiate autonomy and constitute key components of coercive persuasion syndromes./56/ Constitutional protection may thus one day be vouchsafed only to nonintense religions—or at least to religions whose intensity takes conventional, accepted forms.

A number of important Supreme Court decisions regarding new religions are likely to appear in the remainder of the decade. The court probably will have to confront eventually coercive deprogramming and the related issues of alleged coercion, manipulation, and destruction of autonomy in religious proselytization and indoctrination; and it will surely face new questions regarding the innovative financing and varied profitable enterprises of esoteric movements.

POSTSCRIPT

As this paper is being prepared, the U.S. Supreme Court has handed down a landmark decision (May 24, 1983) upholding the right of the Internal Revenue Service to withhold tax exemptions from racially discriminatory private schools, even when the latter operate under religious auspices. Commentary has focused primarily on the implication for civil rights policies; however, there also appear to be significant implications for claims to "church autonomy" and thus for the legal viability of diverse constraints on controversial groups./57/

Very briefly, the majority opinion by Justice Burger appears to endorse a strikingly broad interpretation of the "public policy doctrine" whereby tax exemptions for an organization are contingent on conformity to public policy. Burger's opinion furthermore affirms that a religious tax exemption is necessarily grounded in the *charitable* nature of an organization's endeavors. A contrary claim saw religious, educational and charitable purposes as *alternative* grounds for tax exemption. Justice Burger, however, rejected a literal application of the Internal Revenue Code and affirmed that all tax exempt organizations must be "charitable" in a common law sense of the term which includes serving a public purpose and not contravening public policy.

There is a basis here for challenging the tax exemptions of cults on the grounds that they are anti-social, anti-family, unduly totalitarian, etc. The lack of charitable works could also present a problem. Finally, the "charitable" interpretation of the religious tax exemption strengthens the case for state surveillance of church finances.

Nevertheless, it should be noted that a footnote (#29) in the majority opinion on this case explicitly restricts the application of public policy considerations to religious *schools*. "We deal here only with religious *schools—not* with churches or other purely religious institutions. . . ." Yet, in a new paper, "The Supreme Court Redefines Tax Exemption" (privately circulated and recently submitted for publication), Dean Kelley, Director of the Civil Liberties Office of the National Council of Churches, warns that "a footnote is a weak barrier to the seepage of the Court's 'logic' to all exempt organizations, including churches." Kelley suggests that churches may henceforth conceivably be risking their tax exemption whenever they oppose public policy by counseling draft resistance or giving sanctuary to El Salvadorean refugees. In the recent past, the Internal Revenue Service had already attempted to invoke the "violation of public policy" as a criterion for the denial of tax exemption in *Church of Scientology of California* v. *U.S.*, 9th Circuit Court of Appeals, 1980.

There is another quite recent event (June 17, 1983) which appears to this writer to be highly significant in terms of the evolving pattern of conflicts involving religious movements and the families of devotees. For several years disgruntled ex-devotees have been filing civil suits against movements from which they have emerged and which they claim have manipulated, coerced, and exploited them. A certain pattern has emerged where substantial damages tend to be awarded by juries and overturned or sharply reduced by appellate courts. However, a recent Orange County (California) Superior Court verdict awarding $32.5 million to a former Hare Krishna convert and her mother appears to constitute the largest award by a jury against a religious organization in the history of the state./58/

The plaintiff was a Krishna convert for approximately one year, having joined the group as a fifteen year old minor. During that year the plaintiff was allegedly concealed from her parents, after which she was sent home. In addition to interference with the custody of a minor, the plaintiffs charged ISKCON with falsely imprisoning the ex-devotee through "brainwashing," inflicting emotional distress on her and her mother, and libeling both women. The jury awarded largely punitive damages on all four counts.

Suits against religious movements initiated by apostates are extremely significant for both the future viability of these movements and the evolution of our legal system. Consistent victories against "cults" in these cases will likely result in the legitimation of "brainwashing" or mental coercion as a legal concept. As a case in point, the jury in the Hare Krishna case referred to above appears to have accepted the proposition that the teenage convert had been "coerced" through indoctrination, poor diet (affecting her mind), and intimidation by warnings of eschatological consequences for the loss of one's faith./59/ One must also contemplate the possibility that the routine awarding of vast compensatory and punitive damages to disillusioned ex-converts (and there is no scarcity of these) who claim to have been mentally coerced will emerge as an effective means of destroying unpopular movements.

NOTES

/1/   The term "cult" has no commonly accepted meaning. For our purposes, it may be said to denote stigmatized, unconventional spiritual groups. Such groups are usually, though not always, characterized by the following: (1) authoritarian and centralized leadership revolving around a charismatic figure; (2) communal and "totalistic" organization; (3) aggressive proselytizing; (4) systematic indoctrination processes; (5) recent development or importation to the United States; and (6) largely middle class and youthful clientele.

/2/   For a useful, if somewhat hostile to "cults," overview of the legal issues, major causes and law enforcement trends regarding the alleged "brainwashing" techniques of new religious movements and "deprogramming" tactics of opponents of cults, see Orrin Luckstead and D. F. Martell, "Cults: A Conflict Between Religious Liberty and Involuntary Servitude?" *FBI Law Enforcement Bulletin*, April, 1982.

/3/   Jeremiah Gutman, "Constitutional and Legal Aspects of Deprogramming" in *Deprogramming: Documenting the Issue* (New York: American Civil Liberties Union, 1977): 210–11. See also Robert Shapiro, "'Mind Control' or Intensity of Faith: The Constitutional Protection of Religious Beliefs," 13 *Harvard Civil Rights-Civil Liberties Law Review* 751 (1978).

/4/   For a more extensive elaboration of this viewpoint, see Thomas Robbins, "Constructing Cultist 'Mind Control,'" 45 *Social Analysis* 3, September 1984. See also Thomas Robbins and Dick Anthony, "Deprogramming, Brainwashing, and the Medicalization of Deviant Religious Groups," 29 *Social Problems* 3, February 1982.

/5/   On the evolution of Synanon from a drug rehabilitation program to a social movement and finally to a religious movement, see Richard Ofshe, "The Social Development of the Synanon Cult: The Managerial Strategy of Organizational Transformation," 41 *Sociological Analysis* 2 (Summer 1980): 109.

/6/   The growth of these schools and of their resistance to government regulation is discussed by Peter Skerry, "Christian Schools vs. the I.R.S.," *The Public Interest* 61 (Fall 1980): 18.

/7/   Theodore Kerrine and Richard Neuhaus, "Mediating Structures: A Paradigm for Democratic Pluralism," 446 *The Annals* (November 1978): 11. See also Peter Berger and Richard Neuhaus, *To Empower People: The Role of Mediating Structures in Public Policy* (Washington: American Enterprise Institute, 1977).

/8/   Irving Zaretsky and Mark Leone, "The Common Foundation of Religious Diversity," in *Religious Movements in Contemporary America*, ed. Irving Zaretsky and Mark Leone (Princeton: Princeton University Press, 1974), xxxv.

/9/   On the diversification of evangelicals, see Jerry Rifkin and Ted Howard, *The Emerging Order: God in an Age of Scarcity* (New York: Putnam, 1979).

/10/   See James White, *The Sokagakkai and Mass Society* (Palo Alto: Stanford University Press, 1970).

/11/   Richard Ofshe, "Regulation of Diversified Social Movements," presentation at the Center for the Study of New Religious Movements (1982). For one example, see Irving Horowitz, *Science, Sin and Scholarship: The Politics of Reverend Moon and the Unification Church* (Cambridge: MIT Press, 1978).

/12/   For a discussion of cultural conceptions of autonomy as an underlying issue in controversies over cultist brainwashing, see James Beckford, "Politics and the Anticult Movement," 3 *Annual Review of the Social Sciences of Religion* (1979).

/13/   See the statement of Congressman Richard Ottinger, "Cults and their Slaves," *Congressional Record* (July 24, 1980): E. 3578–79.

/14/   Shapiro, "'Mind Control' or Intensity of Faith?" See also "Cults and the Therapeutic State," *Social Policy* (July 1979).

/15/   Suzanne Gordon, "You Can't Go Home Again," 7 *Working Papers New Society* 4 (1980): 10.

/16/   David Bromley, Bruce Bushing, and Anson Shupe, "The Unification Church and the American Family: Strain, Conflict and Control," presented to the Society for the Scientific Study of Religion, Cincinnati (October 1980).

/17/   Lita Schwartz and Florence Kaslow, "Religious Cults, The Individual and Family," *Journal of Marital and Family Therapy* (April 1979).

/18/   Robbins and Anthony, "Brainwashing, Deprogramming and the Medicalization of Deviant Religious Movements."

/19/   See Dick Anthony and Thomas Robbins, "Cults, Brainwashing and New Religions" in *In Gods We Trust: New Patterns of Religious Pluralism in America*, ed. Thomas Robbins and Dick Anthony (New Brunswick, NJ: Transaction, 191).

/20/   See Dick Anthony, Thomas Robbins, Thomas Curtis, and Madalyn Doucas, "Patients and Pilgrims: Changing Attitudes Toward Psychotherapy of Converts to Eastern Mysticism," 20 *American Behavioral Scientist* 6.

/21/   Margaret Singer and J. L. West, "Cults, Quacks and Non-professional Psychotherapies," in *Comprehensive Textbook of Psychiatry III*, ed. H. I. Kaplan, A. M. Freedman, and B. J. Sadock (Baltimore: Wilkins and Wilkins, 1980).

/22/   Anson Shupe and David Bromley, *The New Vigilantes: Deprogrammers, Anticultists and the New Religious Movements* (Beverly Hills, CA: Sage, 1980).

/23/   Eli Shapiro, "Destructive Cultism," 15 *American Family Physician* 2.

/24/   James Beckford, "Cults, Controversy and Control: A Comparative Analysis of the Problems Posed by the New Religious Movements in the Federal Republic of Germany and France," 42 *Sociological Analysis* 3.

/25/   Beckford, "Cults, Controversy and Control."

/26/   An influential articulation of this point of view can be found in the works of Richard Delgado. See especially "Religious Totalism: Gentle and Ungentle Persuasion Under the First Amendment," 51 *University of Southern California Law Review* 1 (1977). Delgado argues that the combination of *harm* perpetrated on devotees (including psychological harm) and the absence of *informed consent* for the risk of such harms provides adequate grounds for government intervention in the "thought reform" processes of cults. Consent requires a coincidence *knowledge* and *capacity*. According to Delgado, cults initially deceive targeted recruits as to the identity and membership obligations of the group. By the time the recruit becomes aware of the concealed elements of cult life, he or she has been ground down by fatigue, emotional manipulation, and intense peer pressure such that the recruit has lost the capacity to re-evaluate rationally his or her participation in the group. Delgado presents a continuum of remedies which includes, at the stringent extreme, a qualified endorsement of court-ordered deprogramming. For a "moderate" proposal, see Professor Delgado's paper in the present volume.

/27/   For an argument that the diversified involvements of cults such as the Unification Church may warrant the withdrawal of their religious tax exemptions, see Joey P. Moore, "Piercing the Religious Veil of the So-Called Cults," 7 *Pepperdine Law Review* 655 (Spring 1980).

/28/   U.S. v. Ballard, 332 U.S. 78 (1944).

/29/   Richard Delgado, "Awaiting the Verdict on Recruitment," *The Center Magazine*, March/April 1982.

/30/   See William Shepherd, "The Prosecutor's Reach: Legal Issues Stemming from the New Religious Movements," 50 *Journal of the American Academy of Religion* 2. See also Dean Kelley, "Deprogramming and Religious Liberty," 4 *Civil Liberties Review* 22.

/31/   Peterson v. Sorlien, 299 N.W. 2d 123 (1980). For a sharp critique of this decision, see Nancy Grim, "Religious Cult Members and Deprogramming Attempts," 15 *Akron Law Review* 165.

/32/   Weiss v. Patrick, F. Supp. 717 (DRI, 1978).

/33/   Cf. Ward v. Conner, 457 F 2d 45 (4th Cir. 1981), *cert. denied, sub nom* Mandelkorn v. Ward, so U.S.L.W. 3566 (January 16, 1982). See William Shepherd, "Legal Protection for Freedom of Religion," *The Center Magazine*, March/April, 1982. See also the earlier paper by Ellen Babbit, "The Deprogramming of Religious Sect Members: A Private Right of Action Under Section 1985 (3)," 74 *Northwestern University Law Review* 229.

/34/   "Roughly half the time, however, the defense [of necessity] is unsuccessful, usually because the judge does not permit it to go forward" (Richard Delgado, "Awaiting the Verdict on Recruitment," *The Center Magazine*, March/April 1982, 28). For a lengthy, technical, and possibly definitive discussion of the defense of necessity in deprogramming, see Kit Pierson, "Cults, Deprogramming and the Necessity Defense," 80 *Michigan Law Review* 271 (1981). For a vigorous civil libertarian attack on deprogramming and on judicial tolerance of the defense of necessity, see John LeMoult, "Deprogramming Members of Religious Sects," 46 *Fordham Law Review* 559 (1978).

/35/   However, civil actions under the Civil Rights Acts may ensue from coercive deprogramming sanctioned by a court order. Section 1985 of Title 42 covers private conspiracies (according to current interpretation), whereas section 1983 covers instances involving the "color of state law." See Shepherd, "Legal Protection for Freedom of Religion."

/36/   Katz v. Superior Court 73 Cal. App. 3d 952; 141 Cal. Rptr., 234 (1977).

/37/   One such bill was passed in 1980 and 1981 by the New York State Legislature and vetoed each time by Governor Hugh Carey. A similar bill was passed by one house of the Kansas Legislature in 1982. For a brief but vigorous attack on such statutes, see Sharon Worthing, "The Use of Legal Process for De-Conversion," in *Government Intervention in Religious Affairs*, ed. Dean Kelley (New York: Pilgrim Press, 1982). See also Shapiro, "'Mind Control' or Intensity of Faith," and Douglas Aronin, "Cults, Deprogramming and Guardianship: A Model Statute," 17 *Columbia Journal of Law and Social Problems* 164 (1982). Finally, see the papers by Gutman and Shapiro in the present volume.

/38/   See Charles Rosenzweig, "High Demand Sects: Disclosure Legislation and the Free Exercise Clause," 15 *New England Law Review* 129 (1979-80). See also Professor Delgado's paper in this volume, and his longer article, "Cults and Conversion: The Case for Informed Consent," 16 *Georgia Law Review* 533 (1982).

/39/   See W. John Thomas, "Preventing Non-Profit Profiteering: Regulating Religious Cult Employment Practices," 23 *Arizona Law Review* 1003 (1981). See also Richard Delgado, "Religious Totalism as Slavery," 9 *New York University Review of Law and Social Change* 51 (1979-1980).

/40/   Such a statute has been proposed in Nevada.

/41/   See Sharon Worthing, "The State Takes Over a Church," 446 *The Annals of the American Academy of Political and Social Science* 136 (1979).

/42/   See Richard Ofshe, "Shifts in Opportunities and Accountability and the Regulations of Religious Organizations," presented to the Association for the Sociology of Religion, New York (August, 1980).

/43/   See Charles S. Whelan, "Who Owns the Churches?" in *Government Intervention in Religious Affairs*, ed. Dean Kelley (New York: Pilgrim Press, (1982).

/44/   Heffron v. International Society for Krishna Consciousness, 101. Ct. 2559, 2565 (1981).

/45/   Valente v. Larsen, 102 S. Ct. 1673 (1982).

/46/   For a brief discussion of the *Heffron* and *Valente* cases, the latter prior to the Supreme Court ruling, see Barry Fisher, "Current Issues in Government Regulation of Religious Solicitation," in *Government Intervention in Religious Affairs*, ed. Kelley.

/47/   Laurence Tribe et al., "Brief for Appellant Sun Myung Moon," U.S. Court of Appeals, 2d Circuit (November 30, 1982): 42-43.

/48/   "Brief for the National Council of Churches of Christ in the U.S., et al.," U.S.A. v. Sun Myung Moon et al., in the U.S. Court of Appeals, 2d Circuit, (November 30, 1982): 6-7.

/49/   Holy Spirit Association for the Unification of World Christianity v. Tax Commission, 55 N.Y. 2d 512 (1982).

/50/   Unification Church v. Immigration and Naturalization Service, F. Supp., Civil Action No. 81-1072 (D.D.C. September16, 1982), slip. op. at 10.

/51/   Dick Anthony and Thomas Robbins, "New Religions, Families and Brainwashing" in *In Gods We Trust*, ed. Robbins and Anthony: 273.

/52/   Worthing, "The State Takes Over a Church": 150.

/53/   Rosenzweig, "High Demand Sects": 152.

/54/   Richard Stivers, "Social Control in the Technological Society," in *The Collective Definition of Deviance*, ed. F. James Davis and Richard Stivers (New York: Free Press, 1975): 384.

/55/   Rosenzweig, "High Demand Sects": 153. Another writer argues that a convert's absolute freedom of belief is not jeopardized if he is forcibly confined for counterindoctrination (*qua* confrontational deprogramming) subsequent to having been judged to have been an involuntary participant in a cult which employs coercive persuasion: see Aronin, "Cults, Deprogramming and Guardianship."

/56/   See Rosenzweig, "High Demand Sects," and Delgado, "Religious Totalism."

/57/   For a discussion of "church autonomy" and the Bob Jones University/ Goldsboro Christian Schools case (prior to the May 24, 1983 Supreme Court decision), see James McBride, "'There is No Separation of God and State': The Christian New Right Perspective on Religion and the First Amendment," in this volume.

/58/   "Hare Krishnas Ordered to Pay $32.5 Million," *Los Angeles Times*, 18 June 1983.

/59/   "Krishnas," *Los Angeles Times*, 18 June 1983.

NEW RELIGIOUS MOVEMENTS:
CULTURE AND SOCIETY

THE RELATIVIZATION OF SOCIETIES, MODERN RELIGION, AND GLOBALIZATION

Roland Robertson

If new religious movements constitute as important a sociological phenomenon as a number of the most conspicuous students of such movements have claimed, does that not mean that "the world" has changed sufficiently to require a recasting of some basic features of sociological theorizing? Let me be more specific. If it is true that there is, to invoke a favorite phrase of some students of the new religious movements, a "religious ferment" and if we grant that the idea of a religious ferment runs against the grain of much received sociological wisdom, then does that not mean that the matter has to be significantly modified? Should not the comprehension of new religious movements and phenomena of family resemblance (about which more in a moment) lead at least to the consideration that such comprehension necessitates innovation in sociological theory?

Before directly tackling the overall question with which I have begun, it is necessary to say something about the boundaries of the phenomenon indicated by the phrase "new religious movements." In that regard it must be noted that recently the scope of study suggested by the new religious movement concept has been widened to include, for example, the surge of evangelicalism and fundamentalism in America. The reasons for such conceptual expansion would seem to be, first, that the "classical"—that is, mid-1970s—type of new religious movements (for example, the Unification Church, the Divine Light Mission, and Hare Krishna) is not at this time making much headway, and, second, that new religious *trends*, particularly of the kind which would seem to rival the attractions and significance of the classical new religious movements, warrant study as part of the previously identified "ferment." Another aspect of the expansion of scope in the field of study suggested by the new religious movement concept arises in connection with church-state and religion-politics matters. In the second half of the decade of the 1970s the issue of the societal response to new religious movements was increasingly focused along the lines of state interference in and control over the activities of new religious movements, most clearly with respect to the issue of "mind control." Even though much of what has been talked about as a church-state problem in connection with that issue is

more accurately described as a religion-*law* problem, the fact of the
matter is that the new religious movements field of study has by now
developed a specific interest in the church-state *Problemstellung*./1/

Thus the new religious movements field of study has a significantly
broader frame of empirical and, it should follow, theoretical reference
and relevance than was the case in 1975. A pattern of problem shifts
may be discerned. Initially there was concern with a seemingly anomalous, specific phenomenon; however, the boundaries of the latter became
quickly and increasingly fuzzy. Eventually there crystallized the problem of a putative disparity between the restricted scope of the field's
label and the enlarged territory of focus of both its early and late-
coming practitioners. Full recognition of the latter circumstances could
now lead, at one extreme, to the call for a re-narrowing of the new religious movement focus—a plea for purification of a field which has
become contaminated by extra-field concerns. At the opposite end of the
continuum the call could be for abandonment of the new religious
movements focus on the grounds that the new religious movements phenomenon is no longer distinctive or, indeed, significant enough to warrant autonomous pursuit.

My main reason for arguing for something like a midway position on
the continuum of options will become clear as my substantive argument
is unfolded. At this juncture I propose only to state my belief that the
issue-area presently defined, however unclearly, by the new religious
movements interest (particularly in America, the United Kingdom and
other parts of Western Europe) should be analytically cultivated. The
purification option is rejected primarily because the radical limitation of
the new religious movement field to movements of the forms typical of
the early and mid-1970s—even by including therapeutic and, in Weber's
sense, hygienic movements—would defeat much of the purpose of being
interested in such movements in the first place, i.e., the ferment argument./2/ For there are more recent manifestations of "ferment" which
can be fruitfully connected to the new religious movement form of religiosity. The abandonment option should not be taken up for related
reasons, namely, that the focus of ferment might well get lost were we,
for example, to see new religious movements as merely types of religious
movements and thus easily subsumable under study of movements or
movement-organizations, or, to take another example, as subsumable
under a general orientation to the phenomenon of conversion, coercive
persuasion, "brain-washing," or whatever.

Thus even though the new religious movements label may now be
misleading, I claim that in its broadest reach it points toward a significant and manageable range of empirical and theoretical problems. In
essence—but very simply—the latter may be specified as consisting in
tensions between church and state, the politicization of religion, and

religious fundamentalism. Each of these facets of the modern religious situation have been spoken of by mainline new religious movements experts. In my view, however, the latter have not been sufficiently ambitious with respect to the range of sociocultural and historical foci nor with regard to theoretical innovation.

Probably the most significant challenge to the analysts of the new religiosity is the more or less *worldwideness* of the latter. In recent years new religious movements in the narrow sense have been sociologically looked at in a large number of societies, but a much larger number of societies have experienced church-state tensions, often as a result of the revival of fundamentalistic and/or traditionalistic religious standpoints. (In that I define fundamentalism generally to refer to an emphasis upon absolute values and beliefs and the cognitive dedifferentiation of spheres of societal and personal life, I am enabled to categorize, to take a major case, Latin American liberation theology movements as fundamentalist—even though they are not traditionalist.) The tiny number of intellectuals who have sought to explain the worldwide reassertion of religious themes have tended to concentrate on intra-societal and/or psychological "homeless mind" factors— that is, they have sought to produce generalizations about cultural and/or social conditions pertaining to societies as such, or humans in general, which produce the new religiosity (either in directly-causal or in functional-teleological terms). However, the diversity of societies which have, for example, produced church-state tensions (such as the USA, the Phillipines, Iran, Japan, Egypt, Poland, some Latin American societies, and so on) suggests strongly that the purely societal or alienation-from-society foci are inadequate. Simultaneity with respect to religious resurgence in otherwise different types of societies surely requires us to look for theoretical accounts which pivot upon *global* circumstances as such.

GLOBAL AND SOCIETAL IDENTITY

How can we fruitfully establish a mode of analysis which takes us beyond the societal level? In answering this question, we can do no better than consider some relatively neglected aspects of classical sociology which was, of course, pivotally concerned with religion. In their different ways the great figures of classical sociology confronted one particular, central problem: how can societies persist in the face of tendencies which push or pull individuals out of their societal "slots"? It is conventionally thought that in their different ways Max Weber, Durkheim, Toennies, Simmel, and others answered this question by asserting that there were new or, at least, potential forms of solidarity and individual commitment appropriate to what Toennies called *Gesellschaft*. On that kind of interpretation has rested a large part of modern sociological wisdom—even though many have argued that *Gesellschaft* is diffusely the source of discontent and, indeed, of the revival of religion. In particular there has been a strong tendency to address almost continuously over the past forty years the question of societal order, integration and the like./3/ However, I propose, without having the room to cite chapter and verse, that the main sociologists of the classical period did not merely puzzle about the issue of *societal* order and integration and the closely related question of new forms of individual participation (and, on the other side of the coin, the problems and pathologies to which modern societies and individuals are prone). They *also* worked in cognizance of, inter alia, the differentiation of *human* life (or *being*) from societal values (Simmel); the emergence of a "higher international life" and a cult of humanity (Durkheim); and the return of the "primordial gods" via an accentuation of the concern with ultimate values on the part of individuals (Weber).

In that scenario the problem of order as it came to be defined—first Parsons's influence and then in such forms as structuralism, "paradigmism," and cultural Marxism—cannot be sensibly regarded as pertaining solely to society in the sense of the national society. If individuals are now something more than societal members—and if, more generally, there is "something" other than society—then the issues of societal order and membership of society are *relativized*. In fact, there has recently been considerable acknowledgement in various highly ad hoc forms of the increasing significance of such categories as humanity, mankind, human needs, economic, political, and, indeed, spiritual world orders, trans-societal relationship, and so on. What we now need is a systematic recognition of the dimension(s) of extra-societality, and a spelling-out of the implications which the crystallization of extra-societality—to the point where it is even more than a significant residual category—have for the operation of individual societies. In sum, I propose that there is an emergent problem of order at *the global level*—the emergence of that problem being a central aspect of the process of *globalization*. The degree to which this is related to the growth of a world economic system—in the Wallersteinian, Aminian, or Frankian sense—cannot be fully explored here (although I will deal with an approach to religions from a stance approximating that of Wallerstein later)./4/ Suffice it to say that—in line with the approaches of Durkheim, Weber, and Parsons—I consider cultural, including religious values, beliefs and symbols to arise in mutually penetrative relationships with economic-material (and other secular) aspects of life./5/

If there is a higher level—a more fundamental—problem of order than that traditionally discussed in reference to societies as territorially organized and state-guided sociocultural units, then surely we have to think about the problem of societal order in *global-contextual* terms. My most basic proposition in this regard is that once there definitely crystallizes a problem of global order, then the consequent relativization and contextualization of societal order involves a greater consciousness—in a sense a politicization—concerning societal order. I regard, to take a particularly relevant example, the considerable talk (and not just on the part of sociologists of religion) about civil religion as being in large part contingent upon—more precisely, penetrating and being penetrated by—a *world* civil religion *problem*. Rather than seeing societies as running into civil religion problems as a result of parallel developments *inside* individual societies—although such developments may be significant—my argument is that the considerable concern which has been shown in many modern societies about what the society in question "really stands for"—in other words, the question of collective-societal *identity*—arises in large part because of heightened consciousness of the issue of societal identity in a global context where, first, it is no longer clear that individuals are simply members of societies and, second, individual societies are increasingly subject to the application of emergent, but heavily contested, standards concerning what a "good" society looks like./6/

Essentially I am arguing that we are in the throes of a new stage of sociocultural evolution which is taking us past and beyond the stage of purely societal, or even civilizational, evolution. In sum, we now confront the issue of global order and change. Societal order becomes in this circumstance transformed. It becomes in individual cases increasingly contested and fabricated. This does not mean that societies no longer operate in terms of long-standing, centuries-old codes of individual-society relationships, cultural traditions, and so on. Rather, the latter are increasingly subject to internal and external thematization. The problem of global order intensifies concern with societal identities. Societies experience pressure to reach, as it were, into their promordial cores within the context of global norms and emergent "theodicies." On the other side of the coin, the (globally-shared) thematization of the search for particular-societal identities exacerbates the problem of the hermeneutical center of the world as a whole, producing quasi-religious disputes over definitions of "the global situation"—as in Latin American and Islamic attempts to modify the world-cultural scene.

RELIGION AND THE GLOBAL SITUATION

What of religion in this analytical context?/7/ Before specifying my own theses in this regard, I propose to deal briefly with an approach which, indeed, promises to account for modern religious trends in pivotal reference to the theme of "world order." World order is defined by Wuthnow as residing in a "transnational division of labor in which societies and members of societies participate, necessitating recurrent, patterned exchange (economic, political, and cultural) across national boundaries." Stratification into core and peripheral areas is the major consequence of this division. "As with societies, the status of these areas and the relations among them tend to be patterned and legitimated by broad definitions of reality."/8/ We need point here only to Wuthnow's central thesis that strata *within* societies are deeply affected in the econo-mo-political relations *among* societies. "Successive shifts in the relations among nations have created successive shifts in the status and ideologies of domestic interest groups which, in turn, have occurred amidst a chorus of responses at the level of our deepest spiritual and moral convictions."/9/ Even though he announces at one point that a society's religious orientations channel its actions and affect its influence on the world order, Wuthnow's specific emphasis is on the claim that "the chorus of responses" are "deeply conditioned by the instabilities present in the larger world-system."/10/

It should be noted that Wuthnow's approach leaves little or no room for consideration of the ways in which the national *state* and the relationships between states and "their" individuals and groups affect or are bound-up with religious trends./11/ Second, Wuthnow does not address the question of the circumstances under which there will be religious—as opposed to irreligious or a-religious—responses to intra-societal dislocations. Third, in spite of his great concern with relations among and between national societies, Wuthnow does not consider (although he briefly *mentions*) the phenomenon of *ideational* constructions of the relations between nations. It is almost as if he were saying that relations between societies are primarily economic—with political and military ramifications—but that *ideas only enter the picture as intra-societal outcomes of inter-societal relations* (a characteristic weakness of econo-mistic and externalistic approaches to the world-system).

A consequence of Wuthnow's arguments (and of the lacunae in his framework) is that his empirically focused sketches of forms of religious movements could as easily be addressed in terms of intra-societal developments which have been parametrically framed by international-economic processes. On the other hand, his theoretical, generalizing claim veers very strongly toward the extreme *externalist* position—namely, that we can account social-scientifically for virtually all interesting *intra*-societal phenomena as outcomes of the structure of and shifts in the pattern of relations *between and among* societies. I have no intention, however, of upholding an *internalist* position. I seek to promote a way of thinking about the modern world which transcends the old internal versus external (or endogeny versus exogeny) debates—not by trying to render an antinomy as a compatibility, but by rendering the antinomy itself as a feature of the worldwide problem of order. This involves a sociological witnessing of *the simultaneity* of trans-societal and inter-societal issues, on the one hand, and intra-societal matters and indi-vidual-society relationships on the other.

How should religion be located in such a frame of reference? For a start, I suggest that just as we ought to do away with simply external/ internal dichotomies, so we have to relinquish facile religion/non-religion distinctions. Probably the best way of giving substance to this suggestion is by referring to the recent, widespread focus on the relations between religion and politics and between church and state. The problematization of these relationships can best be understood—at least in the early stages of inquiry—by thinking simultaneously about *both* sides of each of these intimately related pairs. In other words, there is no *prima facie* reason for thinking of modern church-state problems as contingent simply upon the resurgence within some societies of the "churches." Surely it is equally important to think of changes or at least trends with respect to the operation of modern *state systems*. Similarly, to puzzle about the recent mixing of religious and political issues is on the face of it as appropriately tackled in terms of the political as it is of the religious dimension. In fact, it is part of the present argument that interpenetration on these fronts ought to take us beyond—but *not* in the sense of sidestepping—the general debate about societal secularization. More precisely, recent empirical linkings of religion and politics may indicate a circumstance in which religion is made more relevant to "worldly" affairs and political arenas are infused with meaning. That does not mean, it should be emphasized, that we should now divest ourselves of an analytical distinction between religion and politics but rather that we should think of these spheres as made societally (and personally significant) via their interdependence. To be sure, in some concrete cases religion and politics may be conflated in such a way and to a point that no operative distinction between affairs of the spirit and those of a *Realpolitik* are possible (thus from one point of view reducing the functionality of the society in question) but we are best advised to think in terms of interpenetration as an analytical benchmark./12/

The core of my thesis in this regard involves what may in simple terms be expressed as the simultaneity of processes of secularization and desecularization./13/ In brief, while the state has enlarged its sphere of operation under the guise of enhancing the *quality of life* and the functionality of the society for which it is responsible, it has at the same time become embroiled in what may be called *quasi-religious* matters on two fronts—one intra-societal, the other extra-societal. In the former respect, the state has become involved in a range of "deep-life" matters such as definitions and raisons d'etre of human life itself, death, old age, and other dimensions of individual and collective meaning, suffering, and reward. In the latter respect, modern states have collectively become increasingly involved in questions of human rights, inequality between and among nations, and so on. In a nutshell, the state has become more and more concerned internally and externally with what Parsons called *telic* matters—that is, matters having to do with "the ends of man."/14/ At the same time, the thematization of the state-run society and of the system of modern states—that is, the consciousness of the "out-there functionality" of society and the system of interrelated societies—propels and amplifies the sense of individuality and personality vis-a-vis the state and raises pressing questions concerning the nature of *humanity*. In other words, at one and the same time the ostensibly secular state has moved into religious territory and the members of modern societies have in various ways become increasingly conscious of the constructedness of the state-run society. The modern state invites religiomoral responses precisely because *it* is increasingly concerned with matters previously lying within the domain of religion-based interest.

There are thus two features of present global circumstances, as I have outlined it, which accentuate or at least open up religious, quasi-religious concerns. On the one hand, globalization involves a "release" from the "security" of life-in-society; on the other, it raises problems concerning both the legitimacy of the world order of societies and the meaning of what mankind "really is."/15/ The first feature involves relativization of society, while the second involves relativization of the self. As I have noted, there are, on the other hand, serious implications of the globalization process *within* societies. As globalization proceeds, pressures are exerted on societies and individuals-in-societies to define the *identity* of particular societies and the attributes of citizenship—matters which social scientists used to think were the special problems of new national societies, but which are now of ubiquitous significance. At the collective-societal level there is thus a thrust in a quasi-religious direction as some take it upon themselves to define in politico-religious terms what "their" society "ultimately stands for."

Civil religion becomes a problem precisely because of the factors which push *individuals* out of a purely societal form of identity formation and accentuate problems of societal identity formation per se./16/ However, I see societal civil-religion concerns as sites of potential religious and religious-ideological conflict. Thus within the USA, for example, the rise of the new fundamentalist Right can be seen as an attempt on the part of adherents to a particular world-view to establish *their* position as the civil religion of America. Fundamentalist revivals in other societies—such as Israel and Iran—may be similarly regarded. Civil-religion talk in America is thus most appropriately seen as an indirect acknowledgement of the *liabilities* of the separation of church and state. Societies such as Israel, Iran, and Pakistan—not to speak of the "secularly religious" USSR—are able to *conflate* religion and politics; their identity formation is not impeded by their constitutions (although it may be impeded in other respects).

At the same time, the implication of the increasing concern with the legitimacy of the world order of societies and concern with the historical nature of mankind raises *world* civil-religion problems. On the ostensibly religious front the most obvious manifestations of the latter are, first, the proliferation of *theologies of liberation* in a number of continental and sub-continental contexts and, second, the rapidly crystallizing interest in world theology. Both of these, but most clearly the first, are manifestations of what Habermas calls

> the repoliticization of the biblical inheritance observable in con-temporary theological discourse . . . which goes together with a leveling of [the] this-worldly/other-worldly dichotomy. . . . The idea of God is transformed . . . into the concept of a *logos* that determines the community of believers. . . . 'God' becomes the name for a communicative structure that forces men, on the pain of loss of their humanity, to go beyond their accidental, empirical nature to encounter one another indirectly. . . ./17/

One example of the "leveling" process of which Habermas has spoken is the fuzzy boundary between some liberation theologies, on the one hand, and ostensibly secular-moral conceptions of the maldistribution of economic wealth and power among nations; another is the Moral Majority injunction that it is a *sin* not to be politically active.

The conjunction of *societal* civil-religion (and, also church-state problems across many sectors of the globe) *and* the incipience of *world* civil-religion problems thus comprises the centerpiece of this analysis of the place of religion in the globalization process. Politicization of theology and religion, on the one hand, and the "theologization" of politics on the other, are core features of this conjunction. Theodical questions—or successor questions to old theodical queries—are high on the agenda of global discourse. Religion is centered in the process of what I call globalization by virtue of both the religious or quasi-religious matters raised as a result of universalistic tendencies involving mankind and relations between societies *and* by the particularizing responses to universalistic tendencies. The fundamentalists who have recently staked claims to interpret and control sociocultural identities of their respective societies are often seen—and not incorrectly—as atavistic relative to the universalizing aspect of globalization. However, they can also be viewed as involved in the process of *revitalizing* individual societies or clusters of societies—engaged in actions designed to grasp the *cores* of societies and provide symbols of effervescence relative to the "iron-cage" aspects of "modernity."

Implicitly I have been addressing a question which has been examined quite a lot in recent years with particular reference to North America: why are the conservative churches growing? However, we need to ask that question not merely on a global scale but also to connect it systematically to religious trends in toto—by regarding religious change in

the modern global circumstance as an *overall movement* which partly
expresses, partly constrains, and partly reflects the general process of
globalization. There are four central elements of the latter: state-run
societies; individual *selves*; *humanity*; and *the systems of relations
among societies*. Particular religious movements may be categorized in
terms of their apparent relevance to—or "appropriateness" in respect
of—one or more of these components of the globalization process or,
equally important, the relationships among them. For example, the New
Religious Right in the American context has particular relevance to
matters concerning the provision of a moral-religious definition of
American-societal identity in a global context in which societal coherence becomes increasingly a matter of internal dispute and comparison
with other societies; liberation-theological movements have particular
(but not sole) relevance to issues concerning relations between societies
(quasi-religious aspects of international justice); some conventionally
labeled new religious movements have relevance to problems about the
relationships between individuals and societies; while others may be best
understood as having primarily to do with extra-societal aspects of the
self (humanity or mankind).

Although I cannot provide here the full-fledged alternative to other
attempts to categorize modern religious movements suggested by my
paradigm of globalization, I believe that such *could* rather easily be
accomplished with particular reference to the components which I have
conceptualized. I seek here only to establish that individuals and societies
are, by virtue of the globalization process, increasingly subject to forms
of "spiritualization" that pivot upon the increasing salience of tensions in
the relationships between individuals and society, between and among
societies, between the self and mankind, between society and humanity,
between self and the system of societies, and between humanity and the
system of societies. One particular consequence of this paradigm for the
study of new religious movements is that it makes it inappropriate to
talk in a facile way about forms of world *rejection*, when in fact much
that may seem to be societally rejective in the religious realm may be
embracive with respect to mankind. In a broader view, much that may
seem to be religiously atavistic—e.g., the recent swings toward fundamentalism in many societies—may actually be "modern," in that such
movements are engaged in "necessary" processes of societal-identity formation within an overall global context.

I have thus been concerned to provide the basic elements of a
general-theoretical framework for the analysis of religious trends across
the globe of which new religious movements are an important part. The
centerpiece of that framework consists in the proposition that societal
order has been rendered increasingly problematic as the world has
become, in a number of respects, a single system. Globalization refers to

the series of interdependent processes that yield a concern with consciousness of the contemporary human condition. Emergence of such consciousness is itself a quasi-religious circumstance—inevitably raising issues concerning the ends of men. One would *expect* that organized religion would be in the forefront of, would be revived by, bursts in the pace of globalization. In a sense we might regard the notion of revitalization as now being applicable to the globe as a whole. In that perspective different types of religious tendency take up different facets of the overall globalization process, with the newer tendencies (including the new religious movements) having relevance to some of the newest of the particular globalization trends. As far as modern history is concerned, the most salient of the latter are undoubtedly the ones having to do with the externalization of society or of particular-societal membership. At the other extreme lie movements whose function seems to be precisely the focusing of concern on societal identity and/or mediating between individual and society. In any case, I claim that new religious movements are best read as exemplifications of an evolutionary shift at the sociocultural level. On the other hand, to study new religious movements in the classic, 1970s sense would be to ignore the *overall movement* aspect of religion across the globe. Perhaps we now need a field of study concerned, in a special sense, with new religious *trends* rather than new movements.

NOTES

/1/   See Thomas Robbins, "Church, State and Cult," 42 *Sociological Analysis* 3 (1981): 209–26. Cf. Roland Robertson, "Consideration from within the American Context on the Significance of Church-State Tension," 42 *Sociological Analysis* 3 (1981): 193–208; Roland Robertson, "Religious Movements and Modern Societies: Toward a Progressive Problemshift," 40 *Sociological Analysis* 4 (1979): 297–314.

/2/   Cf. Steven M. Tipton, *Getting Saved from the Sixties* (Berkeley: University of California Press, 1982). On hygiene utilitarianism, see Gary A. Abraham, "The Protestant Ethic and the Spirit of Utilitarianism: The Case of est," *Theory and Society* (forthcoming).

/3/   On the proliferation of concern with order, see Roland Robertson, "Aspects of Identity and Authority in Sociological Theory," in *Identity and Authority*, ed. Roland Robertson and Burkhart Holzner (New York: St. Martin's Press, 1980), 218–65. See also Roland Robertson, "Societies, Individuals and Sociology: Intra-Civilizational Themes," 1 *Theory, Culture and Society* 2: 6–17.

/4/   For example: Immanuel Wallerstein, *The Modern World-System* (New York: Academic Press, 1974); Samir Amin, *Class and National, Historically and in the Current Crisis* (London: Heineman, 1980); James D. Cockroft et al., *Dependence and Underdevelopment* (New York: Anchor Books, 1972).

/5/ On the concept of interpenetration, see Richard Munch, "Talcott Parsons and the Theory of Action, II. The Continuity of Development," 87 *American Journal of Sociology* 4 (1982): 771–826. On the limitations of the economic emphases of the world-systems approach from a perspective which is not incompatible with the present emphases upon interpenetration, see John W. Mayer, "The World Polity and the Authority of the Nation-State," *Studies of the Modern World Systems*, ed. Albert Beresen (New York: Academic Press, 1980), 109–38.

/6/ Cf. J. P. Nettl and Roland Robertson, "Industrialization, Development or Modernization," 17 *British Journal of Sociology* 3 (1966): 274–911; and J. P. Nettl and Roland Robertson, *International Systems and the Modernization of Societies* (New York: Basic Books, 1968).

/7/ The ideas in this part of the paper have been expressed in slightly different form in Roland Robertson and JoAnn Chirico, "Humanity, Globalization and Worldwide Religious Resurgence," Department of Sociology, University of Pittsburgh, 1981 (to be published).

/8/ Robert Wuthnow, "World Order and Religious Movements" in *Studies of the Modern World System*, 58–59.

/9/ Wuthnow, 71.

/10/ Wuthnow, 60.

/11/ Cf. Theda Skocpol, *States and Social Revolutions* (Cambridge: Cambridge University Press, 1979).

/12/ This position must be distinguished from that of those who now say that a religion/politics discussion is conceptually inappropriate—Daniel H. Levine, *Religion and Politics in Latin America* (Princeton: Princeton University Press, 1981).

/13/ See Talcott Parsons, *Action Theory and the Human Condition* (New York: Free Press, 1978), 233–63.

/14/ Parsons, 352–443.

/15/ This view involved reversal of the claim that the strengthening of state apparati in global context weakens the individual. Cf. Meyer, "World Polity." For a perspective closer to mine, see Donald Bloch, *The Behavior of Law* (New York: Academic Press, 1976), 125–38.

/16/ Cf. Jurgen Habermas, *Communication and the Evolution of Society* (Boston: Beacon Press, 1979).

/17/ Jurgen Habermas, *Legitimation Crisis* (Boston: Beacon Press, 1973), 131. For the view that Habermas's theory of communication leads inexorably to a theology, see Charles Davis, *Theology and Political Society* (Cambridge: Cambridge University Press, 1980).

THE CULTURAL CONTEXT
OF CONTEMPORARY RELIGIOUS MOVEMENTS

Robert Wuthnow

The topic of this essay is the religious movements that flourished so visibly in the 1970s—movements such as the Unification Church, Hare Krishna, Zen, the Children of God, and quasi-religious groups such as Transcendental Meditation, *est*, Synanon, and Scientology. These movements dominated the discussion of American religion for nearly a decade. The groups themselves (at least most them) continue on, not with growing numbers, but with a firmly established organizational and financial base. TM claims to have processed more than 900,000 meditators. *est* has trained close to 300,000. Hare Krishna lists 2,500 full-time monks and priests with ten times that many regular participants. The Unification Church currently numbers 2,500 members in the U.S., but claims more than 2,000,000 members worldwide. Other groups, such as Meher Baba, Arica, Divine Light, and the Healthy-Happy-Holy Organization, have been less visible to the public at large but list memberships equal to the size of many smaller Protestant denominations./1/

Within the past year or two, much of the topical interest in these movements has declined, as other movements, such as evangelicalism and the Moral Majority, have taken center stage. Yet, the new religions continue to be the focus of lively debate, of litigation, and indeed of a vigorous anti-cult campaign. Many of the perplexing questions that were raised by their novel and sometimes bizarre activities, as well as questions of longer standing about the nature of religious movements, continue to be fruitful areas of inquiry. But more importantly, the burning questions that these movements raised about the society at large have by no means gone away. Do these movements signal the decline of the secular humanist ethos? Do they reflect some deeper shift in the focus of American faith? Does their sudden, and largely unpredicted, appearance indicate that our understanding of ourselves and of our culture needs to be re-examined? The new religions have touched only a small minority of the American public directly as converts, devotees or curious bystanders, but all of us are affected by the culture that has produced these movements.

PERSPECTIVES ON THE NEW RELIGIONS

The new religions have been portrayed, both in popular and scholarly accounts, as the antithesis of prevailing cultural values. Robert
Bellah has written that the values, attitudes, and beliefs of the new oriental religious groups, the human potential movements, and even some
variants of the Jesus movement are consonant with what he terms a
"revolutionary" cultural alternative—one that would reject the exclusive
dominance of technical reason and espouse greater harmony with nature
and between human beings./2/ Theodore Roszak, an early proponent of
the new religions in his book *The Making of a Counter Culture*, has
written in a more recent essay that the new religious awareness fundamentally contradicts, and therefore stands in confrontation with, the
secular humanist cultural mainstream. In his view, science, technology,
and politics dominate modern thinking, while the new religions provide
a radical, though pitifully weak, alternative rooted in the wisdom of
ancient, mystical, and hermetic traditions./3/ Jacob Needleman writes
of the new religions as a positive corrective to the dead-end of Western
materialism./4/

On the other side, critics of the new religions have also pictured
them in terms contrasting sharply with the cultural mainstream. The
British sociologist of religion Bryan Wilson perceives a severe element of
trivialization in the new religions, evidenced in his view by their exclusive, nonconventional emphasis on sudden experience, quick conversion,
easy enlightenment, and faddish ritual./5/ Nathan Adler, a psychiatrist
and early critic of the new religions, describes their members as victims
of an "antinomian personality," incapable of thinking rationally, of disci-
plining their emotions or abiding by cultural standards, striking out
instead in wild and frantic experiments expressing a disorganized sense
of self./6/ Harvard's Daniel Bell characterizes the new religions in similar terms./7/ He likens them to an artistic fringe, an enclave of aestheti-
cally oriented, expressive experimenters who have succumbed to the
temptation of letting art stand for reality. Whereas modernity, in his
view, has placed careful restrictions on the role of art in culture, the new
religions have given way to narcissistic self-exploration. The theme of
narcissism has, of course, been emphasized much in other recent writings, such as those of Richard Sennett, Tom Wolfe, and Christopher
Lasch. While these discussions perceive some continuity between the
new religions and the rest of society, in that narcissicism is perceived as
a problem in the general culture, they too argue that in the new religions the cord has snapped, the usual constraints have been broken,
letting rampant, emotional self-titillation come to the surface. More
extreme critics characterize members of the new religions as highly
naive, brainwashed young people who have lost the capacity for critical

reasoning and have succumbed to an alien worldview.

The evaluative tone of these descriptions should not stand in the way of the central observation, shared by supporters and critics alike, that the new religions represent a radical departure from the conventional culture. Indeed, one has not to look far for evidence supporting this conclusion. Superficial acquaintance with the new religions indicates a number of sharp contrasts with the cultural mainstream.

From the outset, the new religions adopted life-styles which deviated from conventional norms, especially in dress, living arrangements, sexual conduct, and religious observance. They experimented with communal living. Some of them moved into wilderness settings to create model communities. They took up oriental and monastic religious teachings, devised their own rituals, borrowed heavily from the occult, espoused mysticism in place of rational cognitive religious doctrines. They evoked, to paraphrase Michel Foucault, a veritable "intrusion of subjugated knowledges."/8/ They criticized Western thought for being oppressive and one-dimensional, arguing that it led only to destruction and despair. They prophesied the end of the modern era and anxiously awaited the coming of an Aquarian age.

Their disenchantment took many forms. The Healthy-Happy-Holy Organization, inspired by the teachings of Sikh religion, withdrew to the wilderness to build a model society tuned harmoniously to the rhythm of nature. The Christian World Liberation Front, like kindred representatives of the Jesus movement, renounced secular life-styles to pursue the simple rigor of apostolic Christianity. Among the Hare Krishna, cultural disenchantment found expression in the movement's portrayal of material luxuries as *maya*—the world of illusion—and in the group's highly ritualistic dancing and chanting.

Other movements expressed their disillusionment in witchcraft, in contemplation, and in blind allegiance to cultic leaders. Perhaps no single event dramatized the tremendous gulf between the new religions and the established culture more than did the tragic mass suicide at Jonestown, Guyana, in November 1978.

The obvious—and convenient—conclusion is that the new religions represent simply the negation, the rival of conventional norms, the antagonist of American culture. The new religions evidently resulted from some temporary breakdown in the social fabric, from severe personal distress, pathological upbringing, hallucinogenic drugs, devious recruitment methods, brainwashing, or, regarded differently, from leadership with extraordinary spiritual gifts or exceptional wisdom about the human dilemma.

Either view is deceptively convenient. If the new religions are products only of pathological behavior or of clear-sighted visionaries, the prevailing culture bears no responsibility for their existence, except perhaps in failing to halt their machinations. Religious ferment is not to be expected except under unusual circumstances. Religious movements are the occasional happenstance, the curious anomaly, or perhaps a model of what the culture is not. There is nothing endemic in the culture itself to produce religious movements of this kind. Nor would we expect to see any of the values of the established culture reflected in these movements.

Both the convenience of the conventional view and the superficiality of the evidence on which it is based should give pause to our reflections about new religions. A more careful assessment, I believe, suggests that the recent religious ferment has been very much a product of broader, more pervasive tendencies in American culture. The new religions, to anticipate my conclusions, bear the distinctive imprint of the prevailing technological worldview. Indeed, they attest significantly to the power of this world-view, in that they initially presented themselves as its stalwart opponents. The understandings that gave rise to the new religions, the different location they came to occupy, and the very activities with which they sought legitimacy all belie the pervasiveness of technical rationality in American culture. Let us turn first to the understandings, particularly of nature and of the social world, that rendered meaning to the appeals of the new religions.

THE LEGITIMATION OF RELIGIOUS PROTEST

Protest against existing social arrangements, whether religious or secular, requires that social arrangements be perceived as objects, as forces exercising an influence on life, but not an inevitable or immutable influence. It is not enough to be victimized by injustice, uncertainty, or outright deprivation. Understandings conducive to collective action also have to be present. In contemporary life, these understandings have been tempered greatly by science and technology.

Traditionally, the concept of nature served as an important metaphor for the inevitable, the realm beyond human responsibility. Events of nature were neither controllable nor the legitimate occasion for social protest. The evolution of science has greatly expanded the category of nature, bringing objects and events more clearly into the natural domain. Nature has, in Max Weber's terms, been "demystified," stripped of divine forces, removed from the category of magic and superstition. The scientization of nature has not, however, led to a proportionate increase in our sense of inevitability. It has instead produced a model for bringing about social change. Knowledge of natural laws serves as the basis for empirical predictions which, in turn, provide leverage for manipulating the material world. Technical rationality consists of identifying procedures, based on empirical evidence, to bring about desired consequences in the material world. The natural realm, in short, has become one for which human institutions can be held accountable.

Like nature, the social realm has also become differentiated, no more the product of simply divine providence or of individual social forces exerting influence over human affairs. The search for abstract laws of social behavior, similar to the laws of nature, has largely come up dry. But the social realm has nonetheless acquired some degree of predictability and, with this, has become an arena over which human responsibility can be expressed.

In the absence of abstract laws, the sense of rationality that characterizes the social world derives in no small measure from efforts to plan and manipulate social arrangements. Borrowing legitimacy from the successes of technology in the natural world, social engineering has emerged as a highly specialized mode of manipulating the social world. Mastery over the social world has come to be dramatized chiefly by the results of social engineering. The effectiveness of social engineering, however, is limited by the growing complexity of modern social life— complexity stemming importantly from the advance of technology itself. As a result, the social realm has become increasingly the arena of unplanned and undesired contingencies. These contingencies appear to defy social engineering and its underlying theories. They occur, seemingly as willful events, impinging forcefully on human affairs with an undisclosed logic. In an ironic sense, therefore, the social world bears signs of "re-enchantment," of being populated by mysterious but objectified forces, even as the natural world has undergone demystification.

The new religions incorporated these understandings of the natural and social realms into their own worldviews. As in science and technology, their universe was dominated to a large degree by the realm of nature, even to the extent of translating religious concepts into naturalistic terms. In focusing on nature they were led to the social institutions charged with the technological manipulation of nature. While they criticized these institutions, they nevertheless took for granted the objective status of the social realm, its rationality, its importance as a factor influencing human behavior, and its capacity to be reformed.

These assumptions provided the mental preconditions for engaging in protest. The new religions' protests were directed not so much at theological issues but at the arrangements and norms of social life. They accepted for the most part the idea that personal betterment, even enlightenment, could be gained by manipulating the social forces around them, for example, by intentionally violating traditional norms, by creating their own communities, and by ritually manipulating their own behavior. They also focused heavily on the undesired contingencies of social life, offering new explanations for these events, and in doing so presupposing the applicability of rationality to all of the social realm. These explanations, in turn, legitimated their own techniques for manipulating social events.

It is significant that the new religions emerged following a rapid increase in the diffusion of natural and social scientific imagery, not only through research but through social programs, the mass media, and higher education. They drew recruits mainly from the more educated segments of society, especially young people with at least some college training, unlike religious movements in the past which have drawn members mainly from underprivileged sectors. Once the social dislocations of the sixties created opportunities for unrest, the understandings associated with the growth of higher education became important in legitimating religious protest.

More specifically, research has shown that young people who thought of life events in terms of social categories of discourse were significantly more likely to participate or be attracted to the new religions than young people whose understandings were different. Those who attributed life events either to God or purely to individual choices were unlikely to approve of social protest in general and religious experimentation in particular. In contrast, those who recognized the objectivity of social forces, the shaping influence of social arrangements, were more likely to believe that protest made sense and that religious movements were acceptable activities./9/

More detailed evidence comes from ethnographic material on the religious movements themselves. Even the movements that were rooted in oriental traditions focusing on the inner life demonstrated a high level of concern with the objective social determination of life events. In fact, contemplative religious illumination appears to have enhanced awareness of social arrangements, making them seem arbitrary, relative, and consequently amenable to experimentation. Mystical experiences can produce insights of many varieties; hence, it is noteworthy that these insights focused so clearly on the social realm. Converts to the new religions also honed their social sensitivities through participation in the student unrest of the period. Weber and Troeltsch notwithstanding, mystical religion and political participation went hand in hand. Social norms came to be regarded as cultural constructions rather than inevitable or divinely instituted patterns of conduct.

Few of the new religions challenged the theoretical basis of the modern scientific worldview. Writers like Theodore Roszak did so, but among members of the religious movements themselves criticisms of science were no more common than among young people more generally. Most of the movements, however, were openly critical of technology and the social contingencies resulting from technology. They pointed out problems in the environment and in the economy. These problems provided symbols with which to dramatize the contingencies of the social world. The movements did not, as one might expect based on the history of religious movements, attribute these contingencies to divine will or individual evil, but used them as occasions for criticizing established institutions. In consequence, the new religions did not become revivalistic movements advocating individual repentance, but became social experiments involving alternative living arrangements and alternative cosmologies purporting to give rational explanations for these contingencies. In a word, religious protest made sense because religious experimenters accepted the assumptions about nature and society that prevail in the culture at large.

THE VARIETIES OF RELIGIOUS PROTEST

A somewhat clearer picture of the cultural conditions influencing the new religions can be obtained by examining the different strategies adopted by the movements and the different patterns of growth and decline that were attendant on these strategies. Looking first at the more authoritarian groups, all of them came to occupy a similar location in the society, even though there were striking differences in their ideologies and life styles. All of them drew recruits primarily from segments passed by in the advance of science and technology or from among the victims of this advance—victims of addicting drugs in Synanon, impoverished minority groups in the People's Temple, and youthful drop-outs from higher education and broken homes in the Children of God and the Unification Church. Like other total institutions, such as prisons and mental hospitals, the movements played a rehabilitative role. They were able to sustain at least moderately sized organizations by providing a function not fulfilled by other social service agencies.

Yet most of these groups ran into difficulty because they did not conform to the social prescriptions governing other total institutions. Their failure to accept the credentialing provisions of the state and theories of therapeutic practice subscribed to by psychiatrists, criminologists, and physicians aroused suspicions of coercion and brainwashing. Their failure to identify themselves clearly as religions or as secular therapeutic groups also raised suspicions, especially concerning fraud and financial exploitation. As a result, two of the groups, the Children of God and the People's Temple, found it expedient to withdraw entirely from the United States. Synanon withdrew into itself, becoming a closed cult-like community, but not without creating serious legal difficulties. The Unification Church expatriated most of its membership but ensured its survival by also making significant changes in its activities. It pursued cultural accommodation by eliminating coercion from its recruitment methods, by abandoning solicitation activities, by sponsoring dialogue with other religious groups, and by sponsoring conferences concerned with the advancement of science and attended by renowned scientists and religious leaders to dramatize its compatibility with the scientific ethos.

The trajectory of the various communal, mystical, and monastic groups was quite different. These groups espoused oriental or medieval traditions and rejected many of the outward appearances of the society. They minimized contact with the larger society by retreating into rural settings and establishing their own self-subsistance economies. In dress and in ritual their members set themselves apart as well, and by instituting extensive trial-socialization periods, rigorous ascetic life-styles, and by limiting the number of new recruits admitted to their communities, they avoided tensions with the large culture. Even these groups, however, borrowed more from the culture than these distancing mechanisms might suggest. The idea of experimentation provided a quasi-scientific rationale for their activities. Members spoke of their involvement as an experiment, a learning experience, a chance to gain knowledge by temporarily manipulating their environment much as one might perform an experiment in the laboratory. The members of these movements were by and large highly educated and many of them had received training in the sciences. In many cases they attempted to reconcile their newly discovered religious views with science. Books such as *Zen and the Art of Motorcycle Maintenance*, *The Crack in the Cosmic Egg*, and *The Tao of Physics* are some of the better known of these efforts. Rather than challenging the scientific worldview, the groups also concerned themselves with phenomena such as ESP for which science offered few explanations. Overall, these movements remained small. The nonmaterialistic life-styles undoubtedly restricted the number of recruits they could attract. But even within these protected enclaves the influence of technical rationality was by no means absent.

Numerically, the most successful of the new religions and quasireligious groups was the so-called human potential movement, including groups such as *est*, TM, Scientology, and Esalen. These groups recruited adherents in relatively large numbers, attracted members who did not give up professional careers and who had received advanced education, yet appeared to offer them something not experienced in other settings. These groups were concerned with inner growth and self-awareness. They exploited territory that had formerly been the domain of psychotherapy and individual counseling and successfully competed for recruits by offering training that was not only as effective but considerably less expensive. These groups also found it expedient not to identify themselves as religions, thus avoiding competing with established religious organizations as well as being able to function in settings denied to religious groups. They participated in settings such as schools and prisons and managed to attract a secularized clientele that had abandoned religious faith.

More than any of the other movements, these groups also appealed directly to science for legitimation. In discussing TM, Anthony Campbell writes that an important reason for Maharishi's success has been the enthusiasm he has shown for relating his teaching, practical and theoretical, to Western science. . . . [H]e has seized every opportunity which has come his way to make contact with scientists, and in the last few years he has enlisted the full-time cooperation of a large number of psychiatrists, biologists, psychologists, and others who are currently helping to relate his ideas to scientific thought./10/

Werner Erhard, founder of *est*, has also eagerly pursued scientists to acquire their confidence and support. Both movements have invited psychologists and neurologists to speak on the structure of the brain, have sponsored experiments among their members, and have published research purporting to show the merits of participation. For the human potential movement more generally, the Association of Humanistic Psychology has also served as an important locus of professional support and research activity.

It is evident in retrospect, then, that the new religions took on the shape they did and enjoyed different degrees of success partly because the culture provided specific locations for them to occupy. These influences are especially evident in the changes that took place over time: the growth experienced by the human potential movement which accommodated itself to the prevailing culture, the changes of emphasis in the Unification Church as it attempted to transcend its early cult-like status, the relative lack of growth and isolation experienced by the more mystical and monastic groups, and the outright demise of the more authoritarian groups. It is also worth noting that the Jesus movement which initially seemed exceptionally promising, particularly since it could rely on the Judeo-Christian tradition for legitimacy, was soon co-opted by established religious organizations. As the counter-culture ended, it proved too similar in its basic message to the churches to survive as an independent movement.

THE TACTICS OF RELIGIOUS PROTEST

The tactics employed by the new religions reveal, perhaps most tellingly of all, the impact of the larger culture. A pragmatic, consequentialist, technical orientation runs through the otherwise diverse practices initiated by the new religions. The groups that survived for any length of time found it expedient to employ techniques producing readily observable results. The Alka-Seltzer generation, reared on products promising instant solutions, demanded nothing less. The new religions became masters of technique. They devised rituals capable of manipulating thoughts and emotions and especially sensory experience. Young people came first for the experience and then stayed on, seeing the ease and effectiveness with which the groups produced results, to learn their teachings. Many discovered religious rituals as a cheaper, legal, and medically safer substitute for mind-expanding drugs. Others found they could gain control over themselves more effectively within a group than alone. In either case, the consequentialist logic of the marketplace prevailed. If the movement produced immediate results, its doctrines were legitimate; if not, alternatives could be found. Allegations that the new religions practiced brainwashing have generally not been substantiated, yet it clearly is the case that the new religions produced tangible effects far more dramatically and rapidly that anything expected in the churches or the schools. Distant and exotic origins notwithstanding, the new religions adapted to American culture by advancing their own version of technical rationality.

The Divine Light Mission, founded in 1971 by the boy guru Maharaj Ji, criticized traditional religions, arguing that enlightenment was neither a spiritual concept nor a metaphoric dimension of faith. It promised enlightenment that could actually be seen, heard, tasted, and touched. In the first three years of its existence it attracted more than 50,000 American youth, teaching them simple techniques for observing an inner light and hearing noises which many claimed to be the voice of God.

The Hare Krishna movement found its ritualized chanting a more effective drawing card than its esoteric Hindu philosophy of life. Even casual participants could feel themselves physically transformed and for the first time submerged in consensual collective activity. More devoted participants found their lives more regimented than any gray-suited executive. The movement offered a highly routinized, comprehensive daily schedule of activities as well as a simplified set of directives codified from the complex doctrines of the Bhagavad-Gita. In one observer's words, it produced "enlightenment by ordeal." Careful planning and sustained effort were no less a part of its orientation than of the proverbial Protestant ethic.

Predictably, the human potential groups bought most heavily into the logic of technique. Groups such as *est* and Esalen were often critics of the material hardware resulting from technology in the world of business, but their own practices extended technology into the realm of self. They codified and sold formalized techniques having consequences such as learning how to "experience one's experience" or, in the terms of one group, becoming aware that "what is, is." These commonplace, but clearly practical, observations acquired importance and legitimacy for their participants because they had been transformed ritually. The common insights of daily life no longer depended upon the faulty intuitions of common sense. They were the objective products of carefully planned and executed procedures.

The new religions and quasi-religions also advanced a concept of self consonant with the extension of technology into the personal realm. The more mystical groups usually retained the idea of true, ideal, or spiritual self, but even in these groups a purely naturalistic concept of self was not uncommon.

Observers of the human potential movement have suggested that it taught participants how to manipulate aspects of self much in the same manner as objects in the environment. Significant portions of the self, especially one's private thoughts and feelings, were objectified and techniques were given for manipulating them. The self, in consequence, became more flexible, capable of sustaining the compromises required in professional life. Under the best of circumstances, the active or true self gained distance, protection, from the person's activities and their subjective implications.

As noted earlier, the new religions were given impetus by the problems or contingencies occurring in the larger society. Some of the techniques which the new religions employed, however, manufactured their own contingencies which the group could then use to reinforce its teachings. Coincidences and other fortuitous events usually ignored or treated casually in ordinary life, such as finding a convenient parking place or a chance meeting among friends, took on great importance. Members of the Divine Light Mission were encouraged to share these "miracle stories," as they called them. *est* discussed them collectively and taught trainees to expect them as a result of their participation. The Children of God and many of the charismatic Christian groups incorporated them into testimonial sessions as evidence of God's provision. By making these events public, the groups essentially multiplied the frequency with which they seemed to happen. The group could then point to them as evidence of the legitimacy of its claim.

The common element in these examples is an emphasis on tangible empirical consequences that can be linked to the techniques practiced by the group. The groups did not legitimate themselves in terms of universal principles or absolute values, but in terms of the short-run consequences of their activities. In this important respect, they echoed suppositions characteristic of the culture at large. Some of them succeeded in rejecting the material comforts of modern life and its stereotypic middle-class norms, but they did not escape the logic of technical reason. The groups that prospered the most made their peace with the technical worldview. Rather than challenging the scientific cosmology, they focused on problems poorly explained in conventional theories and borrowed heavily from the logic of experimentation. The emergence of religious protest itself presupposed conventional understandings of the social world. These understandings assumed an inherent rationality among social events and promised new explanations for the contingencies of modern social life. The new religions exploited techniques having immediate consequences and adopted consequentialist reasoning in support of their practices.

THE RELIGIOUS MAINSTREAM

On balance, the religious mainstream has been far more exposed to the dominant culture than were the new religions. If the logic of technical reason is clearly discernible among the small counter-cultural enclaves that explicitly rejected much of the prevailing culture, we may well ask whether the character of American faith has been changing more generally.

The religious mainstream has imbibed deeply from the spirit of technology. The so-called electronic church is a much cited example. But more subtle indications are present as well. The logic of growth, itself a pervasive feature of the secular culture, has been imported full-scale into the religious realm. Specialized technologies for achieving church growth have been initiated, while programs and doctrines have been re-evaluated in light of their capacity to promote church growth. The experientialist emphasis that emerged more generally alongside that manifested within the new religions, while a useful corrective to purely cognitive religion, has produced a consequentialist orientation to faith, convincing believers that their faith is untrue unless it produces concrete sensory results. Rather than leaving matters of such importance to the mysterious workings of the spirit, techniques have been devised to manufacture religious experience. Harvey Cox, after touring ashrams associated with the new oriental religions, recommended that the churches institute meditation techniques to give members a daily "mini-sabbath" of religious repose./11/ Experiments in multi-media liturgical practice have brought hard technology directly into the pulpit. The churches have also subscribed to the rationalistic mentality that Max Weber warned would increasingly become an iron cage. The means-end calculations associated with rational planning have long transcended the stuffy offices of corporate bureaucracies, finding their way into the child-rearing guidebooks produced by religious writers and studied in church school classes, tracts outlining the four steps to salvation, strategies for fund-raising and evangelism, and sermons showing how to succeed.

Even in conservative evangelical groups, traditionally in tension with science and technology, there are disturbing signs. Tim LaHaye, an evangelical writer whose books sell more than 300,000 copies annually, devotes most of his book *The Battle for the Mind* to a scientific defense of Christianity. Secular humanism, he argues, is unscientific, productive only of chaos, while Christianity is both scientific and rational. The frequency with which he cites scientists leaves the reader wondering where the authority for religion lies, in the pronouncements of God or the pronouncements of science. Social science has also become a source of authority. The periodical *Christianity Today* has discovered the Gallup poll, citing its findings in virtually every issue as evidence of the correctness of evangelical teachings.

A few examples neither document a trend nor suggest that the churches have borrowed too willingly from the secular environment. But the dangers inherent in borrowing uncritically need to be recognized, for the logic of technical reason carries its own conception of faith. Aleksandr Solzhenitsyn in his Harvard commencement address warned the West against relying too exclusively on technical and legal rules, while losing its sense of value and spirit. "Man's sense of responsibility to God and society," he cautioned, "has grown dimmer and dimmer."/12/ If the focus of American faith is, indeed, the pronouncements of science, the spurious sensation derived from technology, the quick formula for salvation, then Solzhenitsyn's warning may well warrant serious reflection.

NOTES

/1/   The figures cited here were obtained primarily from personal contacts with social scientists who have been studying these movements or from published sources compiled around 1979 or 1980. They are, of course, subject to considerable error.

/2/   Robert N. Bellah, "New Religious Consciousness and the Crisis in Modernity" in *The New Religious Consciousness*, ed. Charles Y. Glock and Robert N. Bellah (Berkeley: University of California Press, 1976), 351–52.

/3/   Theodore Roszak, "Ethics, Ecstasy and the Study of New Religions," in *Understanding the New Religions*, ed. Jacob Needleman and George Baker (New York: Seabury Press, 1978), 49–62.

/4/   Jacob Needleman, "Preface," in *New Religions*, ed. Needleman and Baker, ix–xviii.

/5/   Bryan R. Wilson, *Contemporary Transformations of Religion* (Oxford University Press, 1976).

/6/   Nathan Adler, *The Underground Stream: New Life Styles and the Antinomian Personality* (New York: Harper & Row, 1972).

/7/   Daniel Bell, "Beyond Modernism, Beyond Self," in *Art, Politics and Will: Essays in Honor of Lionel Trilling*, ed. Quenton Anderson, Stephen Donadio, and Stephen Marcus (New York: Basic Books, 1977), 213–53.

/8/   Michael Foucault, *Power/Knowledge* (New York: Pantheon Books, 1980).

/9/   The conclusions summarized here are from my book: Robert Wuthnow, *The Consciousness Reformation* (Berkeley: University of California Press, 1976).

/10/ Anthony Campbell, *The Mechanics of Enlightenment: An Examination of the Teachings of the Maharishi Mahesh Yogi* (London: V. Gollancz, 1975), 10–11.

/11/ Harvey Cox, *Turning East: The Promise and Peril of the New Orientalism* (New York: Simon and Schuster, 1977).

/12/ Aleksandr Solzhenitsyn, *A World Apart* (New York: Harper & Row, 1978), 51.

NEW RELIGIOUS MOVEMENTS
AND COERCIVE PERSUASION

Kansas School of Religion
At the University of Kansas
Smith Hall, Rm. 109, Library
Lawrence, Kansas 66045-2164

CULT PROCESSES, RELIGIOUS TOTALISM, AND CIVIL LIBERTIES

Robert J. Lifton

There are two main images that inform one's moral and psychological perspective on cults: totalism, or what I would also call fundamentalism, and civil liberties, the concern for civil liberties that has been raised in connection with the cults. I have not made any systematic study of cults; in fact, I have not chosen to address myself to this area. But because of my earlier book on thought reform, and particularly the notoriety of Chapter 22, "Ideological Totalism," people have used my work in various ways and taken various actions in connection with a reading of my work./1/ A number of people have been in touch with me, including parents of children who had joined cults and young people themselves who have left cults or felt undecided about their future in them. Totalism and civil liberties are both issues that concern me very much, although my work is directed more toward the first, the issue of totalism. Still, the issue of civil liberties is very central to me, because in the past I have fought for causes that are not always popular and understand how important civil liberties are. There is, however, a problem associated with these larger images: in the the name of defending civil liberties, there is often an impulse to glorify the object of one's defenses. Certainly it could be said that some of the cults do some nasty things, but civil liberties are as necessary for people who do nasty things as for those who do nice things. There is confusion in this issue, and discrimination is crucial; however, the American system of civil liberties is such that it is possible to dislike certain cults without making them illegal.

I think anyone talking about the cults does best to identify where he or she lives, intellectually and morally. My own sense of and feelings about the problem are very much influenced by my first study on Chinese thought reform which left me with something like an allergy toward totalism. I happen to think totalism is a very dangerous kind of process in our society—all the more in connection with what I would describe as a world-wide epidemic of fundamentalism in either its political, religious, or combined forms. Within that world-wide epidemic I would place many cults in this country and many religious and political groups on all sides in the Middle East and throughout the world. There are reasons for this epidemic and I will address these later. But because I

come from a civil libertarian background and am interested in nuclear
weapons, and in problems of totalistic attitudes regarding nuclear
weapons, fundamentalism now—including some of the cults—presents a
particular danger, because cults tend to relate their theology to a nuclear
weapon armageddon in ways that, in some cases, may even welcome
that armageddon. During my study on Chinese thought reform in the
mid-50s, I evolved generalizing principles, not simply to condemn the
Chinese communists, but to bring a critical perspective to the process
itself. My way of being even-handed was to bring the subject home into
more familiar patterns or environments in which one could identify
themes of ideological totalism. That is why I developed Chapter 22,
along with other chapters that examined totalistic practices in such
things as McCarthyism in American politics and in training and educational programs. I have since continued to examine ideological totalism,
most recently in work with Vietnam veterans, who demonstrated quick
and sometimes moving transformations in anti-war stances, and more
recently still in a study of the psychology of Nazi doctors. Some of these
issues come back to haunt and inform one. Certainly the issue of totalism
is very alive for my direct work, as it is for the work of many other
people. In terms of my involvement in psychohistory, there is an effort
in my work to evolve shared themes in certain groups that have been
exposed to or have helped to bring about a particular historical event.

The shared themes I have laid out in my work on the concept of ideological totalism apply in some cult situations. Of course, one man's cult
is another man's religion—there is a certain pejorative inference in using
the word. I know that many people prefer the term "new religions," and
I have no special problem with that usage. I tend to speak of cults myself
in terms of a cluster of groups that, for the sake of definition, have these
certain characteristics: First, a charismatic leader who, as in the case of
Jim Jones and the People's Temple, increasingly becomes the object of
worship. Spiritual ideas of a more general kind are likely to give way to
a worship of the person of the leader. Second, a series of processes that
can be associated with what has been called coercive persuasion or
thought reform./2/ A third characteristic of what I am calling cults has
to do with the tendency toward manipulation from above, with
exploitation—economic, sexual, or other—of often genuine seekers who
bring idealism and this kind of search from below.This is a rough model,
and of course one must not judge any environment on abstract generalizations but rather apply them to a particular environment.

IDEOLOGICAL TOTALISM

To develop my analysis of cults, three points need to be covered:
first, the characteristics of ideological totalism and their applicability in

some of these cult situations; next, some larger historical considerations; and finally, some issues of young adulthood. In addition, I will discuss the importance of intense experience, what I call the experience of transcendence (a dimension that is left out in much of the discussion about cults), and nuclear weapons and their possible influence in this whole situation.

The phenomenology I applied when writing about ideological totalism in the past still seems to me to be useful, even though I wrote the book more than twenty years ago. The first characteristic process is what I call "milieu control," which is essentially the control of communication within an environment. If it is extremely intense, it becomes an internalized control—an attempt to manage an individual's inner communication. This can never be fully achieved, but it can go rather far. It is what sometimes has been a called a "god's eye view"—a conviction that reality is the group's exclusive possession. Clearly this kind of process creates conflicts around individual autonomy; autonomy, if it is sought or realized in such an environment, becomes a threat to milieu control. The milieu control within some of the cults tend to be maintained and expressed in several ways: group process, isolation from other people, psychological pressure, physical distance, or unavailability of transportation, and occasionally physical pressure. There is often a sequence of events, such as seminars, lectures, and group encounters, which become increasingly intense and increasingly isolated, making it extremely difficult—both physically and psychologically—to leave.

It is important to note that these cults differ from patterns of totalism that have occurred in other societies. For instance, the centers that were used for reform in China were more or less in keeping with the ethos of the society as it was evolving at the time, and therefore when one was leaving them or moving in and out of them, one would still find reinforcements from without. Rather, insofar as totalistic environments exist with these cults, they are islands of totalism within a larger society which is on the whole antagonistic to these islands. This can create a dynamic of its own, and insofar as milieu control is to be maintained, the requirements are magnified by that structural situation. Cult leaders must go further. They have to deepen the control and manage the environment more systematically and sometimes with more intensity in order to maintain that island of totalism within the antagonistic outer world. Thus I think that in certain cult situations the imposition and the degree of milieu control is closely connected to the process of change. This partly explains why there is often a sudden lifting of the cult identity when a young person who has been in a cult for some time is suddenly exposed to the outside. One can almost observe the process that occurs in some young people who have a very dramatic change from their prior identity, whatever it was, to an intense embrace of the cult's belief system and group structure. Within this process (which I call doubling) a second self is formed that lives side by side with the first self, somewhat autonomously from it. Obviously, there must be some connecting element to integrate one with another; otherwise, the overall person could not be functional, but the autonomy is rather impressive. When the milieu control is lifted by removing the youngster from the totalistic environment, by whatever means, something of the earlier self reasserts itself. This leave-taking may take place voluntarily, or through force (or simply, as in one of the court cases, by the cult member moving across to the other side of the bench, so to speak, away from the other members). The two selves can exist simultaneously and very confusedly for a considerable period of time and it may be that the transition periods are the most intense and psychologically painful as well as the most potentially harmful.

A second general characteristic of totalistic environments is what I call "mystical manipulation" or "planned spontaneity." It is a systematic process that is planned and managed from above but will appear to have arisen spontaneously from within the environment. A great attraction to the process is that it doesn't feel like manipulation, which raises a host of philosophical questions. Some aspects can be rather traditional—such as fasting, chanting, and limited sleep. These have, of course, been practiced by religious groups over the centuries. There seems to be a pattern now in which a particular "chosen" human being is seen as a savior or source of salvation. Mystical manipulation takes on a special quality in these cults because the leaders become mediators for God. In most cults the God-centered principles are put very forcibly, as in the exclusive quality of the cult and its beliefs, as the only true path or source of salvation. This can give intensity to the mystical manipulation and a justification to those involved with promulgating it, and, in many cases, even to those who are its recipients from below. Insofar as there is a specific individual, a leader, who becomes the center of the mystical manipulation (or the person in whose name it is done), there is a double process at work. The leader can sometimes be more real than an abstract god and therefore attractive to cult members. On the other hand, that person can also be a source of disillusionment. If one believes, as has been charged, that Sun Myung Moon has associations with the Korean CIA, and that this information is made available to people in the Unification Church, their relationship to the church can be threatened by disillusionment toward a leader. It is not that simple—direct cause and effect—but I am suggesting this style of leadership has both advantages and disadvantages in terms of cult loyalty.

While mystical manipulation leads to the psychology of the pawn, it can also include a legitimation of deception, so-called "heavenly deception" by the Unification Church, although there are analogous patterns in other cult environments. If one has not seen the light, if one is not in the realm of the cult, one is in the realm of evil and therefore can be justifiably deceived for the higher purpose. For instance, when Unification Church members are collecting funds, it is considered right for them to deny their affiliation when asked. There are young people who have been at centers of the Unification Church for some periods of time without being told that these were indeed run by the Unification Church. The totalistic ideology can and often does justify this deception.

The next two characteristics of totalism, "the demand for purity" and "the cult of confession," are familiar. The demand for purity can create a Manichaean quality in cults and in some religious structures as well as in political structures Such a demand calls for separation of pure and impure, of good and evil, within an environment and, internally, within oneself. Absolute purification is a continuing process. It is often institutionalized, and, as a source of stimulation of guilt and shame, it ties in with the confession process. All movements, at whatever level of intensity, must take hold of an individual's guilt and shame mechanisms to achieve intense influence over the changes he or she undergoes. This is done within a confession process that has its own structure. Sessions in which one confesses to one's sins are accompanied by patterns of criticism and self-criticism, generally transpiring within small groups and with a very active and dynamic thrust toward personal change.

One could raise questions about the ambiguity and complexity of this, quoting Camus when he says "authors of confessions write especially to avoid confession, to tell nothing of what they know." That may be somewhat exaggerated, but it does suggest that confessions occur on varying levels. When a young person confesses to various sins of his pre-cultic or pre-institution existence, he or she can both believe in those sins and be covering over other things that he or she is holding onto and reluctant to discuss. In some cases, this includes identification with one's prior existence, an identification that has not been successfully dishonored by the process of continuous confession. Repetitious confession, then, is often a source of extreme arrogance in the name of apparent humility—so that Camus says, "I practice the profession of penitence, to be able to end up as a judge." The more I accuse myself, the more I have a right to judge you. That is a central theme in any continual confessional process, particularly where it is required in an enclosed group process.

The next three patterns I describe in regard to ideological totalism are "the sacred science," "the loading of the language," and "the principle of doctrine over person." The phrases are almost self-explanatory. I would emphasize especially the sacred science, for in our age something must be scientific as well as spiritual to have impact. This can offer considerable security to young people because it greatly simplifies the world.

The Unification Church is a good example, but not the only one, of a contemporary need to combine a sacred set of dogmatic principles with a claim to science, to a science of man emobodying the truth about human behavior and human psychology. In the case of the Unification Church, even large gatherings of scientists are free to present their own work at these symposia, but the aura of the symposia is of a vast Unification ethos, and, of course, the conference legitimates the intellectual and scientific claim of the Unification Church.

The term "loading the language" refers to a literalization of language—words or images becoming God. We often see a great simplification of a language that seems very cliché-ridden but can have enormous appeal and psychological power around that simplification. Because every issue in one's life—and these are often complicated young lives, in many cases—can be reduced to a single set of principles that have an inner coherence, one can claim the experience of truth and feel it. Answers are available. Lionel Trilling has called this "the language of non-thought" because there is a cliché and simple slogan to which the most complex and otherwise difficult questions can be reduced.

Another pattern of ideological totalism, doctrine over person, occurs when there is a conflict between what one feels oneself experiencing and what the doctrine or dogma says one should experience. The internalized message in these environments is to find the truth of the dogma and subject one's experience to that truth. Often the experience of the contradiction or the admission of that experience can be associated with guilt or condemned in a way that renders it such, in an effort to hold one to the doctrine. One is made to feel that doubts are reflections of one's own evil. Yet despite that, doubts can arise and people, when the conflicts become great, can leave. This is the most frequent problem of many of the cults. In the case of the Unification Church, membership presents more of a problem than money.

Finally, the eighth and perhaps the most general and significant of these characteristics is what I call "the dispensing of existence." This is usually metaphorical. But if one has an absolute or totalistic vision of truth, those that have not seen the light, have not embraced that truth, are in some way in the shadows—bound up with evil, tainted—and do not have a right to exist as full equals. That is why one can deceive them by using the concept of divine deception. There is a "being" versus "nothingness" dichotomy at work here. Impediments to being must be pushed away or destroyed. This can create psychologically a tremendous fear of inner extinction or collapse, should one be placed in the second category of not having the right to exist. However, when one is accepted, there can be great satisfaction of feeling oneself a part of the elite. Under more malignant conditions, the dispensing of existence or the absence of the right to existence can be literalized, and people can be put to death because of their alleged doctrinal shortcomings, as in some cases in the Soviet Union and perhaps in China too. In the fact of the People's Temple mass suicide–murder in Guyana, the use of a suicidal mystique as a consistent part of the going theology intensified this dispensing of existence as an assumed right by a single leader of that cult. Subsequent reports based on the results of autopsies reveal that there were probably as many or more murders than suicides. It is a totalistic impulse to draw a sharp line between those who have the right to live and those who have no such right. That is a terribly dangerous line. It is true that it occurs in varying degrees, but it becomes dangerous in terms of any resolution of common human problems, and everything on this order involving totalism or fundamentalism takes on a double danger in a nuclear age.

One should of course say that, despite these patterns, none of these processes is air-tight. One of my purposes in writing about them is to counter the frequent trend in the culture to deny that such things exist, and also, at the same time, to demystify them, to see them as understandable in terms of what we can say about human behavior.

HISTORICAL DIMENSION

I want to stress the enormous significance of what I call historical or psycho-historical dislocation occurring in contemporary life. This involves the absence or partial loss of the symbolic structures that have tended to organize the life cycle and around which one has developed one's belief systems—whether it be concerning religion or authority, family, rituals of death, or transitions in the life cycle. Many of these symbolizations have lost their power, and they often become burdensome for many of us. In that sense, the cults provide substitute symbols that have intensity and meaning for many young people. When one talks about totalism, one can never take it out of history. One has to relate it to and examine it within an historical context. I would stress in this historical spirit that many of the cults are both radical and reactionary. They are radical in that they raise rude issues about middle-class family life and other undercriticized values in American life. Issues of liberalism, pluralism, and materialism are raised. In that sense, they do represent some continuity with movements of the '60s and early '70s. There is a radicalism that is perceived, and this accounts for part of their appeal for young people, and part, although not all, of the resistance to cults exhibited by many others. The cults also tend to be reactionary in the sense of returning to pre-modern structures of authority and sometimes going so far that they are accused (I think legitimately) of setting up an internal fascism in their authority structure. And their distrust of autonomy and self-definition is really reactionary in the sense that they condemn, violate, and reject a part of Western history that has with great struggle, pain, and conflict evolved from the time of the Renaissance regarding those very principles of autonomy and self-definition. Again, I emphasize that one has to look at each cult situation if one is to evaluate these tendencies fairly.

Another historical idea I would suggest is in tandem with what I wrote about in the late '60s and early '70s. I described a pattern of psychological experimentation in the young that I called the "protean style" after the famous Greek god Proteus who came out of the sea and was notorious for being able to shift into any form of human, animal, or natural shape: fire, flood, whatever. His difficulty was holding onto one shape and to fulfill his assigned task, that of prophecy, he had to be seized and chained. The protean style was very vivid and manifest in the late '60s and early '70s. It involves psychological experimentation with the self, and the capacity to undergo a series of relatively easy shifts of ideas, people, and ways of life—changing from one to another, and sometimes accepting multiple and seemingly contradictory images at the same time. These shifts take place with relatively less psychological consequences today than would have occurred a hundred or two hundred years ago. The protean style has been so prevalent today because it is itself a product of historical dislocation. Several major historical influences have affected or created this dislocation: one that has not been appreciated sufficiently, but which is important for the whole cult phenomenon, is the mass media revolution. This is a major influence and it makes every image and the possibility to associate with every image of the entire 2,000 years of human history available to almost everyone at any moment. I am exaggerating slightly, but everything, at least in image terms, is possible.

The constricted style which the cults embody in many ways is the fleeing from experimentation, often on the part of the same young people. This is the desire for a straight and narrow psychological process in life, partly to escape the confusion of our protean world with its multiple images always battering away at us. The constricted style would seem to be the very opposite of the protean style, but they are two sides of the same coin—both products of an historical moment and of dislocation with great confusion and conflict over what our sense of self should be. One could see the change in actual behavior, for instance, in the shift from the so-called hippie ethos of the '60s and '70s regarding work and its meaninglessness to the present seeming race on the part of many people for a safe job haven. It is partly of course our economic situation under our distinguished present leadership but everybody wanting to be a lawyer or a doctor also has to do with the constricted style which relates to cult formation. For some people, experimentation with the cults is part of the protean search. They go in, try it, experience something, may like some of it and not other parts of it, and leave. Sometimes it is not so easy to leave, and converts are often in great conflict about leaving. The conflict is there over whether, how much, and in what way one wants, or does not want, to extricate oneself, along with the pressures that are applied to persuade one to stay.

A third historical force, of the greatest importance, is the influence of nuclear weapons, and what I call the "imagery of extinction"—the sense we have, at least since the end of World War II, that we are capable of eliminating ourselves as a species with our own technology. This is a central concern of mine, one which I could discuss at length, but I will just suggest a few ways of thinking about the relationship between our imagery of extinction and cult formation. A simple way of approaching this is to look at the history of fundamentalism in the Protestant movement, and the relationship between *fundamentals* and *fundamentalism.*

Fundamentalism in this country was developed in the early twentieth century out of the fear of losing the fundamental beliefs of Christianity. But under duress the protection of fundamentals can give way to a more narrow dogmatic fundamentalism which becomes totalistic—and which the embrace of fundamentals certainly need not be. It is rather like the difference between tradition and traditionalism, in religious terms; the model can be applied generally. With the threat of nuclear weapons, the fundamentals in all our lives are part of that potential extinction. And there is, consequently, a greater susceptibility to fundamentalist formations of a political or a religious kind and an embrace of fundamentalism because of our fear of losing these fundamentals.

To consider the significance of imagery of extinction, we need a model that not only includes immediate everyday experience but also takes into account our broader human consciousness—what theologian Paul Tillich has called "ultimate concern." By looking at ways in which we symbolize life and death, we can get closer to these issues. In my psychological thinking, I use a paradigm that moves away from the Freudian model of instinct and defense and focuses on the symbolization of life and death or death and the continuity of life. Over the years I have applied this paradigm to standard psychiatric syndromes as well as to such larger historical questions as cult formation, fundamentalism, and the nuclear weapons problem. In this paradigm, there is an ultimate dimension involving the individual's broader human ties as well as a proximate level of behavior that we are accustomed to looking at in psychological terms. Death equivalents are associated with the proximate area and are developed even prior to our knowledge of death. The death equivalents are separation, the fear of disintegration, and stasis. These are experienced from birth—first as feeling, later as image, and then finally as a symbolized process. These negative poles—separation, disintegration, and stasis—become the precursors of the idea of death, an idea that appears at the earliest in the second or third year of life. By the ultimate area I mean the sense we require in a normative way of feeling connected to those who have gone before and those who will presumably go on after our own limited life span. This symbolization of historical and biological connectedness, or "symbolization of immortality," as I call it, is necessary to a scientific psychology, even though to date it has been mainly the concern of theologians and philosophers.

The symbolization of immortality can be expressed in five modes. We have a sense of living on in our children and their children; through our works; through our human influences, be they humble or great; through eternal nature; and through the theological mode or through the direct experience of transcendence. All of these are in considerable doubt in our culture today, given our imagery of extinction—mostly from nuclear weapons which represent a potential break in the great chain of being and cause us to doubt the probability of our still being links in that chain. One can hear these doubts in talking to people—people from all strata of the society. We are living in an age of impaired capacity to imagine a human future. This is apparent in the workshops I have held with adolescents and in the more systematic questionnaire studies, especially those conducted by John Mack. The adolescents studied do not necessarily expect to live out their lives. They have doubts about the future. As one fourteen- or fifteen-year-old girl put it, "I just feel we're doomed." And others went on to say "It isn't fair. It gets me mad that these men hold our lives in their hands. They don't know what they're doing." And "They're just like a bunch of kids, a bunch of kids who are trying to see who's got the biggest bomb." So the adolescents are fairly clear on their psychological interpretation. They are not too far from the truth, for who can be certain of any of these symbolizations of immortality, symbolizations of a human future?

This being so, I think there is increasing reliance, to the point of desperation, on the fifth mode of symbolic immortality, a direct experience of transcendence, which is the classical mode of the mystics—"experiential transcendence" as I call it. We see this expressed in the drug revolution in this country, in the seeking of altered states of consciousness, and in many forms of endeavor. This experience has been traditionally provided for in most cultures but is exaggeratedly denied in post-industrial cultures, such as ours. And there is more need for it all the time, even through humble everyday expressions such as the sex experience or athletics, the experience of beauty, dance, or song. There are many avenues to the experience of transcendence that are of the greatest importance because they are the necessary mediators between us and any of the larger forms of connectedness.

One of the most significant functions of cults is the providing of a kind of initiation rite, a group process or community, at a time when one is in early adult life, as is the case of most cult recruits. Such a process fills the need for ritual and symbolic structures not provided by the larger culture. Attempts by the larger culture to provide this are seen as hypocritical or confused, and often for good reason. The cults also provide the experience of "high" or transcendent states, and these are described with great intensity by those who have been involved with cults. These high states are, I believe, connected with what I have been describing—since cults reflect both an increased hunger for them in our culture, as well as the doubt about other forms of connection or symbolization of human connectedness. They are particularly important to young people and to the working out of adolescent and young adult struggles. The cults can be a psychologically attractive medium for the process by which young people move the individual to the historical dimension, as they form an adult identity and become associated with various forms of idea structures or ideologies.

From my perspective, then, cults are not primarily a psychiatric problem. They are a social and historical issue. Of course they raise psychological concerns of great importance and there is a place for psychologists and psychiatrists in understanding these processes, as I have tried to do, in certain limited ways—and in treating people when they need it. I think that the psychological professionals can do the most good in the area of education. I myself feel critical of much of the totalistic inclination in many cults, but I don't think that pattern is best addressed legally. It is best addressed educationally. There have been repercussions already from increased knowledge about cults. That is one reason why the cults have increasing difficulty, in some cases, obtaining members. At least the elements of deception are less easy to maintain and perhaps less present. And there can be more of a personal decision, in many cases, in entering cults. Education about what they are is of great importance and, of course, that education should be as accurate as possible.

Still, not all moral questions are soluble legally or psychiatrically, nor should they be. I think psychiatrists and theologians have in common the need for a certain restraint here, to avoid playing God, and to refuse the notion that we have anything like a complete solution that comes from our points of view or our particular disciplines. When helping a young person confused about a cult situation, at whatever level he or she may be involved in it, it is very important to maintain a genuine personal therapeutic contract so that one is not working for the cult or for the parents. There is the issue that totalism begets totalism—and people talk about the totalism in so-called deprogramming, a process that also seems to have a continuum from intense dialogue to coercive measures (as in kidnapping and keeping people in motel rooms and so on). My own position, which I have stated many times and have conveyed to parents and others who have consulted me, is that I am against coercion at either end. But I think one should see the patterns of totalism inspiring totalism. I can understand the impulse of the parent whose youngster has been made into a zombie-like person. It does not mean that people in all cults become like zombies, but I have seen people in an intense cult situation who are zombie-like—somewhat mute, acting by rote, and expressing themselves in clichés. It is a real moral question of what right one has to interfere with that process. Still I can understand the temptation of a parent to try to interfere with that process. But I cannot condone, in my own morality, the use of coercion or violence.

I will close with some words of ancient Chinese Taoist wisdom. I used them at the end of my original book; they seem relevant here as well. "Only simple and quiet things will ripen of themselves, for a whirlwind does not last the whole morning. Nor does the thundershower last the whole day. Who is their author, the heaven and earth, and even they cannot make such violent things last. How much more true this must be of the rash endeavors of men."

NOTES

/1/   Robert Jay Lifton, *Thought Reform and the Psychology of Totalism. A Study of "Brainwashing" in China* (New York: W. W. Norton & Co., 1961).

/2/   I don't use the word "brainwashing" because it has no precise meaning. One difficulty in some of the writings of Thomas Szasz and others is the assumption that if there is no such thing as brainwashing (strictly speaking, it doesn't mean anything and has had all sorts of misuse and abuse), then there is no such thing as a systematic coercive effort that can be identified to change people. Nor is the identification of that kind of systematic effort, which I call thought reform or ideological totalism, itself illegal. There are several levels of discourse here that one has to keep in mind.

NEW RELIGIONS AND "DEPROGRAMMING": WHO'S BRAINWASHING WHOM?

Lee Coleman

Disapproving parents, in order to justify the forcible removal of their adult son or daughter from a religion they do not like, frequently claim that the young religious convert has been brainwashed. The use of force is justified, it is claimed, because the person's independent thinking has already been stolen by the mind-control techniques of the "cult."/1/

Such an argument could not long sustain itself without the backing of "expert" opinion from mental health professionals. This is because more and more people now recognize that terms like "brainwashing" can be used to invalidate any unpopular idea or activity. (Civil rights advocates, for example, were accused by white southerners in the early 1960s of being brainwashed by northern liberals.) The "anti-cult" movement has indeed been able to gather around it a small but vocal group of mental health professionals who regularly claim—before courts, professional meetings, and the media—to have found evidence of such "mind-control."/2/

This discussion will focus on one particular source of such alleged academic support, namely psychiatrist Robert Lifton's book *Thought Reform and the Psychology of Totalism*./3/ Despite the fact that Lifton in his book is clearly critical of the use of force and total environmental control to change coercively a person's opinion, *Thought Reform* is being used to justify precisely this kind of force and control. In other words, those who call themselves "deprogrammers"/4/ and use *Thought Reform* supposedly to back up their claim that "cults" use "brainwashing," "mind control," or "coercive persuasion," are themselves guilty of employing the very tactics so well described and criticized in Dr. Lifton's book.

Lifton tells us, in Chapter 22, that he wants to consider "the psychology of human zealotry," and he offers a set of criteria against which any environment may be judged—a basis for answering the ever-recurring question: Isn't this just like "brainwashing"? It is this chapter which has been frequently used by "deprogrammers" to argue that "cults" are employing "mind-control." Let us look more closely at this chapter. I will argue that the activities of the kidnappers ("deprogrammers") bear far more resemblance to "brainwashing" than do those of new religious movements.

MILIEU CONTROL

"The most basic feature of thought reform environment," Lifton writes, "is the control of human communication." Such control is clearly most intense when the individual cannot escape from the continuing influence of the controllers, i.e., when he is a prisoner./5/ Who, then, is more guilty of the "milieu control" described by Lifton as the "most basic feature" of coercive thought reform?

Religious recruits may be subjected to intense pressure to adopt a new world view. They are, however, not held as physical captives or prisoners. The clearest proof of this is that even the "anti-cult" movement alleges that the mind, not the body, is being imprisoned. Take, for example, a lawsuit currently being filed against the Unification Church. "False imprisonment" is claimed, yet under oath (deposition testimony) the plaintiffs had to admit that no one ever constrained them from leaving.

"Deprogramming," on the other hand, involves—by definition—the use of imprisonment, followed by a continuous barrage of pressure to renounce one's current activities. Overt physical violence is required to initially carry off the person, and there is always enough "muscle" present to maintain the lockup. Anyone doubting the potential for great bodily harm which is associated with such activities should read the unabashed accounts in Ted Patrick's book *Let Our Children Go.*/6/

MYSTICAL MANIPULATION

Lifton is talking here about "extensive personal manipulation" of a "no-holds-barred character." The totalist feels he has a "higher purpose" which gives him the right to go to extremes, even if such activities "supercede all considerations of decency or of immediate human welfare."

While it is understandable that parents of young adults might feel, with some justification, that their sons and daughters have been the victims of manipulation by the religion, it seems obvious that with "deprogramming" such manipulation is vastly greater because physical confinement is used.

While the recruit to a new (or old) religion may be subject to guilt-inducing pressures if he considers leaving the movement, the kidnapped and imprisoned victims of "deprogramming" *cannot* leave. A favorite tactic of Ted Patrick and his proteges is, in fact, to tell the person he will be held *as long as necessary* until he renounces his faith and his church.

Lifton discusses the "psychology of the pawn" in which the captive, "feeling himself unable to escape from forces more powerful than himself . . . subordinates everything to adapting himself to them. . . . This requires that he participate actively in the manipulation of others, as well as in the endless round of betrayals and self-betrayals which are required. . . ." Once again, Lifton's incisive words fit the situation of the imprisoned victim of "deprogramming" far more closely than that of a religious recruit. Held in a motel room or perhaps the parents' home, the person is made to feel exquisitely guilty. He is made to feel that his current activities are a rejection of parents and family. In fact, the person may have no such hostile feelings towards his family, but in the setting of a "deprogramming," only outright rejection of the "cult" will satisfy the family and their hired helpers.

Another element of the manipulation of the person is the encouragement to deny responsibility for his choices. If only he will acknowledge that he is brainwashed and did not truly choose—by his own free will—to join the "cult," all will be forgiven. All family resentment will then be focused on the "cult," which is solely responsible for any disapproved behavior. This is too tempting for some persons to resist, and it is from such persons that the anti-cult movement recruits its crusading members.

At this point it is well to remember that during the Salem witch hunts, under the pressure of interrogation, many women accused of being witches finally broke down and "admitted" that they indeed were witches. Some even admitted to having fornicated with the devil./7/

Claims of "brainwashing" by some former members of new religions should, in other words, not be considered "neutral." Studies have shown that while many persons freely leave new religious movements because they no longer desire to continue, it is only those subjected to forced deindoctrination who speak of "brainwashing" or "mind-control."/8/ Such persons have indeed succumbed to Lifton's "mystical manipulation" at the hands of parents and their allies.

THE DEMAND FOR PURITY

For those who practice ideological totalism, the world, Lifton writes, "is sharply divided into the pure and the unpure, into the absolutely good and the absolutely evil." As a result, "anything done to anyone in the name of this purity is ultimately moral." Hostile parents and their allies repeatedly have raised charges that "cults" are regularly guilty of deception, fraud, and a host of other illegal activities, because, it is claimed, the "cult" feels it possesses such a higher mission. Such charges, to be taken seriously, should be directed not at "cults" but at a specific group, backed up by specific factual proof. While in some instances such facts have been forthcoming, it has been the very lack of such proof which has forced the anti-cult movement to rely so heavily on the allegations of "mind control."

"Deprogramming," however, is unmistakably an example of the end justifying the means. Crimes (kidnapping and false imprisonment) are committed and then justified as necessary in order to "rescue" the brainwashed convert. I maintain that persons engaging in or condoning such criminal behavior have no solid moral platform on which to make their allegations against new religious movements. They must first renounce their own vigilante tactics.

Lifton has given a brilliant description of another aspect of what may happen to a person subjected to such totalism. He writes:

> The individual thus comes to apply to the same totalist polariza-
> tion of good and evil to his judgments of his own character. . . .
> He must also look upon his impurities as originating from outside
> influences. . . . Therefore, one of his best ways to relieve himself
> of some of his burden of guilt is to denounce, continuously and
> hostilely, these same outside influences. The more guilty he feels,
> the greater his hatred, and the more threatening they seem.

> Such feelings, Lifton aptly warns, encourage 'mass hatreds,'
> purges of heretics, and 'political and religious holy wars.'

> Is this what happens to Unificationists, Scientologists, and
> Hare Krishnas? From what I have seen—and I have known hun-
> dreds of Scientologists and dozens of practicing Unificationists—
> such hatred has not been present, either for their family or others
> outside the church.

> What Lifton's perceptive analysis does seem to describe with
> remarkable accuracy is the attitudes, statements and tactics of
> those ex-members who have, after being subjected to a period of
> ideological totalism (deprogramming), joined the ranks of the
> anti-cult movement. They are now considered experts who "have
> been there." Back in the arms of Mom and Dad, freed of all
> responsibility for whatever choices they made, they are ready to
> further legitimize their new stance by attacking others who have
> strayed from the path of purity./9/

THE CULT OF CONFESSION

Ideological totalists require, Lifton tells us, that the person being indoctrinated "confess crimes one has not committed, to sinfulness that is artificially induced, in the name of a cure that is artificially imposed." While it is quite apparent that many religions, both old and new, include confession as an important ritual, the totalistic type of confession described by Lifton fits remarkably well with the statements and demeanor of those ex-members who have been forcefully de-indoctrinated and then success-fully recruited into the anti-cult movement. Such persons, once their will to resist has been broken, may then "confess" not only that they were brain-washed but that they brainwashed others in the now-hated religion.

As Lifton says, "The sharing of confession enthusiasms can create an orgiastic sense of oneness, of the most intense intimacy with fellow confes-sors and of the dissolution of self into the great flow of the movement. . . ." In their enthusiasm to discredit their former churches, and vindicate them-selves before their families, ex-members joining the ranks of anti-cultists have, unfortunately, contributed massively to the wave of religious bigotry which is now growing in the United States and elsewhere.

Sociologists Anson Shupe and David Bromley have captured the essence of the pressures which lead some victims of "deprogramming" to manufacture "atrocity stories." Shupe and Bromley write:

> . . . to admit that they had made a mistake and to declare no fur-
> ther interest in the given movement was not enough. Consider that
> the parents had been humiliated by the offspring's often hostile and
> sometimes thorough rejection of parents' lifestyle and goals in the
> time preceding deprogramming as well as at least during the initial
> phases of the deprogramming itself. Consider the often substantial
> fees paid for deprogramming and the trouble to arrange it. Con-
> sider also the possible risk of civil and even of criminal prosecution
> that all—parents and deprogrammers alike—faced. These factors
> dictated that the price of re-entry into conventional society had
> now risen, and only public admission of having been brainwashed
> as well as testimony about other allegations of heinous cult outrages
> would suffice to pay for it. Thus, public contrition for having aban-
> doned parental values became the cost of re-admission into the
> mainstream community./10/

THE "SACRED SCIENCE"

Here Lifton is talking about the way that ideological totalists transform their opinions into "scientific truths." Because the totalist is so sure
his beliefs are more "correct" that those of the person requiring reform,
he feels justified in using force to make the person "see the light."

If we ask once again who is more guilty of such thinking—the religions currently being attacked or those who promote what theologian
Dean Kelly has called the "spiritual gang rape" of deprogramming—the
answer is clear. All religions teach that they have found the best way to
the moral life, but none that I know of—including the currently
attacked religions like the Unification Church or Scientology—are guilty
of the degrading tactics of the anti-cult movement. So sure are they of
their moral "correctness" that anti-cultists are quite willing not only to
imprison a religious convert but also to defile his religion.

Take, for example, the lurid examples which fill the pages of the
deprogrammer's bible, *Let Our Children Go*, by Ted Patrick. After
Hare Krishna Ed Shapiro was imprisoned in his parents' home, Patrick
described what happened next.

> 'Get me a pair of scissors,' I said.
> 'Scissors? What for?'
> 'First thing we're going to do is cut that knot of hair off his
> head.'
> 'What? Who are you? What right do you have to go cutting
> my hair? I have a right to wear this. It's part of my religion. I'm
> a legal adult. I'm twenty years old.'
> 'Shut up and sit down, just shut your mouth and listen.'

'I won't listen. I don't have to listen. I want to leave.'
'Well, you're not going to leave. Where's the scissors?'

Patrick then says, "Four of his relatives held him down and I cut off the tuft of hair they all wear on the back of their heads and I removed the beads from around his neck." Ed reacted by smashing whatever objects he could lay his hands on. Next, Patrick says,

> I took him by the arms and flung him into a corner up against the wall, and I said, 'All right, you hatchet-head son of a bitch, you move out of there and I'll knock your goddamned head off!'. . . I had a picture of Prabhupad and I tore it up in front of him and said, 'There's the no-good son of a bitch you worship. And you call him God!'

Such tactics are, Patrick assures us, "the usual line of approach."

LOADING THE LANGUAGE

The anti-cult movement, particularly a small but vocal cadre of mental health professionals, has repeatedly leveled the charge that the "dangerous cults" are guilty of what Lifton called "loading the language." Lifton writes, "The language of the totalist environment is characterized by thought-terminating cliché. The most far-reaching and complex of human problems are compressed into brief, highly reductive, definitive-sounding phrases." "No compunctions," Lifton continues "are felt about manipulating or loading it in any fashion; the only consideration is its usefulness to the cause."

Are the new (and old) religions under attack using language in a reductionistic fashion? Of course they are. As Lifton points out, "this kind of language exists to some degree within any cultural or organizational group, and all systems of belief depend upon it. It is in part an expression of unity and exclusiveness."

But if we wish to see "loading the language" at work in the totalistic way that Lifton is describing, it is the anti-cult movement itself which has developed a vocabulary of deception of remarkable proportion. This has been necessary for one main reason—overt criminal activity had to be rationalized and justified.

Thus, a kidnapping, frequently requiring violent bodily force, becomes a "rescue." The coercion, intimidation, and indefinite confinement which follows becomes a "deprogramming." This bit of linguistic fraud simultaneously implies that the person is a mindless victim of "programming" (robot, zombie) while it diverts attention from the illegal activity taking place.

Adult citizens, clearly of majority age, become "children," as in *Let Our Children Go*. This legitimizes the use of force by parents and their allies and also further implies that the religious recruit is a helpless victim of deception who requires protection.

This list of such manipulative buzz-words is long, but one more will suffice. The very use of the word "cult" is the most obvious example of loading the language. Rather than criticizing each religion as a separate entity, something which requires hard facts, the use of the word "cult" allows all groups under attack to be lumped together. This, of course, is an old strategy of bigotry. Words like "nigger," "kike," "wop," and "greaser" serve a similar purpose. What is remarkable, however, is the ease with which the "anti-cult" movement has been able to inject such loaded words into the vocabularies of otherwise well-meaning persons.

DOCTRINE OVER PERSON

Ideological totalism, Lifton points out here, insists on "the subordination of human experiences to the claims of doctrine." "When the myth becomes fused with the totalist sacred science," Lifton continues, "the resulting logic can be so compelling and coercive that it simply replaces the realities of individual experience. Consequently, past historical events are retrospectively altered, wholly rewritten, or ignored to make them consistent with the doctrinal logic."

To the extent that the theology of any religion requires acts of faith, such faith requires that official versions of truth be accepted, even if this deviates from "the realities of individual experience." This, however, does not amount to ideological totalism because the individual is free to accept or reject such faith.

But when, as in "deprogramming," force is used to intimidate a person into giving up his religious ideas and practices and adopting a new kind of dogma, "doctrine over person" is clearly at work. There is, indeed (quoting Lifton), "the demand that character and identity be reshaped, not in accordance with one's special nature or potentialities, but rather to fit the rigid contours of the doctrinal mold."

Here is a typical way anti-cult tactics may "rewrite" family history. A person who was not particularly close to his family joins an unpopular religion. Becoming concerned, the family tries to initiate far more contact than previously, but it is contact of a very negative sort. Charges of "brainwashing" begin to fill the air, and the person is degraded by being told that he has lost control of his mind. When the person then shuns such contact, the family then portrays their past relationship as an ideal one which was only destroyed by deliberate cult manipulations. The family's own invalidation of the person's choices is completely ignored. And finally, hostility generated towards family because of an actual or threatened kidnapping is laid at the feet of the "cult."/11/

Totalists, it seems, can do no wrong. With their doctrine that "kids" are being "rescued" from "destructive cults" which practice "mind control," they seem quite capable of denying the fundamental insults they are hurling at their own sons and daughters.

THE DISPENSING OF EXISTENCE

Ideological totalists feel so sure of the rightness of their position that they may seek to deny the very right to existence of those whom they see as "destructive." "Totalists thus feel themselves," Lifton states, "compelled to destroy all possibilities of false existence as a means of furthering the great plan of true existence to which they are committed."

Do the new religions seek to deny the very existence of other, more traditional religions? I have seen no evidence of such an attitude in either Scientologists or Unificationists.

Do, on the other hand, anti-cultists seek to destroy all churches they consider "dangerous cults"? They do indeed. Not satisfied with kidnapping individual members or seeking conservatorships based on flimsy allegations of "sudden personality change," the anti-cult movement has repeatedly vowed to destroy these religions outright. They are convinced, as true ideological totalists, that what they find unacceptable should cease to be, even if the traditions and laws of a free and open society must be violated in the process.

CONCLUSION

Despite the clear evidence that the anti-cult movement's use of Lifton's *Thought Reform* is fraudulent, and that it is they who are guilty of ideological totalism, this in no way guarantees that our society will see through the deception. It is up to the rest of us, having penetrated the deception, to educate others about the simple facts about who is and who is not guilty of using force to promote orthodoxy. For this we need no locked doors, no attacks on personal belief, and no denials of Constitutional freedoms. If bigotry triumphs, as it did in Nazi Germany and could here, too, it will be because not enough of us thought clearly and spoke out courageously.

NOTES

/1/   The author considers the word "cult" to be highly derogatory and will only use the term in the context of its use by parties hostile to certain religions.

/2/   For an expert opinion of this phenomenon, and a valuable critique of such "expert" opinions from mental health professionals, see Thomas Robbins and Dick Anthony, "Cults vs. 'Shrinks'" in *New Religions and Mental Health*, ed. Herbert Richardson (New York: Edward Mellen Press, 1980). For examples of articles highly critical of "cults," see John Clark, 242 *Journal of the American Medical Association*, 179–81 (1979), and Margaret Singer, "Coming Out of the Cults," *Psychology Today*, January 1979, 72–82.

/3/   Robert Jay Lifton, *Thought Reform and the Psychology of Totalism. A Study of "Brainwashing" in China* (New York: W. W. Norton & Co., 1961).

/4/ Just as with "cult," I will use the word "deprogramming" only to demonstrate its basically fraudulent nature.

/5/ The other major work on "brainwashing" is Edgar Schein's *Coercive Persuasion. A Socio-Psychological Analysis of the "Brainwashing" of American Civilian Prisoners by the Chinese Communists* (New York: W. W. Norton & Co., 1961). As much as Lifton, Schein stresses that physical confinement or captivity is an essential ingredient of "coercive persuasion." Schein writes of the persons studied: "they were subjected to unusually intense and prolonged persuasion in a situation from which they could not escape; that is, they were coerced into allowing themselves to be persuaded" (18). Generalizing from these studies of American POWs in Korea, he states that coercive persuasion is "applicable to all instances of persuasion or influence in which the person is constrained by physical, social or psychological force from leaving the influencing situation" (269). It seems obvious that the greater the constraint, the more that "coercive persuasion" is taking place.

/6/ Ted Patrick with Tom Dulack, *Let Our Children Go* (New York: Ballantine Books, 1976).

/7/ Take, for example, the confession of Abigail Hobbes, accused during the witch hunts in Salem, Massachusetts. Chadwick Hanson, in *Witchcraft in Salem* (New York: Mentor Books, 1969), writes, "When Lydia Nichols had asked her 'how she durst lie out of nights in the woods alone,' she replied that 'she was not afraid of anything, for . . . she had sold herself body and soul to the Old Boy [devil]'" (94).

/8/ See, for example, T. Solomon, "Integrating the 'Moonie' Experience: A Survey of Ex-Members of the Unification Church," in *In Gods We Trust: New Patterns of Religious Pluralism in America,* ed. Thomas Robbins and Dick Anthony (New Brunswick, NJ: Transaction Books, 1981). Solomon writes that "contact with the anticult movement influences the degree to which one relies on explanations of brainwashing and mind control to account for attraction to and membership in the church" (288).

/9/ As Solomon writes in "Integrating the 'Moonie' Experience," persons forcibly removed "will often arise from the ashes with new-found friends (other ex-members), a rejuvenated parent-child relationship, perhaps a new avocation (deprogramming) and definitely a new reference group and *cause célèbre*—the anti-cult movement" (293).

/10/ Anson Shupe and David Bromley, "Apostates and Atrocity Stories: Some Parameters in the Dynamics of Deprogramming," in *The Social Impact of New Religious Movements* (New York: Rose of Sharon Press, 1981), 195.

/11/ I have personally talked with several members of new religious movements who have described such a course of events. In one case, the father sued the church, claiming that it was not his incessant charges of "brainwashing" which finally forced his daughter to withdraw from him but instead the "mind control" techniques of the church.

COERCION, COERCIVE PERSUASION, AND THE LAW

Herbert Fingarette

I must begin with a few words about the perspective from which the following analyses are relevant to the topic of coercive persuasion in the context of the new religions. I have not done detailed research in connection with the new religions or the concept, specifically, of "coercive persuasion," though I read generally in the field with the intent of getting more involved in the study of these topics. However, I do feel I can bring something positive and specific to thought about the topic. This is because for a number of years my research has covered the area of mental disability, especially in the context of law, and most especially in connection with the criminal law and criminal responsibility. Specifically, I have worked on such topics as criminal insanity, diminished capacity, intoxication, addictions, and on other related notions that one runs across in the law, such as automation, unconsciousness, and involuntariness. Obviously these questions of mental disability and legal responsibility are also closely related to what falls under the rubric of "coercive persuasion."

Moreover, I have more recently been working on the theory of excuses in the law, most specifically on the notions of coercion, duress, compulsion, and undue influence. These are not merely criminal law concepts but are used in a wide variety of legal contexts. And when one thinks of the ways in which people try to importune, plead, deceive, dominate, tyrannize, and otherwise control, coerce, or influence "unduly" other people's minds and actions, then it is evident that all this, too, has close connection with the sorts of thinking that are going on in the area of controversy about "coercive persuasion" in the new religions context, as well as in war prisoner and political indoctrination contexts.

So I thought that I could bring out how the notion of "coercive persuasion" looks to me, as I stand off in the mid-distance, viewing it as a topic still to be explored, balancing what I may lose because of my naïveté about the detail against the fact that I come at it fresh, as an informed outsider, so to speak. Therefore, I shall not try to present a thesis on the topic which is very sharp and precise, but rather to develop an angle of vision on the *legal* aspects of the matter that I think might be usefully suggestive—no more than that, but I hope no less.

First of all, one might ask, what does "coercion" mean in the law?

The answer is that there are various legal tests; they differ, depending on the legal context. The doctrines and the theories relating to coercion are not very clear; there are not only controversies about how to define it but also about the rationale justifying the various legal uses of the notion.

There is, however, a common theme, a thread that runs through all legal definitions, explanations, or accounts of what constitutes coercion and, for that matter, undue influence as well. It is the idea that in coercion the victim's "will" is "overthrown," or "overcome," or "overborne," or "destroyed," or "neutralized," or "subverted"—or something of the kind. The exact language varies but no matter the specific legal context, one finds a constant refrain expressed in some recognizable variant of this idiom: the victim's will was overcome. And that also seems to be the sort of thing that is at issue when there are allegations of coercive persuasion, or brainwashing, or thought reform. In some way, you overcome or destroy or subvert the will of the person. In all these usages, it is implied that the will is not just overcome but is then also dominated by the person who is doing this. So that the victim then becomes a kind of agent, a tool, an extension of the will, of the coercer.

Therefore, in order to bring out the significance of this idiomatic language in law, I want now to run through some of the more specific legal uses of the notion of coercion, and examine these in relation to this basic idiom of the overcoming and dominating of the will. I want to replace metaphor and idiom with a more analytical account.

Let me say at once that while the words, the idiom, the metaphors suggest that the law is here concerned with some kind of profound, perhaps traumatic, psychological event in the mind of the victim, I aim to show that the psychology of the matter is not of the legal essence at all. Even though it appears that the essence of coercion consists in some stimulus that has produced a catastrophic, or at least a very serious, breakdown in the psyche of the victim, and that therefore in order to legally identify instances of coercion, one would have to delve into the psychology of the victim, this seemingly trivially obvious conclusion is radically wrong. Or at least so I hope to show in what follows.

Let me begin by taking up first what is perhaps the most readily thinkable kind of coercion, the gun-at-the-head situation. The gun-at-the-head situation no doubt typically includes some kind of psychological turmoil or even mental trauma in the victim. But one thing that we can immediately emphasize is that the notion of a mental breakdown, a *destruction* of the will, is inappropriate even in this extreme case. The point can be made in a very strong way: it is not only that there need not be a breakdown or that in certain cases there is not such, but that there could not be coercion if there were a mental breakdown of some major sort. What is necessary for coercion is that the victims keep their wits about them, that they pay attention to what the coercer says and act promptly and rationally to obey. Coercion breaks down if the person panics or loses control, if the mind breaks down in its functioning in some way.

If there is no traumatic breakdown in coercion with a gun at the head, what is it that constitutes the "overcoming of the will"? I will quickly run through some of the logical possibilities—even some that are obviously not appropriate for practical purposes—to see if the precise meaning of the "overcome will" can be captured.

One thing that we might mean is that there is no will at all. If something like that *were* the case, then even if the victim committed an unlawful act, the legal implication would in general be that the coerced person would be excusable. For if there is no will, the act cannot be voluntary, and involuntariness is typically a defense in law. But absence of any will at all is obviously not what is at issue here. It does not fit the facts of coercion. An absence of will would exist, for example, in the behavior of someone in an epileptic fit, or in the behavior of someone tripping and falling. And that obviously is not at all the kind of thing factually at issue in the case of coercion. So when we say the will is overcome, we do not mean that the person acts without will.

We might try to go right to the nub of the matter and say that by "overcome will" the law simply means "involuntary." Of course, as we have just seen, we could not mean "involuntary" in the sense that there is *no* will. Then, in what sense can one who acts *with* will be acting *in*voluntarily?

One possibility that comes to mind in the legal context is that there is some kind of mistake or ignorance. If a person was ignorant or mistaken about some fact material to an offense that the person committed, so that in the person's eyes the act did not constitute an offense, then the offending act may be spoken of in law as involuntary. It was not done intentionally or knowingly, hence not voluntarily. This would be an excuse in many legal contexts. But, again, it is obviously not what is at issue in the case of coercion. In coercion we are not dealing with conduct based on mistake or ignorance.

Another thing one might mean in law when one speaks of involuntary behavior is that the person is in some sense irrational. Sometimes the courts do speak of irrational behavior, for example, insane behavior, as involuntary. Of course insanity is an excuse. But irrationality, whether in the form of insanity or any other legally recognized form, obviously does not fit the facts of the coercion case. As noted earlier, coerced behavior in the gun-at-the-head situation is not irrational behavior; quite on the contrary, it is necessarily rational behavior.

Perhaps the behavior is involuntary in the sense that the person is acting under some kind of "irresistible impulse." This is another kind of involuntariness that we run across in the law. The existence of an irresistible impulse could indeed provide a legal ground for excuse. So if coerced behavior were such, this would provide a rationale explaining why coercion is a legal excuse. There are difficulties with this approach, however. First of all, the notion of irresistible impulse is for theoretical purposes a very troublesome notion. The problem is well expressed in the old saying: How do we tell the difference between "He could not resist his impulse" and "He did not resist his impulse"? This becomes in practice a very troublesome issue in the law. Typically, when it comes up openly, as in insanity cases, for example, it involves psychiatric testimony. Since there is no theoretical understanding of how to apply the distinction, what happens is that we get the expert testimony as to the facts about the defendant—facts as to which not infrequently there is general agreement—and yet the experts disagree as to whether the impulse, desire, or mood was irresistible or not. This, of course, is a pretty good sign that what we are dealing with here is not a question of fact, but a question of ideological differences among different schools of psychology and psychiatry.

Now, my point here is not simply that this causes trouble in the courts, but that when we deal with coercion defenses, we do not see this kind of trouble arising. Coercion defenses do not generally call for extensive psychiatric testimony, and do not generate the typical problems and confusions of psychiatric testimony. This, to me, is very good evidence that coercion in law does *not* raise an irresistible impulse type of issue, and that therefore the involuntariness of coerced behavior is not to be understood along these lines.

A close cousin to irresistible impulse and legally much more respectable these days is the notion of loss of self-control. If we stipulate that there was loss of control, then indeed we might in law be on our way towards some kind of legal defense based on involuntariness. Does coercion excuse because coercion is loss of self-control? Again we have to remember that in the case of coercion the victim does not—and must not—lose self-control.

I repeat, for purposes of orientation, that what I am doing here is to look for some way of interpreting "involuntary," having moved from "overcome will" to "involuntary" and in doing so in legal terms that would both fit the typical facts of coercion and also provide a legal excuse. For the object here is to understand what is at issue in law when the notion of coercion is used and to understand it in terms less metaphorical and vague that the idiom of the "overcome will."

An approach to getting at the meaning of coercion is the saying that when there is coercion the victim has "no real choice." Variants of this are that the victim had "no free choice," or had "no fair choice." As far as "free choice" goes, the problem is that this is a phrase that is probably more problematic than the one we want to explain, i.e., "coercion." Certainly the notion of "coercion" and "unfree" are not equivalent. Thus, one can be not free to make a choice and yet not have been coerced: for example, I am not free to talk Swahili, but for reasons that have nothing to do with coercion. Moreover, it is arguable that one can be coerced and yet be free. One example of this that has been offered is the case where one person threatens a second with some terrible mortal threat, and thus induces the latter to perform an unlawful act—the reality being that the person who made the threat never had any means whatsoever of carrying it out. In such a case, the victim was in reality free to act either way, but acted under coercion. One may be a little troubled as to whether this latter example rests on questionable interpretation or misuse of terms. But that is not important. What is important here is that one finds these examples in the literature, that they do have a certain plausibility, that as soon as one tries to link freedom up with coercion, one finds that, rather than clarifying matters, one has introduced a whole new set of problems and controversies. Therefore, I find the notion of "no free choice" to be unhelpful in clarifying the notions of "involuntariness" and "coercion."

What about the idiom, "no fair choice"? Here, I think, we have something that will be useful, especially with further refinement. If a criminal holds a gun at your head, threatens you, and orders you to help him, then you do not have a fair choice. A way of putting this in legal terms is that the person who coerces you has done something unlawful, something "unfair" in a legally cognizable sense. To characterize the choice as "unfair" suggests that there is a plausible basis for viewing the choice, and hence the act, as in law not voluntary; and this in turn would generally warrant being excused. Not every lack of fair choice need arise out of coercion (it might have been deception, for example), but every case of coercion would be an absence of fair choice—i.e., an *unlawful* threat as the decisive reason for the choice.

But something odd has now happened. The crucial element—the unlawfulness of the coercer's threat—is not within the victim's mind but consists of the legal status of the coercer's act. Instead of matters of psychology, we have to do with legal norms and the acts of others. This changes radically the focus of the legal inquiry from what the phrase "overcome will" initially suggested.

Before pursuing this further, let us turn for still further insight to the last of three possibilities embodying the term "choice": the idea that where there is coercion, there is "no *real* choice." Obviously, this is a highly idiomatic approach. It certainly would not stand if taken literally; the coerced person does have a real choice in the obvious sense that the person could refuse to obey. Most writers on this topic agree that it is appropriate to describe the victim as someone who literally does make a choice. It may well be a deliberate choice, and indeed some people— more brave or more foolish than average—do indeed choose to resist.

Yet, there is plainly a certain appropriateness, idiomatically speaking, if one says, "I didn't really have a choice because he was holding a gun at my head." Our question must be: Can we express plainly and more literally what this idiom tells us?

It has been suggested, I think correctly, that what we are getting at here is the absence of a *reasonable* choice. Generally speaking, there is no reasonable choice if refusal means you immediately get your head blown off. One has the power to resist, but it is typically totally unreasonable to do so. If we allow this analysis of "no real choice" as a first approximation, we could make the transition plausibly from "coercion" to "no real choice," and thence to "not voluntary." The law often must rest on the concept of doing what is reasonable, a close cousin to doing what the "reasonable man" would do.

But, once again, this account in the present context results in a surprising, and even a paradoxical insight. It again turns out that involuntariness is not a matter of some psychic process internal to the mind of the victim; the issue turns on the reasonableness of the choice to be made, a very different sort of issue indeed. We have to do here with the standards or canons of reasonableness, which can be quite objective and which in the legal context are typically taken to be objective.

To sum up the preceding analyses: In the attempt to find out what "overcome will" might mean, as used in the legal context of the coercion defense, the two plausible successes in giving it any sense have turned our attention away from the "inside" of the mind of the victim to something "outside," to standards of law and reasonableness. Other and more psychological uses of "involuntariness" in law turned out to have no application in the factual situation of coercion.

The matter can now be developed more positively by looking directly at the classical legal test used for a coercion defense, rather than by focusing on the vague idiom of the "overcome will." The classic test is quite specific: There has to be a well-grounded or a credible threat of imminent death or serious injury for failure to obey the coercer's demand. And, classically, in English and American law, this will be a defense to any criminal charge except murder. Now it is quite true, as I remarked earlier, that a person who is in a spot like this might very well experience great inner turmoil—not a breakdown, but intense emotion. But we need to ask how essential this is to the existence in law of coercion. Suppose, for example, there is an ex-soldier who is experienced in combat, perhaps temperamentally has a devil-may-care attitude, or in any case for one reason or another is unfrightened and is not going through significant emotional turmoil here even though the threat is genuine. He understands quite well that he is threatened with imminent death if he does not obey, and that there is no escape and so, sensibly enough, he obeys. Certainly he has a coercion defense in law, and this being so, it is clear that such a defense does not rest essentially on any inner breakdown or inner trauma. There is no need to show loss of self-control or irresistible impulse. The earlier suggested analysis does quite well here: the legal test singles out a situation in which the victim is unlawfully deprived of any reasonable choice except to obey. So we have eliminated psychology entirely, and we remain with questions of reasonableness and questions of lawfulness as these are interpreted in legal terms.

Let us now test this approach for its generalizability by turning to coercion in a different area of the law, the area of coerced confessions. In the area of coerced confessions, the legal tests of coercion, and the relevant circumstances, are very different from those where a person has committed a criminal act and is claiming coercion as a defense. Making a confession is not a criminal act at all, so there is no question of coercion as a defense to a criminal charge. Here we have a question of doing something under coercion that is lawful but damaging to one's interests. The claim of coercion is a claim that the confession ought not to be admitted in evidence because it was not voluntary. The classic legal tests here are specific and are adapted to this special type of circumstance. The *Bram* test, which still dominates doctrine in this area, was a late nineteenth century case. In substance, it specifies that if the person confessed because of any kind of threat or promise or any improper influence whatsoever, then the confession was coerced, hence involuntary, hence inadmissable. Here we have the other extreme from the criminal defense, for the criminal defense of coercion requires a mortal threat. When one thinks of that paradigmatic gun-at-the-head situation, it is plausible to think of the "will overcome." But the *Bram* test merely requires any kind of improper influence, no matter how slight. Here it would seem no longer plausible at all to talk about overcoming or destroying the will or subverting the will. And yet, the surprising thing is that the courts use this traditional rhetoric in the confession cases, too.

In the famous *Culombe* case, for example, Justice Frankfurter spoke of a "suction process" at work on Culombe's mind. What were the facts? The police had his wife and children come visit Culombe in the jail, and the police encouraged them to appeal to him to confess. Culombe was a person of low intelligence, but he knew what he was doing. He had consistently refused to confess, but his family talked to him and persuaded him that he ought to confess. So he decided to confess, and did so, giving appropriate reasons, and sticking by his decision. I think Frankfurter's rhetoric about a suction process that drained him of will is not descriptively apt. I would say that what happened was that the police unlawfully created a situation in which it became reasonable in Culombe's judgment to confess. According to the legal test, it needed only to be the slightest bit of additional (improper) influence on one side of the issue, so long as this effectively made the difference in deciding to make the confession.

One can imagine someone whose mind is rather evenly balanced, is unsure but has decided not to confess, and then, by some wrongful device, the police presented a situation where now there is just a little bit more reason to confess rather than not. So the person does confess. This does not at all fit the model suggested by the language of the will overcome, destroyed, neutralized, subverted, the language of powerful psychological influences.

Why, then, do the courts continue to use the dramatic rhetoric of the broken will here? I think the answer is along the following lines. It is quite evident that the evil to be corrected is the improper use of state power by police officers to oppress an individual who is at least temporarily under their influence. Basic constitutional principles of individual liberty and of restraint on state oppression make it appropriate to impose strict constraints on police power here. So even mild impropriety, if it could have any influence on something so important as a confession to crime, is impermissible. Hence the confession may not be used if the police have used such influence. But when the specific concept of "coercion" is used as the key element in the legal rationale, the courts must speak in the ways defined by legal precedent. When confessions were induced by torture, the notion of "coercion" and "overcome will" had plausibility. Nowadays, the "improper influences" are often nothing at all like torture—and so the courts have had to explain away the implausibility by speaking of "subtler" forms of "pressure" or "suction." Thus the necessary legal rhetoric is used, but it has lost its sense. (And indeed, the tendency has recently been to invoke "exclusionary rules" explicitly based on impropriety rather than to argue in terms of "coercion.")

Let me now shift to another, very different area of law, in order to complete my survey and decisively demonstrate my point. I refer to the area of so-called economic or business law, and to the legal notion of "economic coercion." Consider the case of a railroad company subject to a tax which it thinks is unconstitutionally being imposed upon it. The company does not want to pay the tax, but, on the other hand, the tax law has an automatic trigger penalty provision, such that if they do not pay the tax properly and on time, they will in effect be shut down instantly. This would of course be a major economic loss to them. So they pay under protest, and then they sue for redress, for return of the tax money, on the ground that they had paid under coercion. The court agrees that it was an unconstitutionally imposed tax, and therefore the company had been unlawfully threatened. The court also finds that the company had no reasonable alternative, that it could never have gotten suitable redress if the railroad had been shut down for refusal to pay up at once. Thus, since the company was unlawfully deprived of any reasonable alternative but to pay, the payment was coerced.

Notice once again that the crucial issues are "objective"—legal and economic. The threat was unconstitutional; the reasonableness of the alternatives was calculable in terms of profit, loss, and procedures for legal redress. Thus, we really have eliminated the psychological element entirely from the concept of coercion here. Moreover, we are dealing with corporations, impersonal (non-psychological) entities. The psychology of the executives who are involved is totally irrelevant. If the president of the company were afraid of something, this might be of some interest, but it need not be so, and is legally totally relevant.

Yet, if one looks at the text of this and other such cases, one finds that the familiar psychological imagery is used. The courts speak of the company being "compelled to yield." The term "coercion" triggers it and by precedent calls for it.

It is true that we might have to do with individuals who are subject to economic duress, for example, an employee who is threatened with being fired by his employer for refusal to sign a waiver. The employee may indeed be frightened and worried. And the courts will always mention this sort of thing, because it does fit the traditional rhetoric of coercion. But even if the employee were cool and calculating about it, it still would be economic coercion if he were unlawfully threatened in such a way that the only reasonable thing to do was to agree. And it remains ultimately a legal question, for the court to decide, whether the options were or were not reasonable.

By now I have taken a long trip through the windings and turnings of law—the reason being that only careful and specific analysis of the law on coercion can convincingly lead one to the correct but counter-intuitive conclusion—a conclusion that not only is likely to be surprising to the non-lawyer but is also likely to be only obscurely appreciated by the law professional. It is, in a nutshell, that the legal concepts and doctrines falling under the rubric "coercion" (or "duress" or "undue influence") do not in essence pertain to psychological questions.

Questions of incompetence and irrationality are pertinent to law, and do rest on psychological evidence, but the recently devised psychological notion of "coercive persuasion" can be radically misleading if one is trying to fix the *legal* status of the phenomena at issue. My impression is that "coercive persuasion" cases will properly fall under the law as to mental incompetence and not the law on coercion. These two are legally mutually exclusive—one who is coerced must be rational in order to be coerced, and "undue influence" can in law only apply if the victim is mentally incompetent. So it is important to keep these notions distinct.

On the other hand, "coercive persuasion" law cases can raise the coercion or undue influence issues—as I see it—if the victim is assumed to have remained mentally incompetent, and if the emphasis of the claim is on the allegation that the influence exerted was in itself unlawful or wrongful in law (independent of whether it is also "coercive.")

Thus, if the persuader talks or acts wrongfully (threatens in an unlawful way, assaults unlawfully, uses deception on material matters, etc.), and if this conduct makes it reasonable to one in the victim's situation to act as the victim did, then undue influence or coercion may exist in law. The legal remedy would depend on the circumstances. But in any case the psychology of the victim would at most be peripherally relevant and never lies at the core of the case.

One may think that the law should be changed so that the psychological dimension is also centrally relevant to coercion, just as it is in the ordinary use of that term. However, I am not trying here to argue about reform of the law but to answer the question whether and how the law of our land, as it is *now*, applies to "coercive persuasion." After all, that is at least a necessary step before one can even consider whether and how to reform the law; and in any case, it responds to a more immediate question in regard to current litigation. Moreover, it is not uncommon for legal terms to develop their own technical meaning and to depart increasingly from the original everyday use of the terms. Sometimes this is undesirable. But often it rises over time and out of real needs and important considerations regarding precision of legal language and justice. In the case of "coercion" I think the latter is the case; the legal technical use is well fitted to the legal context, and has its roots in a wide variety of legal contexts. Hasty change to make legal terms conform to popular usage, without study of the legal contexts that led to the technical use, is likely to do more damage in unforeseen ways than the benefits, if any, of the "cure."

Against this total background of my discussion and with much trepidation and tentativeness, I would like to mention why I think the doctrine of coercion and undue influence are not likely in the long run to be the principal doctrines invoked when cases of alleged "coercive persuasion" in connection with religious sects come before the law. I think this because the legal wrongfulness of the alleged coercer's conduct is so crucial to coercion or undue influence, and because there is such great constitutional restraint on the courts in regard to interfering with or making judgments about religion. Methods of persuasion that might be plainly wrong in law when used in, for example, an economic or domestic context, may very well be protected by the claim that they are intrinsic to religious worship. Beliefs and tactics that most people might consider bizarre in any other context may be protected in the religious context. The reluctance of the courts to interfere—mandated at bottom by our Constitution—places an exceptionally heavy burden on one who would show the conduct to be unlawful; and this in turn makes a claim of coercion very difficult to sustain in the religious context. It seems to me that, on the whole, the more likely legal terrain for such claims would be defined by the claim that the purported victim had been rendered or become mentally incompetent in some respect or degree. However that, too, can be a difficult question to settle legally when one person's mental incompetence is another's religious belief and ascetic practice.

In the end this is a factual question: how gross was the wrong done the victim, or how gross is the incompetence? No doubt after a certain point even the Constitutional restraints on the court dissolve, no matter how insistently a religious rationale is offered.

The law is still in flux on these matters, and I am trying to chart long-term probable trends on the basis of fundamental legal doctrine. Obviously other factors will come into play, too. As I said at the outset, I hoped to throw light from one certain angle, but I have no firm, clean, and overall conclusions about "coercive persuasion." Certainly—as is obvious—I have not attempted to take up here the profoundly important moral, religious, political, and psychological dimensions of this question. And a final but important disclaimer: nothing I have said implies or is meant to imply the soundness or unsoundness of the claims pro or con as to the existence of "persuasive coercion" in particular sects. I have been concerned with determining what law is generally relevant to these claims, not with what the legal decision would be or should be in actual cases.

LEGAL INTERVENTION
IN NEW RELIGIOUS MOVEMENTS

LEGAL PROTECTION FOR FREEDOM OF RELIGION

William Shepherd

The *Prosecutor's Reach* is the working title of the book that I am now preparing./1/ In it I discuss constitutional conflicts in America between First Amendment religious protections of individuals and legitimate interests of government in protecting public welfare. The state prevailed in these conflicts in cases ranging from the Mormon polygamy issue to recent Sunday closing law disputes. *Sherbert* v. *Verner* (1963) and *Wisconsin* v. *Yoder* (1972) marked a turn by the Supreme Court: it allowed the free exercise clause of the First Amendment, when pitted against state interests, to stand by itself; and it established a balancing test by which constitutional religious guarantees may be diminished only where the state can demonstrate that its interest is compelling because abuses are grave, and that its proposed method of regulation is the least onerous available.

Confrontations during the last decade joined new religious group members against government interventional authority. Parents frequently sought to invoke state color of law to sanction both extrication of their adult children from adherence to disfavored religions and treatment of them in order to undo alleged involuntary programming. An appellate court in *Katz* v. *Superior Court* (1977) utilized the *Sherbert-Yoder* weighing-of-interests procedure to relieve five members of the Unification Church from an order placing them under care and discretion of their parents. Analysis of the constitutional issues raised by *Katz* leads to a discussion of the scope of permissible religious deviance, the state's *parens patriae* power, the limits of judicial authority over freedoms of religion and association, the persuasive vigor of arguments condemning cultic mind control, and the usefulness of applying a psychiatric way of thinking about the individual harms and family disruptions attendant upon alternative religious group loyalty.

I disagree with Richard Delgado's various arguments favoring state intervention to extricate and deprogram cult members because even if it were desirable social policy to do so, such interference with the rights of nonconforming religious believers is constitutionally illegal, and it violates

Reprinted with permission from *The Center Magazine*, a publication of the Robert Maynard Hutchins Center for the Study of Democratic Institutions, Santa Barbara, California.

the moral principles—chiefly the rights to equal concern and respect—on which the Constitution is based.

Decisions of courts at all levels throughout the 1970s were negative about claims of deprogrammed plaintiffs against parents and deprogrammers. Parents were not punished for kidnapping, and deprogrammers generally were let off with token payment of either compensatory or punitive damages. Deprogrammers also fared well in criminal proceedings by reliance on the defense of necessity or justification

The problem for those who have suffered pain and injury at the hands of deprogrammers is to fashion a cause of action which courts will recognize as a constitutional ground on which to justify punishment of such vigilante justice. Recently, in cases ranging from late 1978 to the present, a broad new advance in defense of religious freedom has been forged in the courts. Causes of action in favor of deprogrammed plaintiffs have been successfully based on Title 42 of the U.S. Code, Section 1985 (3). (The number was amended in 1976 to Section 1985 (c); I will refer to it simply as 1985.)

This part of the Civil Rights Act was passed in 1871 and popularly dubbed the Ku Klux Klan act. It was part of a package of Reconstruction legislation aimed at protecting the rights of emancipated blacks. It was one congressional implementation of the Fourteenth Amendment of 1868, particularly its Section 1 language to the effect that no laws can abridge privileges or immunities of citizens, that no state can deprive any person of life, liberty, or property without process of law, and that equal protection of the law is afforded to all without exception. The 1985 provision was aimed at rooting out racial conspiracies of whites against blacks. It states that two or more people cannot act on an agreement to deprive any person or class of persons equal protection under the laws, or equal privileges and immunities under the laws, nor can they injure another in person or property, or deprive him of having and exercising any right or privilege of a citizen. Should such injury occur, 1985 concludes, "the party so injured or deprived may have an action for the recovery of damages occasioned by such injury or deprivation, against any one or more of the conspirators." An earlier section of the law, numbered 1983, uses similar language but covers instances in which color of state law is involved.

For many years, 1985 lay dormant. A 1971 Supreme Court case, *Griffin* v. *Breckinridge*, resurrected the section, and broadened its applicability and availablity as a constitutional recourse for causes of civil action. *Griffin* makes viable an argument that the state need not be involved in any way as long as a private, invidiously discriminatory class-based animus is injuriously inflicted by persons in conspiracy against a member or members of a discrete identifiable group such as blacks, women, or Moonies. Under *Griffin*, plaintiffs are required to show (1) a conspiracy; (2) that the purpose of the conspiracy is to deprive someone of equal privileges and immunities; (3) an act in furtherance of the conspiracy; and (4) an injury to another or deprivation of a citizen's rights or privileges. Plaintiffs in these cases must also show that they are members of a group or class so abhorred by the conspirators that such animus motivates the conspiracy.

In racial cases, *Griffin* easily finds a source of congressional authority in Section 2 of the Thirteenth Amendment, empowering enforcement of the prohibition of slavery. In addition—and this is crucial for new religious movement cases—*Griffin* explicitly finds a source of power in any denial of the right to travel interstate. Equally explicitly, it states that other constitutional ways to reach private conspiracies may be possible, and leaves open whether Section 5 of the Fourteenth Amendment (which empowers enforcement of the due process and equal protection clause) is one such source of power. Later courts have split on that last issue.

The broad new advance in defense of religious freedom that has been forged in the wake of *Griffin* can be seen in a few examples of the case law. These cases are affirmations of Section 1985, which agree that, specifically, a deprogrammed plaintiff has fashioned a remedy, stated a cause of action properly, and reached a constitutional source of authority on the basis of which the court can act to redress injuries and to punish conspiring parents and deprogrammers.

Rankin v. *Howard,* an Arizona case which was appealed in 1980, involves an adult member of the Unification Church whose father obtained a possibly fraudulent conservatorship order in Kansas. (Marcus Rankin was not a resident of the Kansas county where the order was granted.) Under the order, Rankin was flown to Kansas, then to Phoenix, Arizona, where deprogramming was attempted under the auspices of the Freedom of Thought Foundation. On defendant's motion to dismiss Rankin's many-pronged suit, the judge ruled (1) that the Kansas judge was covered by judicial immunity, so that Rankin's 1983 color of state law complaint was dismissed; (2) that Rankin had successfully stated a cause of action under 1985; (3) that a religious group may indeed be counted as a class for 1985 purposes; and (4) that Rankin's having been deprived of his constitutional right to free interstate travel is legititimate ground for congressional power to reach the conspiracy. Rankin appealed what was already a substantial victory, and in the Ninth Circuit, Judge Eugene A. Wright gave him a further triumph by ruling that the Kansas judge was not immune if he knew he lacked jurisdiction over a nonresident. For the circuit judge to open the possibility that immunity did not exist in this instance was quite unusual. But as a result, Rankin's 1983 cause of action became allowable along with his 1985 success in the lower court.

Cases involving conservatorships usually try 1983 as a cause of action along with 1985 because action by a judge or the police can trigger the color of state law requirements. Without a conservatorship or some other official state angle, 1985, standing by itself, is the choice.

In *Ward* v. *Connor* (1980), a Norfolk, Virginia U.S. District Court case, a deprogrammed Unification Church plaintiff lost a 1985 cause of action against his kidnapping deprogrammer because the judge found that his church membership did not qualify as a class, that the defendant's concern for the plaintiff disqualified the necessary discriminatory animus, and that an alleged deprivation of his right to travel failed to reach the congressional source of power that would allow the court to act. The Fourth Circuit Court of Appeals reversed all these points. The court refused to consider the Fourteenth Amendment source-of-power issue, but its ruling was another victory for a deprogrammed plaintiff.

Similar circumstances and results obtain in several other cases, including *Cooper* v. *Malko* (California), *Bavis* v. *McKenna* (Maryland), *Augenti* v. *Cappellini* (Pennsylvania), *Baer* v. *Baer* (California), *Greene* v. *Patrick* (New York), and *Dixon* v. *Mack* (New York).

The only genuinely contrary case that I know of is *Weiss* v. *Patrick*, in which the First Circuit Court upheld a lower court ruling that a purely private conspiracy is insufficient grounds for 1985 causes. Also, as in *Peterson* v. *Sorlien*, the court found that consenting behavior on Weiss' part during deprogramming and the good faith of parents was a satisfactory defense.

In *Peterson* v. *Sorlien*, the judge refused to add a 1985 cause to the plaintiff's already-in-motion charge. He also stated, following *Weiss*, that a good faith defense was legitimate, and that the plaintiff failed to show sufficient class-based animus. But there were two strong dissents in the Peterson case, and the trial court's award of ten thousand dollars punitive damages was allowed to stand.

Jeremiah Gutman remarked recently that "if all I have is a hoodlum being engaged by the parent to take the child or adult out of an association because of the objection by the parents to the nature of the beliefs of that association, I believe we can make out a conspiracy under Section 1985 of the Civil Rights Act. With Section 1985, I do not believe you need state involvement; all you need is a class-based animus. The courts have held that an animosity to a group because of its religious affiliation is sufficient."

Although this statement has been disputed, the cases which I have cited bear out its accuracy. If further litigation continues in a similar direction, we can safely argue that the courts have come up with a judicial remedy such that individuals who have been treated injuriously at the hands of hired deprogrammers and admittedly concerned parents can find redress in the courts. No matter what any of us may think is desirable social policy as far as new religious movements are concerned, these cases demonstrate that kidnapping and deprogramming are constitutionally illegal *and* actionable.

It may be that a majority in our society wishes state intervention and private conspiracies of this sort to continue. But legally they cannot. The cases I have cited afford a vivid illustration that the constitutional system in America is not founded on mere majoritarianism. In fact, in Ronald Dworkin's words, the Bill of Rights protects individuals against majoritarianism. Fundamental rights, like the right to equality, may not be abridged in the name of general welfare or general utility. These rights hold also when we find our own children joining what we may consider grotesque and harmful outfits.

We may be justified in saying that an emergency situation exists when our children choose to worship strange gods, to live on low-protein diets, to chant, and to solicit in airports. Society may well be worse off for allowing these things to happen. Grief and distress among families broken up because of them are difficult to ignore. But none of this justifies such drastic intervention as custody orders without right to appearance and counsel, kidnapping, restraint, forcible deprogramming, or illegal civil commitment. People in our society have the constitutional right to be intolerant and dogmatic, and to believe in and peddle mental and spiritual poison, as long as they do so within the law. If we infringe upon the fundamental rights of others to choose and define their own beliefs, we are at the same time undermining our own rights and the fundamental vision of human equality and dignity that was built into the Constitution and which has been elaborated for two hundred years in our best legal decision-making.

The extension of the Civil Rights Act of 1871 by the *Griffin* court of 1971, and its utilization by these recent courts I have mentioned to protect the rights of individuals from injury and deprivation at the hands of those abhorring their way of life, provide another strong plank in the platform of American religious liberty and nonestablishmentarianism.

NOTE

/1/   William Shepherd, *To Secure the Blessings of Liberty: American Constitutional Law and the New Religious Movements* (Chico, CA: Scholars Press, 1985).

THE LEGISLATIVE ASSAULT ON NEW RELIGIONS

Jeremiah S. Gutman

As the 1970s drew to a close and widespread animus toward new religious groups generated political coercion to support restrictions upon religious activities, American legislative bodies became one of the more popular foci of attention. At national, state and local levels, attempts were made to restrict the activities and limit the potentials of disfavored groups to whom it became chic to apply the newly pejorative term "cults."

No attempt will be made in this discussion to tabulate each aborted or successful proposal in the scores of jurisdictions in which they were submitted, but typical devices in the assault upon religion will be examined.

The apparently most innocuous legislative attempt to deal with the asserted danger posed by new religious groups is the simple legislative authorization for an investigation or study. Such legislative activity, however, is only apparently innocuous. It is, to those who recall the inquisitorial nature which has characterized so many American legislative investigative bodies, frightening. Perhaps the name of Representative Goebel of Pennsylvania will never achieve the infamy associated with the name of the late junior Senator from Wisconsin, Joseph R. McCarthy, but his House Resolution 20 of the 1979 session did point his name in that direction. This bill authorized a legislative study of named groups, including the Unification Church, Scientology, Children of God, the Hare Krishnas, the Divine Light Mission, The Way International, and others. Hearings were held to determine whether the churches concerned utilized "improper mind control techniques in their recruitment and subsequent retention of members" and whether they could "undermine voluntary consent" and "interfere with free will." A legislative determination of improper actions by an individual or group is known as a bill of attainder. The Constitution of the United States forbids the Congress from engaging in such practices, and there is little doubt that the Due Process Clause of the Fourteenth Amendment of the Constitution of the United States would be interpreted to forbid state legislatures from engaging in attaint. The Pennsylvania legislative committee thus created did indeed become a forum for the venting of spleen and frustration, a step by the Commonwealth of Pennsylvania toward impermissible entanglement in religious affairs, a first block laid on a road toward legislative interference with free exercise of religion.

Among the tests of neutrality prescribed by the Supreme Court in determining the validity under the First Amendment of legislative or governmental action affecting religion are neutrality, that is, neither supporting nor opposing religion any particular religion, and avoidance of entanglement, that is, involving the government or any agency of government in the internal affairs of a religious body. A bill which is aimed at specified religions unashamedly named in the authorizing resolution is not only a bill of attainder but a clearly non-neutral assault upon specified religious groups, an attempt to have the state legislature involved in an examination of doctrine and activities within the church in order to evaluate and adjudicate their propriety. Neither such official hostility to religions nor entanglement of this kind can be tolerated in the United States.

In the 1981 session, several Pennsylvania legislators introduced a bill, House Bill 406, which would have created "a temporary study commission to study (sic) religious groups which seek to unduly (sic) exert control over children and youth." Apparently having learned from testimony opposing the bill of attainder, the 1981 bill does not name particular religious groups, but would have gone after a class of "groups and individuals . . . which seek to unduly assert control over children and youth which (sic) is hazardous and detrimental to their general and mental health, freedom and life style and which seek to induce, by undue pressure, children and youth to participate in, or join, such groups or individuals through the use of inappropriate suggestions, hypnosis, drugs, unethical physical or social inducements and any other coercive or unacceptable methods." House Bill 406 also qualified as a bill of attainder, because it called upon the study commission to "seek to specifically identify groups and individuals" in the category supposedly defined by the rather bizarre language quoted above. That aside, however, the 1981 Pennsylvania version of a legislative study approach certainly involved impermissible entanglement and, far from being neutral, displayed open hostility to certain religious groups at which the bill was obviously aimed, although the word "religion" and its cognates appear nowhere in the language.

The Pennsylvania approach to harassment of specified or categorized religions also constitutes a violation of the Establishment Clause of the First Amendment proscribing any "law respecting an establishment of religion" and is inconsistent with the Fourteenth Amendment prohibition of denial "to any person (of) . . . the equal protection of the law." To select certain classes of religion for hostile governmental attention not only interferes with the First Amendment "free exercise" of religious liberty by the groups and their congregants, not only limits their First Amendment right "peaceably to assemble," but prefers unattacked respected religions and thus tends toward their establishment while simultaneously placing an unequal legal burden upon the legislative targets.

Not to be outdone by Pennsylvania, Maryland was presented in 1981 with House Joint Resolution 67, "concerning Cults in Maryland." It, too, would have appointed a "committee to study cults and similar movements," making no attempt to define "cult," much less what characteristics would make a "movement" "similar" to whatever a "cult" might be. The Resolution indicated concern that "freedom of thought and independent action is (sic) being denied" to youth by "groups which utilized mind control techniques, which attempt to destroy family ties by turning children against their parents, and which recruit members on school campuses and take them out of the educational process." The Maryland legislators were also concerned with alleged attempts to "interfere with free will." The committee would have been directed to study the activities and techniques of "these cults and other movements" with respect to their influence upon the thought processes and association and to scrutinize internal church activities and fund-raising practices. The fact that the proposed Resolution called upon the committee to "give full recognition and deference to constitutional rights of all persons, to the free exercise of religion and religious beliefs" would not have saved it from the constitutionally fatal infirmities of vagueness, intrusiveness into religious affairs, and lack of neutrality in approach.

In 1981 Massachusetts was presented with a proposed resolution, number 5277, which also would have provided "for an investigation and study by a special commission relative to certain religious groups or cults." Massachusetts House 5272 would have looked into the "social impact of certain groups or cults . . . including but not limited to the Unification Church of Sun Myuing (sic) Moon, the Hare Krishnas, and the Church of Scientology." The Commonwealth of Massachusetts was called upon to look into "the overall impact of the philosophy of such groups upon the citizens of the Commonwealth." Such a resolution, aside from its bill of attainder aspects, its undisguised lack of neutrality and its hostility to specified religious groups, would have launched Massachusetts into an investigation of various philosophies held by the citizens of the Commonwealth and how the ideas and thoughts (I suppose that is what philosophy means) of the citizens might be affected by the existence of the disfavored new religions. The First Amendment to the Constitution of the United States does provide not only for free exercise of religion but protects the rights of all people to think as they will and to express those thoughts as individuals or as participants in peaceful assemblies, whether those expressions be oral or written. It would be difficult to formulate a more fundamental and vicious attack upon freedom of thought than to create a legislative commission instructed to find out how the people of the state are thinking and how their thoughts are being affected by the exercise of free religion, speech, press, and assembly rights of others. Presumably, once the state had such data, it could draft legislation to limit what it perceived as defects in thoughts, flaws in philosophy, and errors in judgment, so that the minds of the citizens could be controlled and kept within limits acceptable to their legislators. Fortunately, House Resolution 5272 never became law.

Other attempts have been made to create legislative kangaroo courts and forums before which persons opposed to religion as such or to certain religious groups could exhibit their hostilities and seek political action against their enemies. It is to be anticipated that further attempts in this direction will be made and that here and there such an investigative committee will actually hold hearings such as those which did in fact take place in 1979 under Pennsylvania House Resolution 20.

The most frightening of the attacks upon unpopular religious groups is that exemplified best by the receivership imposed upon the Worldwide Church of God, Inc. The attorneys general of the various states of the United States are typically charged with supervision of charitably motivated and dedicated activities. Philanthropic and similar organizations are required to register and file accountings, are limited as to overhead, and are subject to audit to see to the correct application of funds solicited from the public for public purposes. In California, the Attorney General asserted the proposition that his state had authorized him to exercise just such oversight and to enforce such accountability not only with respect to philanthropic and similar public activities but with respect to religions. Many of the attorneys general in other jurisdictions expressed concurrence with then-Attorney General Deukmejian. Attorney General Deukmejian, having received complaints from some former and dissident members of The Worldwide Church of God concerning the use and application of church funds, succeeded in having a California court put the church into receivership. To a non-lawyer, that may not sound as dangerous as it does to an attorney. A receiver becomes the boss for all purposes. The receiver takes possession and legally owns all of the property of the entity put into receivership. If the entity is a church, not only the bank accounts, but the houses of worship, the educational properties, the furniture and furnishings, the files, and the sacred objects and vestments become the property of and subject to the exclusive dominion and control of a lay individual designated by the judicial branch of the state government. Such an individual would probably be deemed biased and therefore disqualified were he or she a member of the religious body to be swallowed by the state. The receiver not only controls the property and how it is spent, including how much is paid to the priests and clerks and teachers, but controls all aspects of personnel, hiring, and firing at will—not only clerks, custodians, and teachers, but priests and bishops. Such complete meddling in the affairs of a church is constitutionally intolerable.

The very concept that such a receiver could be appointed is shattering to traditional notions of separation of church and state. Placing a religious organization under the control of a court appointed receiver does not breach the wall separating church and state but demolishes it completely, merging the church one hundred percent with the power of the state. While litigative attempts were underway to correct the outrageous imposition of state power upon the affairs of The Worldwide Church of God, the State of California had the wisdom, through its legislative body, to amend the statute under which the attorney general purported to act to make it clear that the legislature of the State of California did not intend its attorney general to have the power he asserted. Thus, judicial determination, which might have settled once and for all the question of whether or not a state can give its attorney general such power, was never required. Because so many other attorneys general had indicated concurrence with the ideas of Mr. Deukmejian, however, it is to be anticipated that similar attempts will be made in other jurisdictions and that competing bills, both purporting explicitly to grant and to deny such power, can be expected.

Another area of legislative activity with respect to new religions involves attempts to control solicitation. Villages, towns, counties, municipalities, and states in all parts of the country have enacted or given new and often selective attention to previously enacted laws covering time, place, and manner of solicitation of funds by religious groups.

Some states have imposed badge or other identification requirements upon those who seek to raise funds in public to support their religious groups. Many have insisted that evangelists register in advance with police or other authorities. It has been proposed in some jurisdictions that those who solicit funds in public places be licensed and registered, but such jurisdictions frequently recognize the difficulty of applying such a rule to religious organizations and providing an exemption. The problems in this area arise because of the tendency of police and municipal officials to view as religious only those faiths which have wide public respectability and acceptability. Obviously, establishment of religion and unequal protection of law problems inhere in such regulations which are invitations to selective enforcements. Attempts have been made to rule out all door-to-door or public forum fund solicitation with an exception for individuals who have resided in the community a minimum period of time or on behalf of religious groups which maintain a place of worship in the community.

Minnesota attempted to deal with the problem by distinguishing churches which raise their funds by appeals to their own members from those which solicit primarily from the public at large. The former were made statutory beneficiaries of an exemption from the burdens of registration and financial disclosure and reporting which were imposed on the latter. The United States Supreme Court early in 1982 held that, because of the "clearest command of the Establishment Clause . . . one religious denomination cannot be officially preferred over another" and

that, because the "constitutional prohibition of denominational preferences is inextricably extricably connected with the continuing vitality of
the Free Exercise Clause," such "favoritism among sects" demands that
the law embodying such "religious gerrymandering" be held invalid.

It is much easier for religious organizations and proponents of religious
liberty to deal with state-wide bills and acts than it is with local ordinances
and their administration. The Minnesota statute was promptly and vigor-
ously attacked in the federal court. Attempts in other state legislatures to
burden evangelical solicitation have been widely publicized and opposed.
County, city, town, village, and other government subdivision regulations
are less visible, and small communities often have such homogenity of population that it is easy unconstitutionally and arbitrarily, even in the absence
of ordinances, to harass and eliminate outsiders, particularly those seeking
to persuade that established ideas and religious adherence should be re-
examined and new ideas explored and novel affiliations considered. The
remedy for such interference with freedom of exercise of religious and
related constitutional liberties can be secured only if the affected groups or
local outraged individuals secure a wider publicity for local unconstitutional actions. Such wider publicity can best be secured by initiation of litigation or by calling such matters to the attention of state-wide and national
organizations such as the American Civil Liberties Union and its affiliates
and Americans United for Separation of Church and State. When the
oppression is on a broader scale and state-wide, it is typically easier to generate public attention and to rally opposition to unconstitutionally oppressive or unwise impositions upon religious freedom and to prevent their
enactment by state legislatures before the problem of enforcement arises.

Some opponents of new religions analogize the evangelist to a door-
to-door salesman and seek to impose restrictions upon religious fund
solicitation parallel to those placed upon commercial entrepreneurs. In
some jurisdictions it has been required, and in others it has been proposed, that the evangelist be made gulity of a criminal act for failure
initially to identify herself or himself as speaking on behalf of a named
organization. Some government authorities, such as fairground operators
and airport managements, have succeeded in convincing courts that
accepting religious contributions in a public area constitutes a traffic
hazard and an interference with pedestrian flow which justifies criminal-
izing acceptance of such donations. Since the Supreme Court of the
United States recently agreed with this alarming idea, the so-called
"booth requirement," at least in a state fairground, it would be surprising
if booth requirements were not imposed in many airports, other passen-
ger terminals, publicly operated shopping centers, the concourse under a
publicly owned office building such as the World Trade Center, sports
arenas owned or operated by public authorities, and similar places of
assembly in which one would have thought until recently that the First

Amendment went, with all of its rights and burdens, with all who entered.

Similar in concept and origin to the requirement that there be forthwith identification of affiliation of the solicitor is the deceptive recruitment legislative construct which Congressman Ottinger has proposed. An unfiled bill under discussion by Mr. Ottinger would create a new federal felony, punishable by up to five years imprisonment and a five thousand dollar fine, to be visited upon anyone who "with intent to persuade . . . any individual to become affiliated with . . . any organization, knowingly . . . conceal(s) any material fact . . . in promoting affiliation by such individual with such organization and . . . attempt(s) to coercively persuade such individual from . . . contacting any individual not affiliated with such organization . . . by means of any communication in interstate commerce. . . ." This proposed addition to the Crimes and Criminal Procedures section of the United States Code would criminalize evangelical and recruitment contact, not only by religious but by other membership organizations. Its thrust and structure constitute an invitation to selective enforcement against unpopular and minority groups, including particularly the unnamed targets, the new religions, which the proponent frankly identifies as "cults" whose alleged abuses are assertedly addressed by this bill. The "Deceptive and Coercive Organizational Practices Act" would snare within its net the pastor who entices youth to his community center with promises of ice cream and cake but really secretly harbors the hope that they will join his flock. While this bill may never be dropped into the hopper of the United States House of Representatives, the draft has been so widely circulated since Mr. Ottinger recognized in mid-1981 that his earlier conservatorship approach, discussed below, "might violate an individual's rights of freedom of speech and religion," that copies or variants will be appearing in state and other legislative bodies.

The most notorious of the legislative assaults upon religious liberty are the conservatorship bills. Most American jurisdictions have categorized people with various degrees of differing infirmities in an effort to protect them and society. A typical state structure will provide for the appointment of a conservator or guardian of the property of someone who does not have or has lost the capacity to manage his or her own affairs. This type of arrangement is often invoked with geriatric patients. The next step up the line might be the appointment of a conservator or guardian of the person who is unable to care for personal needs, to make decisions about where to live, is likely not to remember to eat or otherwise care for personal needs. Once more, it is the aged and physically infirm with respect to whom someone else is given the authority to make such intimate decisions.

For those suffering more severe disabilities from which there is little or no prospect of recovery or amelioration, there may be an adjudication

of incompetence and the appointment of a committee or fiduciary variously designated as guardian or something else to become legal owner, as
trustee, of all of the property of the incompetent who, as a result of the
adjudication, no longer has legal status to make any decisions about her
or his property or affairs unless the committee concurs. The final and
most extreme status is for those whom the state in its wisdom designates
as requiring involuntary incarceration and therapy. It is now the law in
the United States that incarceration without therapy is a denial of basic
constitutional rights, so that the warehousing of annoying or disruptive
individuals merely to preserve the superficial calm of society is no longer
possible unless at least the facade of treatment is erected to mask the
incarceration.

To some people, it is a symptom of poor mental health to accept on
faith without proof assertions concerning any factual matter, such as the
existence of a god or gods, the origin of life and matter, and miraculous
performances by saintly people. Some of the people with a view of this
kind are members of psychiatric and allied professions and have been
heard to diagnose such disorders as religious syndrome. There are others
who, while they themselves may not be adherents of any religion, recognize that the First Amendment and basic human dignity, even in the
absence of the First Amendment, require that an individual be permitted to believe without interference by the state or any agency of the
state what appears best to that individual. Even those who perceive an
inconsistency between rational thought and faith can recognize the right
to faith. Civil libertarians insist upon such a right, and the First Amendment guarantees it.

The conservatorship bills which have arisen in the United States
Congress and in states including Connecticut, Illinois, New Jersey, New
York, Ohio, Oregon, and Texas share the concept that the existing mental status categories described above are not adequate to deal with adults
who join new religious movements. They therefore seek to create still
another stigmatized group of persons legally deprived of the right to act
and make important decisions on their own affairs, unable to associate
with whom they please, incapable of believing what they think best and
what seems right to them, and, most importantly, not free to go where
they please and associate with those chosen by themselves.

If a person falls within one of the varying definitions of incapacity
proposed in such bills, a conservator or guardian would be appointed to
take charge of the individual. The conservator decides where the individual lives, with whom the individual associates, what the individual
reads. The conservator becomes the jailer, censor, the dictator over all
aspects of the individual's life. What does a person's family have to
allege (not to prove but merely, under some bills, baldly to allege) to
trigger such massive intervention by the state? Such things as (1) being

associated with a group which practices deception in recruitment or which requires unusually long work schedules; (2) exhibiting sudden and radical change in behavior, lifestyle, habits, or attitudes; (3) showing mentational changes; (4) losing free will; (5) undergoing psychological deterioration; (6) losing substantial capacity to understand; (7) being exposed to a systematic course of coercive persuasion which undermines the capacity to make independent judgements; (8) suffering psychological deterioration; (9) experiencing an abrupt and drastic alteration of basic values; (10) showing blunted emotional response or regression to childlike levels of behavior; (11) losing spontaneity or originality in language; (12) suddenly changing personality, values, goals or associations with others (13) becoming impaired in the ability to evaluate information critically or to form independent conclusions.

Among the items such bills would call upon a court to consider in finding the proposed "conservatee" worthy of the benefits of the law are drastic weight change, cessation of menstruation, diminished rate of facial hair growth, and cessation of perspiration. One bill would deem incapacitated a person who has undergone a radical change in mood, habits, thought, or perceptions, if such a change coincides with continuing and regular association with a disapproved group. Some of the proposals see the need for a conservator for one subjected to peer pressure and would provide a conservator for a person whose mood changes are coincident with association with a group which systematically misrepresents ideals.

These bills share much in common. They share fuzziness of language, use of buzz words arising in ignorance and prejudice, lack of definition, and incorporation of vague and undefined scientific-sounding phrases. They seek to base imposition of Draconian restrictions of liberty upon standards both vague and elusive. These bills would visit a punishment upon an individual for exhibiting symptoms which the law finds undesirable and detrimental to the individual but allegedly having their genesis in practices and techniques alleged to have been engaged in by others. Even if one gets over the vagueness problem and is sympathetic to the alleged plight of an individual who only thinks that he or she has found happiness, and even if one deplores the asserted techniques and conduct of those who are charged with having brought the individual to such a state of affairs, the conservatorship bills visit punishment upon the "victim."

To the extent that these bills deal with alleged deceptive and misrepresentational practices respecting ideals, beliefs, and convictions of a religious group, a court would, at the hearing on the application for appointment of a conservator, be required to look into the substantive nature of the ideals and beliefs and examine the "truth" of the statements made on behalf of the group. It has for decades been the law in the United States that judicial inquiry into the nature, truth, or falsity of the tenets or claims of a religious group is forbidden.

The conservatorship bills would punish by deprivation of basic freedom those who have experienced what some psychologists call the conversion syndrome, that is, having undergone a spiritual experience, a religious awakening, having been born again.

Fortunately, such bills have nowhere passed the legislature, except, to the dismay of many of its citizens and religious leaders, in the state of New York where Governor Hugh L. Carey in two successive years was compelled to veto the legislation as an attempt unconstitutionally to interfere with religious and other constitutional liberties. It is, however, not the end of the battle, and conservatorship bills can be expected in other legislatures, perhaps revised and disguised but nonetheless easily and quickly recognizable by those who are sensitive to civil liberties.

The animosity toward new religious groups is certainly no less in 1985 than it has been in recent years. That attempts to enact laws founded upon one or more of the models discussed above will be repeatedly made in the same and additional legislative bodies is certain, just as it is predictable that ingenuity will create models for the continuing assault upon new religions—an assault which, while aimed at those groups, is in reality an attack upon religion itself.

CULTS AND CONVERSION:
THE CASE FOR INFORMED CONSENT

Richard Delgado

Extremist groups' use of powerful techniques of coercive persuasion ("brainwashing") to produce obedient followers raises perplexing issues of criminal responsiblity, free will, and the limits of governmental intervention. At times, such conditioning has been raised defensively, as in the trials of Patty Hearst and Larry Layton, and the courts-martial of returning POWs. At other times, allegations of coercive persuasion have been made in an effort to induce state action, such as legislation or court orders aimed at prohibiting or reversing extreme forms of conditioning.

Earlier commentary has explored the criminal responsibility of the coercively persuaded defendant, as well as numerous problems raised by proposals to regulate the proselytizing and conversion activity of "cult" groups like the Unification Church, People's Temple, and The Way. This article analyzes one aspect of the latter controversy—the proposal to recognize a requirement of disclosure in religious conversion, similar to that imposed in medicine and human experimentation. Under the proposed rule, religious proselytizers would be free to convert, indoctrinate, and condition members of the public only after disclosing certain information to them and obtaining their assent. As with informed consent requirements in general, the principal aim of such a rule is to strike a balance between the legitimate interests of converters and the rights of potential converts to select their own religion or nonreligion.

Values of self-determination already play a significant role in the debate about religious cultism. On a rhetorical level, defenders of these groups ask why young adults should not be free to join whatever religious organizations they desire. Opponents respond that free choice is exactly what these groups deny. Constitutional analysis of state intervention raises consent issues, as do tort and criminal actions brought by cult members after unsuccessful deprogrammings, and suits by ex-members against cult leaders for unlawful imprisonment, slavery, intentional infliction of emotional distress, and fraud.

This article was originally published in 16 *Georgia Law Review* 3 and is reprinted by permission.

This article argues that these autonomy values, already invoked by both sides of the debate, should be extended and institutionalized in the form of a requirement of informed consent to religious conversion. First, it will show that such a requirement is necessary, to prevent injury to specific interests of converts, as well as plausible, in that the context in which it is proposed recognizes and protects disclosure and freedom-of-choice values. It explains why such a requirement has not been developed, and why it is appropriate for it to be recognized now. A composite model of the cult-joining process, drawn from descriptions of the recruiting practices of cult groups, is then put forth and analyzed to identify the points where consent problems arise. Final sections consider the remedies available to enforce an informed consent requirement, possible objections to such a requirement, and answers those objections.

I. NECESSITY AND PLAUSIBILITY
OF AN INFORMED CONSENT REQUIREMENT

Proponents of an informed consent requirement in a novel area should be able to show: (1) that the requirement is needed to avoid injury to legally protected interests; (2) that autonomy values are recognized in the setting in which the requirement is urged; and (3) that the current absence of such a requirement does not imply a social judgment that it should not exist.

A. Harms That May Be Averted by Means of an Informed Consent Requirement

Psychological studies, legislative hearings, civil and criminal actions, and first-person accounts by former cultists indicate that a number of harms may befall members of these groups: These include: physical injury from malnutrition, inadequate sleep, overwork, and inattention to medical needs; pecuniary loss, psychological injury, including guilt, suicide, maturational arrest, psychosis and neurosis; impairment of autonomy and decisional capacity; and loss of opportunity by the convert for normal personal, career, and social development.

Not every cultist suffers these harms, or regards them as such. Some thrive under the demands of cult life; others rise to positions of leadership where they wield influence and power over religious empires. Many find contentment, even joy, in the group and view any costs associated with their conversion as acceptable. Others, however, leave cult life—voluntarily, by expulsion, or by forcible retrieval and deprogramming—sick, angry and disillusioned. Many state that, had they known of the group's identity or nature, they would not have joined. These risks, comparable in many ways to those of consensual medical treatment of human experimentation, suggest the need for similar legal protection.

Informed consent rules exist, in part, to protect persons against risk. The existence of risk in religious conversion is thus one ground in favor of such a rule in that setting.

B. The Setting—Insiders, Outsiders, and the Government

It is necessary next to examine the setting in which a disclosure/consent requirement is proposed to see whether it is consistent with the values recognized therein. In some settings, an informed consent requirement would be inappropriate or pointless, while in others, important interests in physical or psychological integrity are at stake, making such a requirement both plausible and desirable.

Values of self-determination are deeply rooted in our societal views and legal treatment of religion. Although some religions stress passive values such as faith, suspension of disbelief, and uncritical discipleship, the legal system has always required that religions treat each person *as though* commitment to membership is an affirmative act that is his or hers alone to make.

The early framers saw religious freedom in these terms. For example, in drafting the preamble to Virginia's statute on religious freedom, Jefferson wrote: "God made man's mind free, and deliberately chose that religion should be propagated by reason and not by coercion." Locke, whose writings strongly influenced the early colonists, regarded freedom of choice as an essential ingredient of religious liberty. He characterized religion as "the inward persuasion of the mind," and the church as a "voluntary society of men, joining themselves together of their own accord."

Modern case law also protects truth-tellings in religious matters, although the scope of required disclosure varies. Some recent cases treat religiously motivated deception no differently from ordinary fraud, perhaps on the theory that fraudulent behavior cannot be religious. Other cases apply a "sincerity" test, under which religious persons or groups may utter falsehoods if they sincerely believe that the utterances constitute religious truth. A middle-of-the-road position, illustrated by *Founding Church of Scientology* v. *United States*, probably represents the majority view in insider-outsider dealings. *Founding Church* concerned the FDA's seizure of allegedly mislabeled E-meters used by the organization for "clearing" adherents. The court found that "[I]n order to raise a religious defense to a charge of false statement [here misbranding], the person charged with the alleged misrepresentation must have explicitly held himself out as making religious as opposed to medical, scientific or otherwise secular, claims." Thus, Scientology was permitted to market E-meters, and to make exaggerated claims for their therapeutic efficacy, so long as it did so in religious terms. If the Church had marketed the devices in secular terms—had failed to hold itself out as a religion—the mislabeling would have been punishable.

Case law concerning insider-outsider relations shows a less sustained concern over exploitation and nondisclosure, perhaps because members are deemed to have consented to normal transactions within the group. Even here, however, courts have developed doctrine to protect church members against overreaching by persons in leadership positions. Holding religious advisors to be "fiduciaries," courts have carefully examined gifts, wills, and other transfers of property by members that inured to the leaders' benefit.

In church-government cases centering around various types of religious exemption, courts have also imposed requirements of honesty and disclosure. Thus, schooling, drug, tax, and selective service decisions hold that, to qualify for an exemption, a religious group or adherent must possess the requisite belief sincerely and not merely as a cover to gain the desired benefit.

A small body of authority suggests that a right against imposed religiosity exists independent of any physical or psychological harm that might result from it. In *Campbell* v. *Cauthron*, for example, inmates in a penal institution had been exposed to volunteer religious witnesses on Saturday and Sunday. Permitted to enter the prison by the administration, the witnesses sang, prayed, and preached to their captive audience. The Eighth Circuit forbade these practices, holding that "[f]orced inculcation. . . even by volunteer witnesses, would . . . contravene the Free Exercise Clause." Prison officials were required to "take steps. . . to insure that no inmate is subjected to forced religious indoctrination."

C. Current Absence of Informed Consent Requirement

The proponent of an informed consent requirement in a novel setting must not only show that the requirement is plausible and helpful, but also that society has not already considered and implicitly rejected it. It might be argued that, if a requirement of informed consent to religious conversion were desirable, it would already exist—religious conversions have been part of human experience for thousands of years.

Two considerations, however, suggest that this negative inference should not be drawn. First, until recently, religious groups recruited relatively openly and honestly. It is unlikely that an early Christian, a Renaissance-era Catholic, or a contemporary evangelical could have been inducted without knowing that the group he or she was joining was religious. This is no longer true of all groups. Moreover, if a traditional-type religious recruiter misrepresented his or her cause, the problem had a simple solution: the recruit, on learning of the misrepresentation, could simply leave. With present-day cults, this option may not be available.

After luring the convert-to-be to a "guest lecture," "work camp," or "Peace Corps" meeting, some cult organizations apply classic techniques of coercive persuasion to minimize the chances that the recruit will defect once the group's identity is known. This combination—deception to gain a foothold and coercive persuasion to consolidate it—presents dangers that the legal system has only begun to confront.

Another reason to reject any negative historical inference relates to the increased understanding of the mechanisms of psychological manipulation and the recent knowledge that cults use these manipulative techniques. Before the recent studies of Lifton, Meerloo, Schein, West, and others, little was known about coercive persuasion of the sophisticated type employed by cult organizations. The legal system lacked the understanding necessary to frame rules, or even to appreciate the need for innovation. Early efforts to restrain cultic abuses thus relied on models of physical domination—unlawful imprisonment, kidnapping, intentional infliction of emotional distress, slavery and peonage. But these have proven effective only in extreme cases of exploitation. More subtle means of mental and physical manipulation require new approaches.

II. THE CULT JOINING PROCESS

A. A Paradigm

Judicial and legislative records, as well as first-person accounts of cult experiences, draw a composite picture of the process by which a typical young person becomes a member. Usually, the youth is just above the age of majority and is physically and psychologically normal. The home life is ordinary: there is no apparent pathology of any sort. The youth is often a college student, or at some other "in-between" period of his or her life— uncertain, at loose ends, anxious (all normal experiences).

The approach is made by an experienced cult recruiter of the opposite sex. Approaching the target individual at a college dormitory, social function, library or bus stop, the recruiter smiles, makes eye contact, and strikes up a conversation on a disarming topic suggested by the location, the recruit's clothing, books, or equipment. The proselytizer is taught to concentrate on youths who are alone or who look preoccupied. The recruiter next elicits a subject of concern to the target, such as war, race, poverty, the impersonality of the universe, or the moral ambiguities of modern life.

The recruiter professes interest and surprise: by coincidence, he or she belongs to a group that has the same concern. The friends share a house together near the campus. Just that evening, in fact, they are holding a dinner and discussion. There will be a guest speaker and a free meal. The recruit is urged to attend.

At the meeting the target person finds himself or herself surrounded by other smiling young people of about the same age who demonstrate great interest in his or her clothes, ideas, and experiences. He or she is showered with flattery, smiles, hand-holding, and feigned affection. Later, a rousing speech is given on a vague but stimulating topic, and a simple meal is eaten. The group does not identify itself. At the end of the initial meeting, the group pressures the new person to attend a longer (often three-day) workshop in the group's country retreat. The workshop is presented as an opportunity for the recruit and his or her newfound friends to "get to know each other better" and for him or her to learn more about the group.

At the retreat, held in an isolated setting, the recruit encounters additional warmth and friendship, but also a barrage of speakers, classes, songs, chanting, games, and "struggle sessions." There is little time for rest, privacy, and reflection; a more experienced cult member accompanies the recruit at all times. Diet and hours of sleep are severely restricted, while a constant sensory barrage and nonstop activity maintain the recruit in a state of narrowed attention.

Topics such as the spiritual world, guilt, salvation, and the identity of the organization and its leader are introduced in carefully staged sequences, as the cult perceives that the recruit is "ready" for them, and in physical circumstances designed to make withdrawal difficult and unlikely. If the recruit expresses doubts or shows curiosity about the group or its objectives, he or she is told to suspend them, as these matters will be addressed later. When the person finally does gain this information, he or she is unable to act because of impaired judgment resulting from sleep deprivation, peer pressure, guilt, and excitement. The final act of commitment is made when the young person, isolated from friends and family, and surrounded by cohorts who press him or her to make a commitment, is anxious about sin, identity, and salvation, and frantic for a framework within which to solve these frightening problems.

If the target person commits himself or herself to the group, additional indoctrination takes place. Physiological depletion, anxiety, isolation, and repetitious lecturing and chanting serve further to distance the individual from earlier behavior and thought; meanwhile, cult leaders press him or her to reorganize life into simplistic patterns of right and wrong, good and evil, us and them. The person's past recedes in his or her memory, replaced with a new, intense preoccupation with the group and its part in cosmic struggles.

The convert's estrangement from the past is accelerated by shifts in language and thought patterns. Words acquire new meanings. Critical thinking is discouraged, along with humor and metaphor. Converts are taught to feel, not to think, to obey, not to reason. When the process has continued for a number of weeks or months, the recruit may be deemed ready for the duties of a full-time member: fundraising on the streets, work in a cult-operated business, or scavenging for edible garbage. The new member appears simplistic in his or her thinking patterns, stereotyped in his or her responses, unresponsive to relatives and former friends, and indifferent to events in the outside world. He or she has become a cultist.

B. The Paradigm Analyzed: Consent-Negating Features in Cultic Induction

The above account contains several features that call into question the adequacy of the convert's consent.

1. *Traditional Consent-Negating Features.* Cult conversion practices often include such traditional consent-negating features as deception, coercion, physical or mental debility, and abuse of a fiduciary relationship. In determining consent in extra-risky settings, modern courts have looked to additional factors: the irreversibility of the process or change, its intrusiveness or far-reaching quality, and the unpredictability of effect. As these are often present in the cult-joining situation, the case for an informed consent requirement strengthens.

2. *Unique Elements in Cult Conversion.* There are other elements peculiar to the cult-joining process that have not yet been discussed by courts. One is the cults' maintenance of an inverse relationship between capacity and knowledge, the two key ingredients of informed consent. At early stages, the recruit's decisional capacity is relatively intact. He or she may be anxious about some adolescent crisis, lonely or confused, but is generally not clinically incompetent or pathological. However, knowledge of the cult's identity and of the obligations of membership is missing. If this information were disclosed at the time of initial contact, many recruits would react by leaving. The cult therefore keeps these elements secret until the recruit can be expected not to react negatively. Information is parceled out only as the cult perceives that the person has lost the capacity to respond according to his or her ordinary frame of reference. Knowledge and capacity are thus maintained in inverse proportion.

A second, related feature unique to cult-joining is segmentation of induction into steps or stages, with only nominal consent given by the recruit before progressing from each stage to the next. Thus, at the time of initial contact with the recruiter, the recruit consents to go to the evening gathering. At the first meeting, he or she consents to attend a longer retreat. Toward the end of the retreat, he or she agrees to sign up for an even longer workshop. At each stage, the intensity of the indoctrination and the convert's dependence on the group increase. The ultimate effect is a commitment to a journey, each step of which is nominally consented to, but whose ultimate destination is concealed until the penultimate step—at which point the individual has been so prepared that committing his or her life and fortune to the group seems a small and insignificant step. Both features—the maintenance of an inverse relationship between knowledge and capacity, and the segmentation of the joining process—deprive the convert of the chance to exercise a fully autonomous decision to join or not to join.

C. Policy Analysis

As has been seen, cultist conversion activity poses dangers to the physical health and emotional well-being of some persons without full consent. We have also seen that the informed consent requirement is a plausible way of addressing these problems and is consistent with the liberty values of the religion clauses. In considering whether to institute such a requirement we reasonably might wish to know further: (1) how well the policy values of informed consent would be served by enforcing such a requirement in religious conversion, and (2) how well the requirement would function in relation to the nonliberty values of the religion clauses.

Informed consent requirements serve a number of purposes: protecting the individual's interest in psychic and bodily integrity; preserving a sense of shared venture between the consent-giver and the consent-obtainer; and promoting the visibility and scrutiny of the treatment in question. Requiring informed consent in religious proselytizing would promote each of these values. Insisting that the future cultist be offered information about the cult advances the goal of personal control over major decisions; it promotes closer identification between proselytizers and their targets, and encourages shared decision-making power. By requiring disclosure, and allowing tort suits where disclosure is not made, public awareness of cult conversion and its consequences should increase.

In addition to the generalized disclosure/free choice values discussed earlier, many of the underlying values of the religion clauses would be further advanced by an informed consent requirement. These values include strife avoidance, neutrality, religious pluralism, avoidance of "ignorance and corruption," and protection of liberty of conscience.

An effective informed consent requirement should lessen societal strife in several ways. At present, the only forms of redress available to a disenchanted leaver are to become a deprogrammer, to campaign actively against cults, or try to persuade a government agency to "investigate" them. A private action in tort, based on the informed consent doctrine, would provide the recruit with a direct legal remedy. For parents, the only recourse presently open is abduction and deprogramming. If the radical changes brought about in their children were seen as freely chosen, many parents would be less alarmed and retaliation and self-help should diminish.

At the same time, the goal of official neutrality with respect to religious affairs would be advanced, as a value neutral criterion of consent would replace existing criteria more prone to subjectivity and bias. Informed consent would also promote religious pluralism, by which a sect must "flourish [according to] . . . the appeal of its dogma." By denying aggressive religious factions access to recruiting techniques that bypass decision-making faculties of would-be adherents, the requirement protects the "free market" value of the religion clauses. Furthermore, it helps prevent exploitation and corruption in religious recruitment and protects integrity of conscience. The requirement would thus promote the concerns that underlie disclosure/consent requirements, as well as those that animate the religion clauses.

III. FRAMING AND EFFECTUATING THE INFORMED CONSENT REQUIREMENT

We have seen that a requirement of informed consent is needed; we now turn to the specific form such a requirement would take. Because the constitutional interests of proselytizers are at stake, the requirements should be no more onerous than that which is necessary to protect the recruit's interest in free choice. It would seem that both interests can best be accommodated by a requirement of interactive consent, mediated by the recruit so as to give him or her control over the scope of disclosure. The recruiter's initial duty would be to offer material information at the point when conversion activity begins. Not every individual will wish to hear it; some will wish to delay the receipt of information; some will want more information, others less. If the subject expresses an interest in learning detailed information about the group's practices, the converter would be under a duty to disclose it. If the convert indicates a desire not to receive information, however, the proselytizer's duty is discharged and the conversion activity can proceed.

What would constitute the required initial disclosure? The converter should, at a minimum, be required to reveal that the group is religious, to give its most widely known name or identity, and to offer to provide further information. From this point on, the convert controls the scope of inquiry, with the converter's only duty being to respond honestly and fully to all questions, or to discontinue the conversion attempt.

If a cult breaches the duty to obtain informed consent, and the individual succeeds in disengaging from the organization, he or she can sue in tort. General damages would be recoverable for the affront of involuntarily imposed religiosity; special damages would be available for any lost wages, medical expenses, loss of of consortium, and emotional distress. If the failure to inform is willful, punitive damages should be available as well. If the principal remedy—private actions in tort— proves inadequate, legislatures could enact further protection: a "cooling off" period, a requirement that religious proselytizers wear identification badges, or provisions for the filing of documents requesting rescue. In addition, educational authorities could launch campaigns designed to acquaint school-age youth with the recruitment patterns of cult groups and make them aware of their legal rights.

After an individual proceeds nonconsensually to membership, the analysis becomes more problematical. Private suits can be brought only after the recruiter breaches the requirement and the harm materializes. If, however, the breach and the subsequent inculcation of cultic values are successful, there will be no plaintiff to bring suit: the victim's preference rationales will be altered so that he or she identifies with cult values and perceives the earlier nonconsensual induction as harmless and perhaps even necessary to free him or her from the shackles of the material world.

In many cases, the conversion will be temporary and will "wash away" if the individual is deprogrammed or simply removed from the cult setting for a brief period. When this happens, the person's desires vary as a function of time and relief from reinforcement. At time A, the individual professes to be happy as a cult member and demands to be left alone. At time B—perhaps only a few hours later—he or she expresses relief and gratitude over being freed. To make matters even more difficult, both choices will seem "rational" in that the individual can justify them by reference to broader values he or she holds or claims to hold. The choices are thus neither insane nor incompetent, just variable.

How should courts treat these situations of rapidly fluctuating preferences? One possibility would be to treat time-variable consent as evidence of selective incompetence, as some courts have done in amputation cases, and appoint a proxy decisionmaker. Another would be to adopt a "first in time" or "last in time" approach, in which the original or most recent values of the person in question are respected. A third approach would disregard justice considerations and make the decision on utilitarian grounds. A fourth approach would decide on grounds of intrapsychic freedom, or long-term autonomy: when in doubt, opt for the treatment that most respects the individual's potential for autonomous exercise of his or her faculties. A fifth approach would assume that a person can have only one "real" preference over a very short time-span, and endeavor to provide criteria for what that preference is. A final approach would attempt, by counseling or carefully controlled deprogramming, to move the wavering individual to a neutral third ground, from which he or she would be able to evaluate the two choice systems and decide freely between them.

The difficulty with all postinduction remedies is that, unlike preinduction remedies and especially informed consent, they operate in the realm of religious belief. Preinduction remedies only affect conduct, as they regulate the recruiter-recruit relationship at a time before belief is formed and conversion fixed. As is discussed more fully later, religiously motivated conduct is regulable on a showing of compelling state interest. Religious belief, on the other hand, is highly, perhaps absolutely, protected. Should protection of religious belief extend to belief that is inculcated through disapproved means and without a conscious, informed choice on the part of the believer? An argument can be made that appellate decisions protecting free choice in religious matters imply that unchosen belief is not protectable, or at least not protected absolutely. The issue seems never to have been litigated and should be regarded as an open question.

The only decision by a higher level court dealing with religious manifestations of questionable origin and authenticity is *Peterson v. Sorlien*, a December 1980 decision of the Minnesota Supreme Court. In *Sorlien*, the parents of a young cultist tricked her into leaving the cult to visit the home of a family friend. There she was confined and confronted with a team of deprogrammers who attempt to engage her in "reality-inducing therapy." For three days, the young woman strenuously objected, adopting the fetal position and blocking her ears with her fingers to avoid hearing what the deprogramming team and her parents were saying. Later, she talked with the deprogrammers, reconsidered her choice of religious lifestyle and remained with the parents and deprogrammers, roller skating, taking trips, shopping, playing softball, swimming and picnicking. She had many opportunities to escape but did not do so. Later, she initiated contact with her boyfriend, a cult member, with the object of convincing him also to leave the group. A meeting was arranged, but subsequently the young woman rejoined the cult and filed a civil suit against her parents for unlawful imprisonment.

The court found that at least thirteen of the young woman's sixteen days outside the cult had been spent voluntarily with her parents and deprogrammers and that during her stay in the cult the woman had acquired a new temporary identity. The court found that "cult indoctrination . . . is predicated on a strategy of coercive persuasion that undermines the capacity for informed consent," that in such settings "consent becomes a function of time," and that other social institutions do not undermine consent so extensively. Under these circumstances the court found the young woman's acquiescence "dispositive" and announced a new test of consent in cult situation: where parents remove the child "and the child at some juncture assents to the action in question," the entire course of conduct is deemed consensual and no unlawful imprisonment occurs. The United States Supreme Court denied *certiorari*, allowing the decision to stand.

IV. OBJECTIONS TO A DUTY OF INFORMED CONSENT

Objections could be directed toward both the feasibility
and constitutionality of a requirement of informed consent.

A. Objection Based on Feasibility

Feasibility-related objections to a duty of informed consent include
that religion is not rational and that an interruption to obtain informed
consent will render conversion impossible.

1. *Irrational Nature of Religious Experience.* It might be argued
that religion is not rational and that a requirement of informed consent,
which assumes a cognitive model, is therefore inapposite. Persons do not
become adherents to religions by weighing their respective advantages
and disadvantages; they commit themselves out of faith, obedience, and
discipleship.

Although some religious groups may view conversion as an involuntary act, it does not follow that they may use methods of induction that
abridge consent. The legal system is not required to adopt the religious
group's view of conversion. Allowing religious proselytizers to define
their own limits invites abuse, and is unnecessary. In the closely related
areas of public fundraising, courts have imposed limits to control religiously based fraud. The requirement of interactive consent seems no
more onerous that those other rules and is aimed at protecting an interest of even greater importance.

2. *Disruptive Effect of the Requirement.* It could also be argued that
an informed consent requirement would constitute an unreasonable barrier to religious conversion, as any break in the proceedings would slow
the emotional momentum, "destroy the mood," and make conversion
difficult or impossible.

If the brief delay necessary to give informed consent causes some
persons to decide not to proceed to membership, this is an acceptable
price to pay to protect against an even greater evil of nonconsensual conversion. Cult followers may disagree, believing that the person who
rejects conversion loses something of inestimable value. This weighing of
costs and benefits, however, is not theirs to make. The Constitution
directs that choices of religious belief and affiliation be made by the
individuals directly concerned. Others may disagree with these choices,
but are required to respect them.

B. Constitutional Objections

Another group of objections focuses on the constitutionality of
informed consent under the First Amendment.

1. *Free Exercise of Religion.* A requirement of disclosure interferes
with the free-exercise right of recruiters by imposing restrictions on the

way they induct new members. Informed consent requirements in medicine and human experimentation also interfere with the right of doctors and researchers to practice medicine or carry out research, but, unlike religion, these areas are not expressly protected by the Constitution.

Restrictions on religiously motivated conduct are not unconstitutional per se, but are subject to a balancing test in which the court weighs the state's interest in restricting liberty against the religious person's or group's interest in performing the acts in question. The religious interest ordinarily will receive broad protection, but this is lessened to the extent that courts determine the underlying motivation to be insincere, or the conduct noncentral to the system of belief and practice. For its part, the state's interest must be legitimate, compelling, and achievable by no less onerous means.

(a) *Compelling state interest.* Two related state interests support a requirement of disclosure: the interest in averting nonconsensual religious conversion, and the interest in protecting the public against secondary effects of fradulent religious proselytizing. As mentioned earlier, case law and constitutional theory demand that religious choices not be imposed; such choices are left to the individual. Imposed or nonchosen religiosity is constitutionally and morally offensive. Protection of free choice in religious matters would thus appear to constitute a compelling state interest.

A state may also wish to protect the public against the indignation and demoralization that can result from deceptive religious recruitment. This interest was cited in dicta in *United States* v. *Ballard* and *Cantwell* v. *Connecticut* and received explicit protection in more recent cases stemming from Hare Krishna activity in airports and at country fairs. Although most of these cases have centered around dishonest fundraising rather than recruiting of new members, the state interests are similar in the two areas.

International Society for Krishna Consciousness, Inc. v. *Barber*, decided by the Northern District of New York in August 1980, is a recent example. In *Barber*, the director of a county fair and others were sued for restricting the members of the Hare Krishna sect from soliciting freely among the public and for confining the cult's aggressive proselytizing (called "Sankirtan") to a booth. The sect charged that the restriction was unreasonable and violated their civil rights under 42 U.S.C. 1983.

The court found that the sect had engaged in a pattern of deceptive practices extending over a period of years. The Krishnas wore disguises, such as that of Santa Claus, violated their agreement with the fair officials to wear identification badges, and slurred the word "Krishna" to make it sound like "Christian." They invented fake purposes and nonexistent programs, told young couples that they had been selected as the best-looking couple on the fairgrounds and would receive a prize, and deliberately miscounted change by folding bills in half. They hid their identification badges or wore badges belonging to other groups. They focused on the handicapped, servicemen, young couples with children, and others deemed easy "marks" and sold records with photographs of leading recording stars on the cover, although the contents consisted only of Krishna chants and wails.

The Krishnas defended these practices by characterizing Sankirtan as their religious duty. Further, even if the member of the public did not know that he or she was giving to a religious organization, the member received spiritual benefit—the greater the donation, the larger the benefit. The Krishnas justified their deception by religious paternalism: "It is the task of the doctor or the mother to give . . . the medicine because she knows it's best. So we are approaching conditioned souls because they in their own right will not turn to Krishna." Among themselves they described nonbelievers as "diseased," "dogs," or "misguided," who need to be relieved of their material possessions as a first step toward attaining spirituality.

The Krishnas' arguments were unavailing. The court found that the state has a compelling interest in regulating fraudulent speech, even under religious auspices. Moreover, the booth restriction was a reasonable means of insuring "authentic[ity] and honest[y]" in the Krishnas' dealings with the public. Criminal prosecutions for fraud were not less onerous alternatives; the fluidity and mobility of the attenders at county fairs made it unlikely that a victim would remain to press charges. Other federal decisions have ordered similar protection for the public against deceptive religious fundraising. A common remedy is a requirement that the group identify itself or wear badges.

(b) *The cult's or recruiter's interest.* The interest of religiously motivated persons or groups in expressing their beliefs by action is entitled to considerable deference in our constitutional scheme of values. It is not protected absolutely, though courts will seek to accommodate it when doing so does not require sacrificing an even greater social value. The degree of protection is lessened, however, when a court finds that the motivation behind the act is insincere or nonreligious, or when the conduct is not a central element or tenet of the group's doctrine or way of life.

(i) *Sincerity.* A court could find that a cult's interest in inducing conversion without informed consent is insincere. First, it could hold that, in this setting, deception and non-disclosure establish insincerity. In opposition, the recruiter's organization might argue that its religion compels deceptive recruitment, and that its members are following this mandate sincerely. The court then would be faced with deciding whether sincere religious deception is legally protected. The weight of case law, reviewed earlier, suggests it is not.

Insincerity could also be found if a court determined that the dominant motive of a group or sect in recruiting new members is nonreligious—financial or political, for example. Conscientious objector or other exemption-related cases show that an admixture of political or economic motives will weaken a free exercise claim. Since many cults are intensely preoccupied with money and power and shape their recruiting accordingly, a court could find the requisite sincerity missing.

(ii) *Centrality.* Another element that courts consider in deciding the degree of deference due free exercise claims is centrality. The closer a course of conduct comes to the theological core of a religion, the more sympathetically courts will view claims for exemption. Because regulating consensual recruitment does not endanger the ability of a religious group to exist, preach, conduct its ceremonies, or adhere to its system of beliefs, it seems unlikely that a court would characterize the group's nonconsensual recruiting techniques as a central element or practice. Admittedly, a group deprived of the ability to recruit nonconsensually loses a powerful method of increasing its size; however, ordinary means of recruiting—preaching, revivals, advertising, door-to-door canvassing, and handing out leaflets—remain available to it. The group's interest in using extraordinary rather than ordinary means of induction would not seem to constitute a "central" element in the constitutional sense.

(c) *Least restrictive alternative.* If the state's interest is strong enough to prevail over the group's interests, the means by which it acts still must be no more onerous than necessary. It is difficult to conceive of an effective means of assuring free choice in religious affiliation less onerous than a requirement of disclosure. Informed consent of the proposed interactive variety is less intrusive than that applied in other areas, in that the scope of disclosure is as narrow as the subject desires. When the target person desires to be converted, the brief delay required to inform him or her of the group's identity and religious nature would constitute only a momentary interruption and might be necessary in any event.

2. *Excessive Entanglement.* A further concern is that a requirement of informed consent poses risks of excessive entanglement. Designed to protect both free exercise and nonestablishment values, the prohibition against excessive entanglement bars interference of religious and state authorities with each other's spheres of influence. In our case, the concern would focus on what has been called "administrative entanglement"—the unnecessary intrusion of regulatory procedures into the spiritual realm. This entanglement is likely to be found when the government invades an important area of church autonomy or governance, acts from no clearly neutral principle, or resorts to dogma or doctrine in resolving a dispute.

An informed consent requirement would seem unlikely to contravene the rule against excessive entanglement. Unlike intervention in property disputes, defrockment, or challenges among splinter groups, a court's enforcement of an informed consent requirement does not invade an area of church governance or authority; the cult's organizational/doctrinal integrity is not endangered to any significant extent. Further, the principle on which the court proceeds—that individuals should have the right to choose their beliefs and affiliations—is religiously neutral. Finally, in finding a breach of informed consent in a given transaction between a believer and a nonbeliever, the court is not required to decide among competing religious principles of dogmas. The only matter to be determined is a nonreligious one—whether the target person received the information he or she was due. The requirements of informed consent would therefore seem unlikely to contravene the prohibition against excessive entanglement.

3. *Disparagement of Religious Belief.* Courts, like all arms of government, are constitutionally barred from questioning the verity of religious doctrine. The leading case, *United States* v. *Ballard*, in holding that truth of religious claims could not be presented to the jury in a mail fraud case, declared:

> Heresy trails are foreign to our Constitution. Men may believe what they cannot prove. They may not be put to the proof of their religious doctrines of beliefs. . . . [I]f one could be sent to jail because a jury in a hostile environment found these teachings to be false, little indeed would be left of religious freedom.

Thus, although the *Ballard* jury properly could decide whether the defendants believed that they could perform miracles and transmit messages to and from God, it could not be permitted to decide whether these beliefs were, in fact, true.

More recently, a California appellate court held that a conservatorship order, granted to remove members of the Unification Church for deprogramming, violated the prohibition against evaluating church doctrine. "When the court is asked to determine whether that change [of lifestyle] was induced by faith or by coercive persuasion, is it not in turn investigating and questioning the validity of that faith?"

Would an informed consent requirement constitute an impermissible disparagement of the validity of religious doctrine? To ascertain whether it would, let us for a moment detach the question from the religious context and consider it instead in connection with consent to medical procedures. Suppose a critic of informed consent to medical experimentation argued that the requirement derogates medical authority and expertise, questions the scientific basis of medical judgments, and hence should not be imposed. This criticism would be seen as fundamentally misguided. Informed consent is required in medical treatments and human experimentation, not because we fear that the doctor's judgment is likely to be medically erroneous, but because the decision to undergo treatment is one that is for the patient alone to make.

The doctor is competent to tell the patient his or her diagnosis and prognosis, as well as the various forms of treatment and their costs and benefits. The doctor's expertise ends at this point. The patient then must decide whether to incur the costs of treatment in the hope of achieving certain gains. With regard to this decision, the physician has no peculiar competence. One patient may prefer the risk of rapid death at the gain of some days or weeks of mental clarity, unclouded by drugs or debilitating treatment. Another might cling to life more tenaciously, willing to risk pain, mental disorganization, or disfigurement in return for a higher probability of cure. Respect for human values and personal autonomy dictate that these decisions be lodged with the individual patient.

The situation is no different with respect to religion. The would-be converter is free to present religious claims to anyone who will listen. He or she is free to attempt to convince others to abandon friends, family, careers, previously held values, loyalties, and property, for life in a religious commune or sect. Courts must permit them to do this; but they need not allow believers to impose lifestyles or values on persons who do not choose them. With respect to this decision, religious converters have no special competence, and their interest in a rapid and easy conversion must give way to the right of potential converts to make their own decisions.

4. *Freedom of Speech.* If an informed consent requirement is constitutionally permissible under the religion clause, it should also be permissible under the free speech clause of the First Amendment. An informed consent procedure only interferes with the converter's right to speak with would-be converts if they would otherwise refuse to speak with the recruiter. It is difficult to maintain that proselytizers have a constitutional right to engage in extended conversations with persons who do not wish to speak to them. When a would-be convert does, in fact, wish to speak with the converter and become converted, the obstacle of a momentary delay to give informed consent would be *de minimis.*

The current debate about the proselytizing methods of religious cults is highly polarized. Critics emphasize the dangers of cult membership and the deviousness of the techniques cults use to induce it, arguing that these factors justify harsh action aimed at the cults. Cult apologists, on the other hand, argue that no remedy is necessary or even constitutionally permissible, and that the occasional damaged victim is the price we all pay for religious liberty.

This article proposes a moderate solution that concedes the right of cults to exist and to proselytize, but seeks to insure that the decision to join a cult is made by, not for, the individual convert. The solution, a convert-mediated requirement of informed consent, would require that religious proselytizers disclose key information to target persons before initiating conversion attempts. Most mainstream religious groups, and a few cults, already do this; the requirement would affect only those that do not. The principle enforcement mechanism would be private suits for damages.

The proposed requirement, although novel, would be consistent with the historic values of the religion clauses, as well as with those of informed consent generally. Moreover, it can be defended against criticism that it is unfeasible and would impermissibly entangle the state with religious affairs. It represents the least onerous method of protecting individuals' decision-making authority and guarding against unwanted or imposed religiosity. It promises to lessen social strife and self-help. It is a remedy to which courts and counsel should give careful attention.

INDOCTRINATION, PERSONHOOD, AND RELIGIOUS BELIEFS

Robert N. Shapiro

Religious beliefs are absolutely protected under the first amendment. And constitutional principles are easier to state than to apply.

Take the case of Young Adult, a twenty-one-year-old who had graduated from high school with a string of successes and an attitude that appeared buoyant. His early college career did not proceed smoothly, though, and by his sophomore year he was no longer happy. In the local shopping mall, during the spring term, he was approached by a member of the Holy Unconventional Church. A leaflet and a long speech offered Young an open and blessed existence without the cares of the world, if he joined the Church. The Church, he was told, gave one inner peace and provided a link to the Source of All Being.

Young accepted an invitation to a Church lecture and sacred banquet, where he heard and met Father, the leader of the Church and the professed presence of the Source. Father said that Young could find the Source of All Being if he left home and joined the Church. All family ties would have to be broken, material possessions left behind. Becoming a Brother in the Church would require a monastic existence, and instruction that would not be easy, though it would be deeper and more lasting than any lessons that college offered.

Young visited the Church on two other occasions, attending worship services and talking further with Father and several members, before joining. He wrote a note to his parents to say that he had entered his new religious training, and he called once to tell them he was doing fine. They did not understand, and tried to convince him to leave, alternately yelling at him, scolding, commanding, and pleading. None of that surprised Young, since he had not gotten along with his parents for some time.

The first two weeks of Young's religious training were the most intense. He spent all his time in a sparsely furnished room with writings of the Church, and was told that he should not leave. There was no radio, television, or telephone. He saw Church members every few hours

An expanded version of this article originally appeared in 56 *Southern California Law Review*, 1277–1318 (1983). This adaptation is published with the permission of the *Review*.

who discussed the teachings of Father. and quizzed Young on Church doctrine. Young ate two meals a day, alone for the first week and then with other trainees, but always in silence as the rules required.

After the first phase of training, Young was transferred to a farm of the Church where he and other trainees worked in silence in the vegetable garden and later retired to study Church teachings and answer questions on them. Once a week, all trainees spent a day in a cleansing fast and extended prayer, keeping an all-night vigil beforehand. A deep sense of commitment developed in Young who wanted with increasing fervor to become a Brother. He did so in a ceremony that included his baptism and adoption of a new name, Deep Believer.

Deep knew all teachings of the Church by heart. At the Church's direction, after his baptism he lived communally with several other recently admitted Brothers and Sisters. They traveled for the Church, proselytizing in various cities, approaching people as Deep had originally been approached.

It was on one of these missions that Deep saw his parents. He had no particular desire to talk with them, but they insisted on asking questions about his activities and involvement in the Church. At their request Deep agreed to stay at home during his mission in the city, and later that day they returned to pick him up. Instead of driving home, however, Deep's parents drove him to the house of a family acquaintance whose son had also left for the Church. There were gathered several other people, only some of whom Deep recognized, but all began to talk to him about the Church, since all had been touched by it in some way, most often by having a child leave home to join.

One of the guests was Pointed Questioner, a psychologist with extensive experience with deconversions from new religious groups. All others left the room eventually so that Pointed Questioner could talk to Deep alone. At first, Deep refused to cooperate in any way; he remained silent except for periods when he quietly chanted Church doctrine and stared straight ahead. Pointed's initial questioning continued for two hours on the first day. After Deep refused to move and spent the first night in the same room, another two sessions of about an hour each on the second day yielded similarly scant information.

On the third day, Deep's attitude changed. His willingness to answer questions at least allowed Pointed to administer some tests. Pointed asked Deep to draw a person; Deep's drawing revealed a fragile outline of a figure. When Pointed showed Deep some pictures and asked Deep to make up a story based on them, Deep's was brief and simple. Similarly, Deep responded curtly to a Rorschach ink-blot, and his answers completing sentence fragments referred mostly to the immediate surroundings, often in. a sad tone. Eventually, Deep's concentration began to wander; he was irritable for a time, then assumed a calm attitude and recited

Church dogma in answer to any further questions.

After these tests, Deep's parents filed a petition in the local probate court for appointment as his temporary guardians, saying that Deep had been a victim of brainwashing. Pointed appeared as a witness and explained that Deep had been exposed to a process of coercive persuasion. The psychological tests revealed a borderline personality, someone uncomfortable with himself and seeking to restore himself by finding a place in a different reality. Deep had thus entered into something like a trance, a condition of psychological bondage to the Church. His responses to many questions were simplistic, revealing a child-like and regressive personality. At times Deep exhibited a virtually flat affect, showing no interest whatever in the questions; at other time, he was unusually cheerful.

In all, Pointed characterized Deep as being in mind control, a victim of psychological kidnapping. Pointed proposed therapy that would involve stress examinations to bring Deep back to himself. The examinations would challenge Deep, Pointed explained, to bring some changes in himself, by checking out his logic, testing his ability to act on his own behalf. While such examinations could evoke anxiety, they offered the best way to lead Deep back to reality.

Deep's situation is hypothetical, but it reflects actual cases./1/ A California Superior Court judge, for example, appointed the parents of five adult members of the Unification Church as temporary conservators of their children in response to assertions that the children were victims of "mind control" by the Church./2/ Parents of an adult member of Hare Krishna in Massachusetts applied for an extension of their temporary guardianship over their adult son so they could continue psychiatric examinations to determine if the son was suffering from a mental illness resulting from brainwashing. They proposed a "mind control probe" which would include stress examinations./3/ In another case, in Vermont, parents brought a suit against the Unification Church, claiming enslavement of their daughter and requesting that the Court determine her competency "to make decisions regarding her future."/4/

In Arizona, after a father was appointed temporary guardian of his child and authorized to administer "counseling" for the ward to treat a condition resulting from adherence to beliefs of the Unification Church, the child (an adult) brought a Section 1985 civil rights suit claiming a conspiracy to force him to renounce his religious affiliation./5/ More litigation against parents occurred in Minnesota where a daughter sued her parents and others for false imprisonment and intentional infliction of emotional distress in trying to persuade her to leave The Way Ministry./6/ In another Section 1985 suit in Rhode Island, an adult daughter sued her parents and others, alleging involuntary deprogramming away from the Unification Church./7/

These cases have been resolved in both directions./8/ None, however, has carefully analyzed either the claims being made or their legal foundations. All acknowledge the principle that religious beliefs are absolutely protected under the First Amendment, and that religious conduct may be regulated only to further a compelling interest of the state,/9/ and then only in the least restrictive manner possible./10/ Too often, those principles are stated as incantations, and merely precede one conclusion or other rather than leading to it.

The purpose of this essay is to provide some of the analysis that is missing from court opinions and commentary. Understanding the claims that are made in deprogramming cases will be an important first step; accordingly, Sections I and II discuss the possible meanings of assertions that someone has been brainwashed, and the different ways in which such a condition can be caused. These are novel claims, unlike others in the law. Since the claims concern asserted religious beliefs, the analysis must be carried out against the background of the constitutional understanding of religion, set forth in Section III. Only then can possible results and remedies be discussed, in Section IV, and wider implications considered, in Section V.

The analysis will show that many claims about brainwashing assert no more than that an individual has changed, and that someone else does not like the change. The more serious and unprecedented meaning of such claims is that an individual has become a robot as a result of coercive influences. If those influences are applied without consent *and* if the result is an incapacity to adopt or affirm religious beliefs, then the state may intervene to restore that capacity. That narrow case is the only way around the absolute constitutional protection for religious beliefs because it is the only case in which there are no authentic beliefs at all.

The claim that someone has been changed into a robot is obviously a drastic one. Moreover, the understanding of what constitutes a religious belief is very broad. Thus, although the many conversions to new sects, especially by young adults,/11/ upset families and distress friends, the problems such conversions involve may not be legal problems. In that case, the courts should stay out.

I. MY CHILD HAS BEEN BRAINWASHED: TYPES OF CLAIMS

The general claim justifying deprogramming, or some other intervention in an individual's thinking processes that is either directed by the state or undertaken with its authority, asserts that the sect adherent has been changed. The change has been caused, the argument goes, by a process described as brainwashing or coercive persuasion, in a manner drastic enough to warrant deliberate efforts to change the person back. This claim can have different meanings. In its weak form, the claim says, "This is not the same person that I knew; someone has changed my child into a different person." At its strongest, the claim is far more drastic: "This is not a 'person' any longer; someone has changed my child into a robot."

A. *Type-I Claims*

What does the weak claim (we may call it a Type-I claim) mean? "This is not the same person" would be trivial if "same" meant "unaltered." Everyone changes over time, both physically and mentally. Some degree of change is compatible with sameness or identity of a person.

Philosophers define personal identity in a variety of ways. Although different theorists assert the primacy of mental or of bodily continuity,/12/ our actual concept of a person who remains the same over time seems to involve a being with both memories and a material body/13/: some mental and physical continuity is necessary to personal identity. "Continuity" may be defined as simply the absence of a radical break, but a more complex view sees identity as a function of "connectedness," so that different selves exist if successive stages of an individual are disconnected psychologically./14/ Under both approaches the question remains as to the degree or quality of change that is required before identity itself can be said to have shifted. That is, what degree of change is compatible with the concept of sameness?

Robert Nozick has recently looked at this question from a new perspective. Identity in general—whether of persons or otherwise—may be analyzed in terms of the "closest continuer." An entity x is the same as y if x continues y (temporally), if nothing else continues y more closely than x does, and if x continues y "closely enough."/15/ Whether Nozick's test simply restates the theory based on continuity (since it refers to that criterion at each step) or combines the identity theories based on continuity and connectedness (since a judgment about a later y continuing the earlier x "closely enough" to be called the same requires an evaluation of the connectedness of x and y), his theory provides a useful analysis for cases where allegations of brainwashing clash with claims of religious freedom. Does the convert to a new sect cease to be the same person that he was before conversion? If so, in what sense has his identity changed; and what difference does any change make in terms of the way that person should be treated?

Some examples without the complications of religious conversion can focus these questions. In the case of the Ship of Theseus, a wooden sailing ship of ancient Greece is changed by the removal of a single plank. Is it the same ship? Yes, according to Nozick's criteria: and yes again, if a second and even a third plank is replaced, and many more, perhaps even to the extent of all planks. But what happens when the replaced

planks are stored on the side, and then a new and identically designed
boat is built with the original planks, next to the "continued" ship built
by replacing planks? What is the *closest* continuer? Though the progression, plank by plank, yields successive ships that we might deem "close
enough," when we build the second (rebuild the first?) ship, we find two
continuers, and no clear answer about the continuing identity of the
original ship.

Bernard Williams poses a similar problem in the case of a hypothetical
person./16/ Is the individual A the same person after an operation that
produces total amnesia? At least on Nozick's theory of the closest continuer, A is still the same. What if, further, the amnesia is accompanied by
certain changes in A's character. Next case: the changes of character are
produced together with certain "memory" beliefs which happen to be illusory, not fitting the life of any actual person. Then, what if the character
traits and "memory" are appropriate to B, an actual person? In two more
stages, the character traits and memory are transferred to A "from" a second individual B, though B remains the same; and at last B is not left the
same, and in fact the character traits and memory of A and B are
exchanged.

We may reach a stage, along this progression, at which we would no
longer say that A has remained the same. Indeed, if A in advance were
told the progression and its final stage, and were informed that one of
the original A and B would have some pain inflicted on him, which
would A choose? Does bodily continuity or continuity of memory count
for more in determining continuity of self? Or, despite those continu-
ities, is there a psychological disconnectedness in these examples that
indicates changed identities?

These classical philosophical conundrums bring us to the edge of
personal identity and help us to understand the Type-I claims. The convert to a new sect does not exchange identities with anyone else. There is
both bodily continuity and memory continuity. In Nozick's terms, the
later stage continues the earlier, and no other person continues that individual more closely. The only question is whether the later stage continues the earlier closely enough to be called the same. The convert has
certainly changed outlooks drastically, and has adopted dramatically
different values. If the continuity is not close enough in some sense, if
the convert is disconnected from his former self, then a different person
might have emerged from the process of conversion.

We should remember that even "normal" individuals sometimes
change drastically. If we call them "different people" after the change,
we usually do so metaphorically, as a description and not as a prelude to
state-authorized treatment to change them back. For example, consider
the diligent student who has always achieved highly at school but then
takes a vacation to a different climate, where he discovers relaxation in

(say) the South Seas and becomes a sailing bum. Or, by contrast, what about the confirmed surfer who suddenly "finds" capitalism and forsakes his board for a briefcase, his swimsuit for a three-piece? Whether we judge that such an individual has kept the same identity may depend on the level at which we ask the question: *continuity* is preserved, and so is identity on one theory; *connectedness* may have been broken by the dramatic shift, and identity with it.

What matters for purposes of this discussion, though, is that no one would expect the state to conduct or authorize deprogramming of either the South Seas sailing bum or the New Capitalist. Even if they are deemed to be "different people" from their former selves, becoming-a-different-person is one thing that individuals are allowed to do. In the case of religious conversion, any other result would be surprising. Conversion involves psychological and emotional changes which may be drastic enough to lead others to see the convert as a different person in casual conversation. That becomes the "change" that supposedly justifies deprogramming.

The application for temporary guardianship of Deep Believer may rest on those sorts of perceptions. Deep may be a different person from Young as far as his former acquaintances are concerned—"Have you seen Young lately? He's changed so much you'd think you were talking to a different person"—but the same conversation might be made of him had he just finished the Dale Carnegie course. Moreover, Deep (like any other convert) may not be able to explain the change analytically.

Deprogramming might be proposed because he is "incapable of fully understanding the conditions to which he has been subjected that account for his recent change of attitude."/17/ Yet even if he has become a different person in some sense, he is no different from a convert to an established religion, the Dale Carnegie graduate, the South Seas sailing bum, or the New Capitalist. And whatever else *those* "changed people" must deal with in terms of others' reactions to their new selves, they need not worry about deprogramming.

There remains the element of coercion: someone allegedly *causes* the convert's change. The consequences of that claim for the analysis will be considered below, in Section II, but the simple fact of altered lifestyle does not justify deprogramming. To the extent that more is asserted, the claim becomes a stronger (Type-II) claim, and must be analyzed separately.

B. Type-II Claims

In the movie *Invasion of the Body Snatchers*, alien beings produce "pods" that develop into bodies identical to humans with the same psychology except for the lack of all emotions. These new pod-people replace their duplicate originals, which shrivel and disappear, not by death (or murder) but in a succession of synchronized stages in what seems to be the same person. Professor Nozick analyzed the distressing effect of the movie through the closest-continuer scheme./18/ If the pod-people did chase and murder the originals, that would have a certain criminal horror. But the synchronized replacement of successive stages of an individual produces a worse horror: Nozick's closest-continuer theory asserts that the pods must be the *same people* as the originals, and we do not want that to be the case. Something is missing from the pod-people which makes us resist the conclusion that the pods are in any significant way the same as the originals.

The pods are not close enough continuers of the originals to be called the same. The lack of affect means not so much that there is no continuity of the same person, or even sufficient connectedness, but that there is no longer any person being continued, no connectedness at all. The pods are non-persons, so the notions of sameness, continuity, and connectedness become irrelevant.

And so with brainwashing. The claim that someone has changed, is not the same, can mean that the person is *no longer a person* at all. This is a robot.

The inquiry must shift, in analyzing this Type-II claim, from criteria of sameness to criteria of personhood. Philosophers again differ in defining personhood, and again the difference concerns the relationship between the two most obviously important elements, mind and body. Descartes thought of the mind as logically independent of the body, so that the essential feature of a person is mental only./19/ By contrast, A. J. Ayer's physicalist theory ties states of consciousness to the particular body with which the person is identified./20/ Strawson sees the "person" as unanalyzable and primitive, prior to the notion of consciousness altogether./21/ Or a person may be *all* of the various ways by which personhood can be characterized: the body (as victim of a crime, for example), the appearance (a "comely person"), the self-conscious and rational individual, the source and subject of rights and obligations, the entity that takes roles and discharges functions, the being capable of verbal communication and of reciprocating. A synthetic view of a person combines a physical body, whose actions are controlled only to a limited extent by instincts, with a consciousness of the indeterminate nature of the physical self./22/

In all of these descriptions, *preservation* of one's personhood depends upon preventing the substitution of another individual's judgment for one's own. Thus, one way to summarize the views of personhood is in the negative: a person is not a robot. If a robot is defined as an entity—even one with a high degree of intelligence—programmed from outside, then a person is an entity programmed from within./23/

Type-II claims maintain that an entity who was a person at a previous time has ceased to be so. The former person has lost the capacity to program himself. Specifically, he has become incapable of adopting or affirming religious beliefs.

If Deep Believer's parents make such a claim, they are not merely saying that he has abandoned a former way of life, that he has been attracted to a new mode of living, or even that his new lifestyle involves unquestioning faith and absorption of dogma. Rather, they assert that the new faith has been implanted and that Deep is incapable of adopting it as his own. He is like the pod-people in *Invasion*. When a doctrine of the Church is recited, it is not being stated "by" Deep. It does not reflect an authentic belief of his own. It comes from somewhere else.

Thus, when all the facts are sifted, vastly different kinds of claims may emerge from a case like Deep's. The Type-I claim may be primarily emotional—"my child is now a person who is different from the one I knew before, and I do not like that"; a change in one individual is objectionable to some others, and those *others'* dis-ease lies behind the attempt to change the individual "back." The Type-II claim, on the other hand, makes a frightening positive assertion that challenges the alleged victim's very existence: someone who was a person is no longer one. On that basis rests the attempt to bring the individual back to personhood.

II. CAUSATION AND BRAINWASHING

A spectrum of causes may lie behind the actual changes involved in a person's conversion. Such changes may be voluntary or self-induced. Or, if involuntary, the changes may have weak or strong causes. The less severe of the involuntary-causation theories asserts that conversion to the new religious sects occurs because of deception: potential converts may be lured into a situation in which persuasive forces come to bear without the convert's knowledge of what, exactly, he is being converted to. This is something less than a brainwashing claim. The stronger involuntary-causation claim follows the classical coercive persuasion model./24/ Whether a potential convert is approached directly or deceptively, he is then allegedly deprived of sleep, railed at, regimented in diet and daily routine, shut off from all contact with the outside world, and thereby brainwashed into a new mode of thinking.

A. *Voluntary Change*

It is not unusual for an individual to try to change his behavior or beliefs. Anyone who has read self-improvement books, attended sessions about the power of positive thinking, made a New Year's resolution or undertaken an organized weight-loss program can verify the possibility of attempting (if not achieving) self-induced change. One can also consent to coercive influences, for example, by entering a seminary or monastery. To be valid, such consent must be both voluntary and knowing. Even "voluntary" entry into a religious order, however, involved some unanticipated coercion in the initiate's relinquishment of the old self, no matter how strong the individual's motivation to become a priest or monk. In a different field, a medical or psychiatric patient's knowledge of a procedure to which he consents is always limited to a certain degree, no matter what the prior disclosure. Yet the gap in knowledge is not deemed to prevent informed agreement to enter the religious order or undergo the treatment, and "informed" consent in those cases is legally effective.

Some procedures may be so severe as to raise the level of required disclosure and prior knowledge. Psychosurgery, for instance, could eliminate the possibility of knowing consent to any future procedure and might therefore be allowed only in the most unusual circumstances. Not only the physical changes wrought by psychosurgery but also the drastic effects of psychological treatments like behavior modification raise fears that the capacity to consent or deny consent to future influences could be impaired. That capacity is sufficiently important to warrant close protection. But whatever the level of knowledge required to validate consent as "informed," when such a finding is made, it should protect the individual from attempts to change him back.

At the actual time of consent, one must have both sufficient knowledge and a capacity to give that consent. If a convert's capacity is alleged to decrease as knowledge increases—so that capacity clearly exists only when the prospective convert is relatively unfamiliar with the training that lies ahead—the "match" of sufficient knowledge and capacity must still exist at *some* time, to validate the convert's choice. But as explained below, the choice need not be articulated in closely analytical and rational fashion.

Converts to new sects often look for a new belief system even before they choose their particular sect. For a young person confused about ultimate principles and values, the prospect of a closed meaning system in a group where the authority structure is clearly defined is attractive because such a system would eliminate the kind of moral ambiguity that makes that individual uneasy in the first place. Thus, the observation by a psychologist in one case that the adherent was "maintaining himself in mind control"/25/ was at least a suggestive contradiction in terms: although anyone who "maintains" a specific attitude cannot be having his mind controlled by anyone else, one can consciously submit oneself to an authoritarian system that prescribes appropriate thoughts as well as actions (compare conventional church dogma or Talmudic rules). The voluntary submission to indoctrination in that case should preclude later questions about the convert's valid "ownership" of the resulting beliefs.

B. Deception

By definition, one does not know that a deceptive practice is occurring. No effective consent to the process of change is therefore possible. But the nonvoluntary origin of the beliefs induced by deception does not automatically expose them to being erased by deprogramming. Nor should such origin even raise a presumption that the "victim" is presently incapable of holding those beliefs as his own.

There are subtle and unannounced methods of persuasion practiced every day. We are bombarded by commercial and political advertising, and even education is predicated on a community sanctioned form of "brainwashing-in" of socially acceptable ideas. Plato thought that the educational system should be designed to produced beliefs that the state found acceptable;/26/ recently Frances Fitzgerald has shown how the writing of American history textbooks can shape the way generations of students think about the past;/27/ and the Supreme Court has explicitly stressed the inculcative role of schools./28/

If ideas are to become the target of deprogramming, their involuntary origin must be coupled with a present incapacity to affirm them as one's own. And if the weak (deceptive) form of causation results in a Type-I change, the convert is not incapable of adopting or affirming his present beliefs.

Young Adult was approached by someone who offered a blessed existence through the Church. If the proselytizer had offered a course in self-improvement and the banquet and lectures tried instead to convert Young to a religion, the deceptiveness of the introduction would not justify deprogramming as long as the neophyte retained the capacity to adopt or reject beliefs. Even if a severe discontinuity in a convert leads us to say he has become a different person, he has not ceased to *be* a person. Why should he be deprogrammed?

Consider an agnostic who happens to attend a service at church or temple during a time when, coincidentally, the minister or rabbi is in the midst of a spiritual *crise*. Even though the preacher would not for the moment believe in any of the religious tenets he set forth, he might feel an obligation to continue outwardly the same because of duty to his flock. The agnostic suddenly finds himself attracted to the faith, and adopts it. The "deception" hardly undermines the convert's faith.

The intentional deceiver should not endanger a convert's ideas any more severely, as long as the convert has the ability to adopt or affirm his own faith after any deception. Whether the seeker thinks he is going to find true conventional religion and ends up being converted to a new sect, or believes he is going to a new sect and ends up a committed Catholic or Jew, if he retains all the elements of personhood, then despite the change of his outlook he can adopt or ratify the beliefs as his own.

Thus, deception in itself does not justify deprogramming. Of course, as a social policy, deception should be discouraged and fraud is thus a crime. The deceiving party is punished directly, but punishment should not extend to the deceived. If deception yields a Type-I change, the convert's belief can nevertheless be affirmed as his own. If deception results in a Type-II change—though it is difficult to understand how non-coercive deceptive persuasion could render a person a robot—the inquiry resembles that of a classic brainwashing case. Those cases must be considered next.

C. Coercion

Despite an involuntary origin, beliefs may still be adopted as one's own—witness Saul on the road to Damascus and every sudden convert since. In the case of long-term "coercion," such as a child's being forced to recite catechism or attend religious school, the beliefs formed are not subject to deprogramming. The result should be the same even in the case of intense coercive persuasion as long as that process fails to remove the *capacity* to adopt or affirm beliefs as one's own.

Not all coercion is illegal. One is entitled to try to convince others of one's beliefs by peer pressure, shame, or even threats of divine retribution. Even in cases involving proscribed coercion by force, the victim's will is not extinguished. Rather, the force or threat makes the victim *exercise* his will differently from usual. Certain uses of force are discouraged and punished by being made crimes.

It is a different kind of coercion, however, that extinguishes another person's will and results in what is commonly understood as brainwashing. In that case, the capacity to affirm religious beliefs may be dissolved, and the strong claim of causation would be linked with the strong Type-II change in the victim, from person to robot. The extremity of both the origin and the result should alert us to the extraordinary nature of the argument: someone has ceased to be a person as a result of intense outside influence, and because of that change the state is asked for authority to change the individual "back to" a person, that is, authority to change the individual's mind and mental processes.

In the case of A, the devout adult adherent of religion X who is forcibly abducted by fanatic adherents of religion Y, coercively persuaded over weeks, converted to Yism and transformed into a Y proselytizer, the involuntary origins of A's new religion are clear enough. If A affirms his adherence to Yism, though also acknowledging that coercive persuasion brought him to Yism in the first place, the present capacity to affirm and adopt beliefs should protect those beliefs from state-authorized modification.

A's case hypothesizes actual coercive persuasion, whereas Deep Believer may not have been exposed to that sort of force. The inquiry in

Deep's case might not reach this stage of the analysis. If it did, however, the state would be justified in authorizing treatment only if the present capacity to affirm or adopt beliefs were lacking.

The problem for the convert—A or Deep Believer or anyone—comes in trying to prove (a defense against conservatorship proceedings, for example) that he retains the capacity to affirm his beliefs. The fact of having adopted a belief, albeit a new and unusual one, cannot prove incapacity to choose beliefs: it contradicts the conclusion. Nor can the content of a religious belief show that a person is incapable of choosing religious beliefs in general; religious beliefs may not be probed in this way. Finally, the intensity of the new belief should not be used to support allegations that the new beliefs are programmed in and therefore not authentic beliefs.

Sharpen the hypothetical. Suppose that a drug is involved rather than coercive behavior: someone is kidnapped and forcibly given a drug that leaves him unchanged except that he chooses a new religion to which he adheres without question, chanting, proselytizing, and forsaking former beliefs and modes of living.

If the drug leaves the individual in the same condition as the coercively persuaded A in the previous hypothetical case, the response obviously remains the same. Or if the drug takes away the capacity to affirm and adopt religious beliefs, the inquiry ends: that is precisely the situation in which some therapeutic measures—yet to be defined—would be justified. But the administration of a drug with those effects also changes the nature of the inquiry. Outside coercive influences may produce certain *symptoms*, such as a change of religion, which may or may not indicate continued capacity to affirm or adopt religious beliefs; the drug may be *defined* as something whose essence *is* the deprivation of the ingestant's ability to make choices about religion. To that extent, the drug case over-sharpens the hypothetical.

What if someone gives himself a drug that changes his religion? Again, Type-I and Type-II results must be examined separately. In the first case, there remains an individual capable of affirming choices—a "person." Thus, even though the individual might not have come to the new religion by a conventional route, the administration of the drug followed by affirmation of its results does not justify compelling a change of those beliefs in turn. The result should be the same even if the person took the drug by mistake, or out of sheer curiosity after finding it on a shelf: the continued capacity to affirm beliefs protects the beliefs that are in fact adopted.

In a Type-II situation, the individual would take the drug with the knowledge that it would change his beliefs and also leave him incapable of affirming the resulting beliefs or changing them further. The voluntary origin should afford some protection—as discussed above, one can consent to coercion. But society has an interest in keeping its citizens capable of adopting or affirming beliefs. Thus, laws prohibit the ingestion of *any* mind-altering drugs, unless medically prescribed. The same policy, though not required analytically, might extend to ban a drug whose only effect is the change of one's religious beliefs and subsequent incapacity to adopt others, or even a drug that changed religious beliefs but left the capacity to choose one's religion intact (the Type-I situation). In all cases, criminal sanctions should prohibit the coercive administration of any such drug by another individual.

With all the caveats noted above, then, a case for some sort of deprogramming treatment does emerge. The situation in which any treatment is appropriate, however, is narrow and extreme. An individual must have been involuntarily subjected to persuasive influences, and as a result of the coercion the individual must presently lack the capacity to adopt or affirm a genuine belief.

What is the test for such a condition? How do we recognize a robot with the shell of a human being? If an individual acts like a person, that individual should be deemed a person. Moreover, in applying that test, we must acknowledge that an intensely religious person may act in very unconventional ways./29/ The specific issue to be determined is whether an individual has the capacity to adopt or affirm religious beliefs. As long as that capacity remains, the manner in which it may be exercised should not matter, nor even *whether* it is exercised. The judicial determination of such capacity will be just as sensitive and as difficult as that about capacity in other areas—to care for one's property or one's person, for example—and it will also have to be made against the limitations just mentioned.

If the test for personhood seems trivial, one need only look at some of the claims of would-be deprogrammers to realize how much such a measure is needed. The mind control exerted by some sects is said to be so subtle that it cannot be detected by usual methods. Someone under its influence may react to standard psychological tests in ways that seem perfectly normal. So an adherent's new cheerfulness is offered as proof of the alleged brainwashing, and stress examinations are proposed to tease out further evidence. The proposed test would at least bring some common sense back into the inquiry. And it would avoid the danger of trapping a convert so that only a renunciation of the new religion could prove independence of mind.

The preceding analysis of both the types of causes and the types of results in so-called brainwashing cases can be set out as shown in the chart on the opposite page.

The cause of change may be voluntary; or if involuntary, it may take either a weak form (deception) or strong (coercion). The resulting change is either a Type-I case (the changed-person) or Type-II (the robot).

CAUSE OF CHANGE

		VOLUNTARY	INVOLUNTARY/WEAK	INVOLUNTARY/STRONG
TYPE OF CHANGE	I: CHANGED PERSON	No Deprogramming	No Deprogramming	Continued Capacity To Affirm Beliefs No Deprogramming
	II: ROBOT	With Knowledge: No Deprogramming	Deception Eliminates Informed Consent: Treatment May be Allowed	Treatment May Be Allowed

Neither a voluntary process nor a weak involuntary cause (deception) that produces a Type-I change justifies deprogramming. Even when the involuntary origin of beliefs takes a strong, coercive form, the continued capacity to affirm beliefs (a Type-I case) should prevent any interference by the state with the adherent's beliefs.

More difficult are the Type-II cases. When an individual voluntarily takes a drug that renders him incapable of changing his beliefs subsequently, there might be reasons of policy that weigh in favor of deprogramming. Principles of informed consent, however, suggest that the voluntary submission to a process (or ingestion of a drug) that renders one incapable of further choosing one's beliefs should insulate the resulting beliefs from subsequent change by an outsider. Since informed consent is critical, in a Type-II situation any deception resulting in a robot would justify an attempt to restore the individual's capacity to adopt or affirm religious beliefs. The most drastic case, of coercive changes that yield a Type-II robot, would also call for a course of treatment that could restore the ability to choose.

Human lives do not fit neatly into categories, of course. The case of Deep Believer will have to be sorted out to determine whether Deep's conversion was voluntary; if voluntary, whether the process of initiation was undertaken with sufficient knowledge to validate any consent to coercion; if involuntary, whether Deep subsequently affirmed the new beliefs independently, or whether Deep became a programmed robot. Those are not easy questions for a judge to resolve. At the least, a judge must not apply criteria that would force Deep to renounce his new religion in order to prove he had adopted it voluntarily. Deep does seem to have adopted a belief system that gave new meaning to his life, but evidentiary questions cannot be resolved in the hypothetical case. As they are answered, with proper regard to the permissible limits of inquiry, the facts as determined will fall into some portion of the preceding analysis.

Four of the six matrix cases would preclude deprogramming. The two cases with a firm analytical basis for attempting to restore an individual's capacity to adopt or affirm religious beliefs both involve Type-II changes. Only in the robot-situation may the state properly intervene.

That situation is entirely new to the law./30/ Indeed, where has it arisen in any context outside *Invasion of the Body Snatchers?* In nearly all conceivable cases, then, the matrix emphasizes that deprogramming is simply not justified. There may be a case in which the justification actually exists, in which an individual has become a robot; but that case has not yet walked out of a science fiction script.

III. BELIEFS, RELIGION, AND RELIGIOUS BELIEFS

While the bare meaning of brainwashing claims must be deciphered as the first step in any analysis, those claims implicate a broad context of religion. The adherent seeks the protection of the First Amendment for what he asserts to be his religious beliefs, while others attempt to justify intrusion by asserting variously that the claimed religious beliefs are neither authentic as beliefs nor religious in nature.

A. *Beliefs and Mentation*

A right of privacy exists under the Constitution, and, though it has been variously defined, at its core lies "the principle . . . of an inviolate personality."/31/ Whatever else it involves, the constitutional right of privacy protects an individual's inner thoughts against intrusion by the government./32/ Claims of brainwashing or coercive persuasion aim to bring the government into this area by alleging "menticide," the disruption of mentation by a third party.

The government's exercise of power to control directly its citizens' minds is unconstitutional. In a case involving a prosecution for possession of obscene films in the accused's own home, the Supreme Court rejected the state's assertion of a right "to protect the individual's mind" from the effects of obscenity, a right that would allow the state to control the moral content of a person's thoughts./33/

The justification offered for deprogramming is no more compelling. The state, it is argued, has an interest in maintaining each individual's mental health, an interest strong enough to override the individual's right to his own thoughts, whatever they be. Society does run more smoothly when everyone behaves predictably, but that does not automatically justify the state in redirecting the individual's divergence from the desired norm.

In particular, the state cannot enforce its interest that its citizens function at the maximum level of their capacity. Where the state sought to administer antipsychotic drugs to a non-institutionalized incompetent and no emergency was involved, the Supreme Judicial Court in Massachusetts recently held that the fundamental right of the individual to privacy, including the right to refuse treatment, was not outweighed by the state interests of preserving life and ensuring a maximum level of mental functioning. As *parens patriae*, the state may desire to "remove obstacles to individual development," but even treatment that restores competence to the incompetent is not automatically justified. The state's desire to maintain and improve the capabilities of each individual is usually shared by its citizens, as a matter of their own preference. But it may not be forced upon them. Anyone has the option to ignore what the "reasonable person" would adopt (especially when religious views are involved); and, at least when an actual life-or-death crisis does not arise, that choice must be respected.

The state is allowed considerable leeway in training its citizens. The function of public education, for example, is indoctrinative: the Supreme Court has recently acknowledged again the role schools play in exposing students to many uniform lessons as they grow up./34/ The state may not coerce an individual, however, to adopt particular views. Neither can the state rummage around among an individual's beliefs and wander about the individual's mind to select "out" certain beliefs deemed unacceptable. One's inner thoughts would then be shaped not only by the beliefs proscribed, but also by the sheer threat of the state's "confiscation" of any thoughts at all. If the danger sounds farfetched, think about the proposed treatment of the adherent to the new sect.

The state is allowed to commit an individual upon a showing of mental illness, when coupled (in nearly all states) with a finding of "dangerousness" to self or others. One of the necessary predicates for commitment thus concerns an individual's actions, or propensity to act, and not merely his beliefs. Moreover, commitment does not automatically constitute a finding of incompetence, and competent individuals have the right to refuse treatment. Indeed, even the incompetent may refuse treatment. Thus, the window for state intervention with one's beliefs is extremely narrow even before we turn to the area of religion.

B. The Constitutional Understanding of Religion

The cases of United States v. Seeger and Welsh v. United States set forth the Supreme Court's most extended discussion on the constitutional understanding of religion. Seeger preserved the constitutionality of the conscientious objector provision in the Selective Service Act which requires that the objection be based on "religious training and belief." The Court defined religious beliefs as those "which are based upon a power or being, or upon a faith, to which all else is subordinate or upon which all else is ultimately dependent." We can identify such a belief by asking whether it "occupies a place in the life of its possessor parallel to that filled by the orthodox belief in God of one who clearly qualifies for the exemption"; the Court also required that the belief be "sincere and meaningful."/35/

Tied as it is to an orthodox belief in God, such an understanding is compatible with traditional definitions of religion. But the parallel-position standard does not require theistic tenets in a religion, and in Welsh a set of beliefs that rested entirely on ethical and moral concerns met the test./36/ In that respect, the modern constitutional understanding of religion accords with at least one major strand of modern theology. In Seeger, the Court quoted Paul Tillich, equating "god" with "the depths of your life, . . .the source of your being, . . . your ultimate concern, . . what you take seriously without any reservation."/37/ Religion provides an ultimate ordering principle for a believer and gives a deep coherence to that individual's life.

The constitutional boundary of religion is crossed, according to *Welsh*, when beliefs rest "solely upon considerations of policy, pragmatism or expedience." Justice Harlan further distinguished religion from philosophy, understood as "mere adherence to ethical or moral beliefs in general,"/38/ and thus identified religion by an intensity of conviction. Protection for one's religious faith does not require an individual to articulate an explicit set of beliefs or present a clear basis for beliefs; and a court cannot be "microscopic" in its review of claimed beliefs to determine whether they are religious. Rationality and logic may be entirely absent. But conviction there must be, a faith which binds the individual to an ultimate concern.

The hallmark of religion thus becomes the willingness to stake one's all on the belief system one adopts. That attitude reflects the fact that the religion orders the individual's world for him, and not just intellectually so. If an individual holds a *religious* belief, then *because* of such a belief, the world makes some sense. Without it the world would, figuratively, fall apart. Tillich makes the same point in *The Shaking of the Foundations:*

> [I]f the foundations of this place and all places begin to crumble, . . . only only two alternatives remain—despair, which is the certainty of eternal destruction, or faith, which is the certainty of eternal salvation. 'The world itself shall crumble, but . . . my salvation knows no end,' say the Lord. *This* is the alternative for which the prophets stood. This is what we should call *religion*, or more precisely, the religious ground of all religion./39/

C. Protecting Religious Beliefs

Religious beliefs are absolutely protected under the first amendment./40/ This is an extraordinary provision in a Constitution that balances and weighs competing interests. Indeed, a balancing test applies to regulation of religious conduct and the burdens otherwise placed on one's religion by more general statutes. *Sherbert* v. *Verner* permits such regulation in the face of a compelling state interest./41/ But no asserted interest of the state can justify regulation of the beliefs themselves: there is no balancing to be done.

Religious beliefs cannot be used to establish mental illness as required for involuntary psychiatric treatment, because religious beliefs cannot be examined for their truth or falsity. Even in established religions, many beliefs are bizarre by any rational standard. Recent court cases have tested whether creationists' belief in the literal truth of *Genesis* qualifies as science,/42/ but no one has suggested not only that "creation science" be barred from public school curricula but also that the creationists themselves be committed for their fundamentalist tenets. Similarly, for some, Jesus' rising from the dead or God's speaking to Moses from a burning bush is an article of faith; yet others' opinion that such beliefs are absurd does not allow them to try to have the believing Christian or Jew committed. The worship services of many conventional religions include rote elements, from the *credo* to the *sh'ma*. At a more intense level, monks may be required to repeat litanies many times a day. Deep Believer learned Church doctrine by heart, and chanted prayers when his faith was questioned. But Deep and other adherents to new sects are no more mentally ill, because of their faith, than believers in established religions, and enforced psychiatric treatment is no more appropriate in the former cases than the latter.

The government may restrict individuals in ways that indirectly affect thoughts or beliefs—as in cases where access to mind-altering drugs is restricted despite religious objections, or when the showing of obscene films is controlled or banned and so individuals are deprived of sense data to "process" privately. But it may not try to change directly the religious beliefs themselves which are absolutely protected. For in cases where deprogramming is proposed, the beliefs are the chief objectionable feature, and they are the focus of the state's attention.

The fact that speech is involved does not lessen the protection. If the speech simply declares the religious belief, it differs from thoughts only in its "visibility." As belief made manifest, declarative speech deserves exactly the same protection as is accorded to belief itself. When speech does more than declare beliefs, the state may assert interests of its own to weigh against additional individual interests as proselytizing for the religion and spreading the faith. Doctrinally, that balance can be struck in favor of reasonable time, place and manner regulations, as long as the least restrictive regulations are imposed. The Supreme Court has recently held, for example, that a state regulation was reasonable enough, although it confined all booth-renters at a state fair to their own booths in presenting their ideas and selling their wares, and in doing so had the effect of preventing Hare Krishna adherents from practicing *sankirtan* which calls for proselytizing as a religious tenet./43/

State regulations of the content of religious speech, however, would be tantamount to controlling the thoughts and beliefs themselves. If an electroencephalogram could project an individual's thoughts on a screen, the state would never be allowed to inspect those projections and regulate the underlying thought processes. Declarative speech is nothing more than an audible projection of beliefs.

Ironically, those whose intensity of beliefs dominates their lives, those who take their religion with unreserved seriousness, are said by some to be non-persons *because* of the intensity. The argument contradicts itself, and in a case like Deep Believer, it seems incorrect as a matter of fact. His new faith gave deeper meaning to his life than he had experienced previously. All that is proved by the argument against the intensity of his beliefs is that most of us only give lip service to religion—to intensity, ultimate concern, and unreserved seriousness—without adopting such features in our own lives or honoring or even tolerating them in others.

Thus, the constitutional right of privacy and the constitutional understanding of religion afford to religious beliefs a protection that narrows severely the kind of inquiry than can be made about them. An individual must adopt beliefs as his ultimate concern, if they are to rise to the level of religion, but the specific beliefs may not inspected for their truth or falsity. The beliefs must be sincerely held, but that requirement should be one primarily of congruence: one must believe what one professes to believe at that time, and only a demonstrable difference between one's actions and one's professed tenets can reveal a noncongruence. Finally, the intensity of one's religious beliefs should bring added rather than decreased protection.

The only other ground on which to challenge religious beliefs—and the only ground on which such challenges are seriously made, in the case of adherents to new sects—is to assert that they are not beliefs at all, i.e., authentic beliefs of the believer's own, but rather involuntarily programmed responses of a robot. And so the legal analysis bring us back to where the philosophical analysis began.

IV. RESULTS AND REMEDIES

A. *Deprogramming*

Deprogramming is seen by its proponents as a kind of treatment which aims to restore to an individual what he has supposedly lost in the process of his conversion. But the very pervasiveness of the claimed affliction calls into question whether any limited psychological remedy is possible. Classical models of brainwashing involve several stages: cleansing the mind and ridding it of old beliefs (washing); an infusion of new beliefs; and (re)freezing the mind to adopt the new pattern of thought. And the proposed "cure" in a case like Deep's resembles the disease; the deprogramming seems little different from the brainwashing itself.

Psychosurgery might someday become sufficiently exact to connect or disconnect specific neurons or thought patterns. Such a technique would enable the "unfreezing" of a single mental pattern, in particular the adherence to a set of (religious) beliefs. That result would accord with the professed goal of deprogrammers, to "free" the adherent's mind and enable a choice of religion without allegedly coercive influence. But even the least drastic result of "successful" treatment would be readoption of the same religion. Such testing of religious beliefs is flatly banned by the Constitution.

Especially in its early forms, deprogramming was often stressful and confrontational. Renunciation of beliefs in the face of those methods should not be taken as proof of prior brainwashing. Such reasoning would have all the logic of medieval methods of trial: if an alleged witch survived her dunkings, for example, she had to possess magical powers and so was guilty, whereas her drowning would prove her purity and innocence. So with the supposed victims of brainwashing: surviving an assault on beliefs only proves to the skeptics the strength of the brainwashing, while deconversion from a faith shows that the abandoned beliefs were merely temporary, implanted and inauthentic.

That argument relies on the dubious premise that deprogramming can "work" only on those whose beliefs are not their own, and that a faith adopted without initial coercion cannot be shaken. The premise would not even be tested, perhaps, if Young Adult had converted from a casual Unitarianism to a dogmatic, evangelical Catholicism. If it were, though, might not a barrage of questions, concentrated demands of proof of the new beliefs, blasphemies against the adopted tenets and constant derision, in solitary confinement, all have the effect of weakening the new faith? A constant believer, after such treatment, might be deemed a saint, but society does not require that degree of faith of every adherent.

Even if deprogramming is limited to the most benign form, of unfreezing beliefs (rather than unfreezing-changing-refreezing), it effects an actual change in the individual's patterns of thought. Presently, the only permissible method for changing an individual's pattern of thinking requires the strict requirements of civil commitment proceedings and further proceedings concerning competence and enforced psychiatric treatment. To commit someone against his will, one must prove mental illness and dangerousness to self and others, and as discussed above, religious beliefs cannot be used to find someone mentally ill. Indeed, even a Type-II case of brainwashing may not cause a recognized mental illness.

If mental illness and dangerousness are established independently, any treatment that follows commitment still cannot aim to change or have the effect of changing religious beliefs. In *Winters* v. *Miller*, the Court of Appeals for the Second Circuit found that a mentally ill patient may refuse medical treatment on the basis of religious beliefs./44/ Such an individual must obviously *have* religious beliefs, and thus also the capacity to control his mind sufficiently to form or adopt those beliefs. Even for the mentally ill, then, involuntary psychiatric treatment must be carried out in a way that does not impinge on religious beliefs, without an independent finding of incapacity in that respect.

A finding of mental illness is exactly what parents do not want for their children's records. Thus, they attempt to end-run the commitment, or even guardianship, statutes. But if mental illness is not available as the ground for state action, what is? The grounds most often evoked refer either to the unstartling assertion that someone has changed or to the novel and far-reaching claim that someone has ceased to be a person. In either event, conventional psychiatric treatment is not appropriate. In the one case, no treatment is called for. In the second, new kinds of psychiatric treatment must be tailored to restore personhood, specifically the capacity to choose religious beliefs, without dictating of what those beliefs will—or more importantly, will not—consist. Otherwise, deprogramming simply becomes reprogramming.

B. Persuasion—and Coercive Persuasion

If persuasion induces someone to join a religious sect, persuasion may draw that individual away from the new adopted tenets. And persuasion, by any lawful method, is available to anyone as a means of attracting someone else to or away from, a particular set of beliefs. To be sure, not all religious conversions occur because a listener is rationally persuaded of the soundness of a creed, and then systematically adopts it. Religious conversions may happen suddenly, and adherence involves faith as well as rational thought. Those features of religion may increase the difficulty of "deconversion," but they do not pose any legal obstacle against attempts to persuade one to leave a faith behind.

Religious indoctrination, like secular moral education and the inculcation of all human values, is part of the fabric of one's entire life. If one acquires religious conviction during childhood, conversion away from that faith may be less likely to occur. Conversely, a seemingly sudden conversion may reflect equally long-growing dissastisfaction with the religious values and beliefs to which one has been exposed.

Adherents to new sects are seekers, and established religions may have to ask why the seekers find answers elsewhere. One objection to the new sects is that their doctrines are simplistic: ultimate answers are by nature not easy answers, and what someone claims to regard with unreserved seriousness should be worth taking seriously. If established religions find others' answers too easy, they face a challenge to their own skills of persuasion and attractiveness of faith. That challenge is not played out in court, however.

Entirely different questions arise if coercive persuasion is established along with the victim's resulting inability to adopt or affirm religious beliefs. For the victim, the goal must be to restore that *capacity*, and the treatment must not state or imply any specific religious views or espouse any particular tenets. New research, focused on this specialized question, may be needed in psychology and psychiatry before any such treatment becomes possible.

As far as the perpetrator is concerned, if coercive persuasion and resulting lack of religious capacity could be proved, prosecutions might be possible for the existing crimes of kidnapping or unlawful imprisonment, or civil suits might be available for assault and battery, intentional infliction of emotional distress and the like. These principles apply equally to religious sects and deprogrammer alike: if religion provides no license to commit a crime or tort, neither does parenthood. Thus far, such legal actions have been largely unsuccessful. One response—a problematic one—might be to create new crimes and offenses, such as "mental kidnapping" or a federal tort of enslavement. Another response might be to recognize that the perceived problem may not be, generally, legal one. At the extremes, there might be actionable legal wrongs, but the majority of cases concern societal dis-ease for which courts are not best physicians.

V. THE RELIGION OF THE REPUBLIC AND NEW SECTS

Our society is not comfortable with new religious sects. They differ both from established, familiar religions and from the "religion of the republic"—a nondenominational civil religion which emerged early in this country's history as its political system and social values were raised to the level of the sacred./45/ Against these norms, vigorous sectarian religions may not accomodate themselves to the expectations of the state, and may even become an authority competing with the state. The tension resembles that between competing civil authorities in conflict of laws situations where it is resolved in each case by making one law control while the other recognizes the limitations on its authority./46/ In resolving the tension between religions and civil government, the religious demands upon an individual's *actions* may be balanced against state interests, and real limits might be appropriately imposed on certain activities of religious sects. But religious *beliefs* are like a sovereign nation whose law supersedes all others.

The supremacy of religious belief jars when the belief runs counter to the principles on which civil government and secular society rest. America was founded on a rationalist Enlightenment model within which freedom of religion would operate./47/ Accordingly, each citizen would always want to improve the self, and that process would involve some degree of education, effort, directedness, and individuality. The antithesis of these qualities is communal action and subsumption of the self in the entire group, a non-rational mode of thinking, and simply-being rather than going-directly. The Founding Fathers would perhaps have not much liked new sects. But the freedom of religion they established prevents the preferences of some from controlling the beliefs of others.

Intrinsic to our society and constitutional scheme is not only freedom of religion but also freedom of thought. The marketplace of ideas must remain open, unfettered by government action, and the state may not prescribe an orthodoxy of belief in any respect. It would be a mistake, however, to transform *freedom* of thought into a *requirement* that all thought and all mental processes be rational, and further to impose that requirement on freedom of religion. Religious belief may be logical and rational, but not necessarily so; neither must one choose one's religion in a logical way. A misunderstanding of these principles lies behind a proposed requirement that an adherent "fully understand the conditions to which he has been subjected that account for his recent change of outlook"/48/ and a willingness to have the state direct or authorized "treatment" and change of claimed religious beliefs if that rational and articulable understanding is not forthcoming, even though the believer may not "appreciate the value" of the therapy.

Freedom of religion means not only the freedom to adopt a belief system by rational choice but also the latitude to adopt beliefs—any beliefs that one regards with unreserved seriousness—for no rational reasons, for no reasons at all, for positively irrational reasons. The state can no more compel an explanation of one's thoughts or beliefs than it can compel the adoption of certain beliefs in the first place. While the state can keep the marketplace of ideas open and unfettered, an individual or group may opt out of the market, may opt instead for closed belief systems. And while society may hope that individuals will want to improve themselves and develop their maximum capacities, it cannot enforce that hope.

To collapse religious freedom into a requirement of rational thought subjects religion to societal norms under which divergences become unacceptable. New sects, for example, are said to "manipulate guilt,"/49/ yet established religions' doctrines of sin and damnation are not mentioned, nor is the guilt-based work ethic on which so much of secular society depends. Similarly through this lens

> a religion becomes a cult; proselytization becomes brainwashing; persuasion becomes propaganda; missionaries becomes subversive agents; retreats, monasteries and convents become prisons; holy ritual becomes bizarre conduct; religious observance becomes aberrant behavior; devotion and meditation become psychopathic trances./50/

Labels can just as easily transform religious beliefs into illnesses. To remove these dangers, the state is barred from dictating an orthodoxy in belief.

The hard edges of most established religions have been smoothed by long exposure to societal concerns, and in this country the religion of the republic and established religions have come to be fashioned in one another's image. Many sects that are generally accepted today, however, once faced oppressive government action. Christianity itself was originally an unconventional sect which after a period of persecution became Rome's official religion. New sects cause fear in part because they are new.

If freedom of religion is to mean anything, new sects must be protected for their very difference of lifestyle and thinking (or nonthinking). Beside the constitutional reasons, the new sects may have some positive social effects as mediating structures and therapeutic groups. This is not meant to paint an unrealistic rosy picture of new sects and their impact on society. If their tenets offer a source of ultimate meaning to some individuals and order some individuals' worlds, they cause others great pain, especially families and former acquaintances. But the longevity and difficulty of the conflict between religion and the family do not transform the problem into a legal one. Even if a belief is not religious, the state cannot control an individual's thoughts, whatever they concern, and may not confine someone in a non-criminal case in the absence of mental illness and dangerousness to self or others. In all these matters, a bias always works in favor of the individual. In the criminal law, the bias dissolves the construct of free will in certain instances: we recognize exceptions for volitional impairment resulting from epilepsy, for example, and sometimes for momentary inability to appreciate the consequences of one's actions (but not for the "accretion" of volitional impairment from a deprived economic background). The limitations on culpability *keep the state out* of individuals' lives. In the areas of belief and religious belief, the presumption is also exclusionary: the state may not tamper with beliefs unless there is proven mental illness and dangerousness *and* incompetence, and those categories are not permitted to attach to religious beliefs themselves.

New categories should not be created to let the state in to fiddle with a person's thoughts. The Constitution builds high protective walls; the individual beliefs are not subject to majoritarian preferences. Society may hope for a certain kind of self-improving individual, and established religions may accommodate themselves to the secular expectations of society at large and conform to the religion of the republic. But society does not always get the kind of person it wants, and adherents to new sects do not necessarily adhere to the religion of the republic as well. The religious beliefs they do adopt are absolutely protected. Individuals may drop out of cults as they drop out of society itself; the new sects may soon be no force to reckon with at all. But in the meantime, an individual's adoption of an unorthodox creed does not justify the state in tinkering with that person's mind.

NOTES

/1/   In addition to the cases cited in notes 2-7 below, certain elements of Deep Believer's situation are also drawn from the hypothetical case of *Barns* v. *Barns,* prepared by the Board of Student Advisors for the final round of the Ames moot-court competition at Harvard Law School in 1977. For other discussion of such cases, and the problems they raise, see generally Richard Delgado, "Religious Totalism: Gentle and Ungentle Persuasion Under the First Amendment," 52 *Southern California Law Review* 1 (1977), hereafter cited as "Religious Totalism"; Comment, "'Mind Control' or Intensity of Faith: The Constitutional Protection of Religious Beliefs," 13 *Harvard Civil Rights-Civil Liberties Law Review* 751 (1978), hereafter cited as "Constitutional Protection," by the author of this essay; and Note, "Conservatorships and Religious Cults: Divining a Theory of Free Exercise," 52 *New York University Law Review* 1247 (1978), hereafter cited as "Conservatorships."

/2/   Katz v. Superior Court, 73 Cal. App. 3d 952, 141 Cal. Rptr. 234 (1977).

/3/   *In re* Shapiro, No. 471805 (Middlesex P. Ct., Mass. Nov. 4, 1976).

/4/   Schuppin v. Unification Church, 435 F. Supp. 603 (D. Vt.), *aff'd,* 573 F.2d 1295 (2d Cir. 1977).

/5/   Rankin v. Howard, 457 F. Supp. 70 (D. Ariz. 1978), *rev'd on other grounds,* 633 F.2d 844 (9th Cir. 1980), *cert. denied,* 451 U.S. 939 (1981). The plaintiff sought relief under two separate sections of the Civil Rights Act, 42 U.S.C. Section 1983 and Section 1985. Liability under the former requires state action in depriving an individual of rights under federal law or the Constitution, while Section 1985 liability instead requires a conspiracy to deprive a person or class of persons of legal rights. In *Rankin,* the District Court found a lack of state action and thus dismissed the Section 1983 claim, but it did not dismiss the Section 1985 claim. The Court of Appeals' reversal concerned the Section 1983 claim which it remanded for trial with the Section 1985.

/6/   Peterson v. Sorlien, 299 N.W.2d 123 (Minn. 1980), *cert. denied,* 450 U.S. 1031 (1981).

/7/   Weiss v. Patrick, 453 F. Supp. 717 (D. R.I.), *aff'd mem.,* 588 F.2d 818 (1st Cir. 1978), *cert. denied,* 442 U.S. 929 (1979).

/8/   The Court of Appeals in California overturned the temporary guardianship that was imposed by the Probate Court. Katz v. Superior Court, 73 Cal. App. 3d 952, 141 Cal. Rptr. 234 (1977). The parents' petition in Massachusetts to extend their guardianship was unsuccessful. *In re* Shapiro, No. 471805 (Middlesex P. Ct., Mass. Nov. 4, 1976). In Vermont the declaration for competency was refused because it would otherwise end-run the special requirements for state competency proceedings. Schuppin v. Unification Church, 435 F. Supp. 603 (D. Vt.), *aff'd,* 573 F.2d 1295 (2d Cir. 1977). The Section 1985 claim in Arizona was recognized as stating a cause of action, Rankin v. Howard, 457 F. Supp. 70 (D. Ariz. 1978), *rev'd on other grounds,* 633 F.2d 844 (9th Cir. 1980), *cert. denied*, 451 U.S. 939 (1981). By contrast, the Rhode Island Section 1985 claim was dismissed, on the factual finding that the plaintiff's daughter who was complaining about alleged deprogramming had willingly stayed home and listened to arguments about her Church membership. Weiss v. Patrick, 453 F. Supp. 717 (D. R.I.), *aff'd mem.*, 588 F.2nd 818 (1st Cir. 1978), *cert. denied*, 442 U.S. 929 (1979). A similar conclusion was reached in the Minnesota case. Peterson v. Sorlien, 229 N.W.2d 123 (Minn. 1980), *cert. denied*, 450 U.S. 1031 (1981).

/9/   Braunfeld v. Brown, 366 U.S. 599, 603 (1961); Cantwell v. Connecticut, 310 U.S. 296, 303 (1940); Reynolds v. United States, 98 U.S. 145, 166 (1878).

/10/   Sherbert v. Verner, 374 U.S. 398, 402, 406 (1963).

/11/   The analysis here assumes that a convert has reached the age of majority. Situations involving minors are complicated by the convert's age. See Wisconsin v. Yoder, 406 U.S. 205, 232 (1972). But minors as well as adults possess constitutional rights that the state must protect, including rights of religious belief. See generally "Constitutional Protection," supra n. 1, at 778–83.

/12/   Compare, e.g., John Locke, *An Essay Concerning Human Understanding*, ed. Peter H. Nidditch, 4th ed. (1700; Oxford: Clarendon Press, 1975) with A. J. Ayer, *The Concept of a Person* (New York: St. Martin's Press, 1963), 16–19. See also John Perry, "The Importance of Being Identical," in *The Identities of Persons*, ed. Amelie Rorty (Berkeley: University of California Press 1976), 67.

/13/   See Terence Penelhum, *The Encyclopedia of Philosophy* (1967), Vol. 6, 95, 101, s.v. "personal identity"; cf. David Lewis, "Survival and Identity," in *The Identity of Persons*, supra n. 12 at 17.

/14/   Derek Parfit, "Personal Identity," 80 *Philosophical Review* 3 (1971). See also Comment, "The Limits of State Intervention: Personal Identity and Ultra-Risky Actions," 85 *Yale Law Journal* 836, 840–41 (1976).

/15/   Robert Nozick, *Philosophical Explanations* (Cambridge: Belknap Press, 1981).

/16/   Bernard Williams, "The Self and the Future," 79 *Philosophical Review* 161, 172 (1970).

/17/   Richard Delgado, "Religious Totalism," supra n. 1 at 59 Cf. Thomas Robbins and Dick Anthony, "Deprogramming, Brainwashing and the Medicalization of Deviant Religious Groups," 29 *Social Problems* 283, 285–86 (1982).

/18/   Nozick, supra n. 15, at 58–59.

/19/   Rene Descartes, "Meditations on First Philosophy," in *Philosophical Writings*, trans. and ed. Elizabeth Anscombe and Peter Thomas Geach (London: Thomas Nelson & Sons, Ltd., 1954).

/20/   Ayer, supra n. 12 at 82, 116.

/21/   P. F. Strawson, *Individuals* (London: Methuen, 1959), 102; P. F. Strawson, "Persons," in *The Philosophy of Mind*, ed. V. C. Chappel (Englewood Cliffs, NJ: Prentice-Hall, Inc., 1962), 127, 135–37.

/22/   Roberto Mangabeira Unger, *Knowledge and Politics* (New York: Free Press, 1975), 55–56, 199.

/23/   The development of artificial intelligence may test this definition. See generally John C. Haugeland (ed.), *Mind Design* (Cambridge: MIT Press, 1981). Increasingly, computers can be programmed to modify their own programs. See Douglas R. Hofstadter, *Godel, Escher, Bach: An Eternal Golden Braid* (New York: Vintage Books, 1979), 629-32, 679-80, 692-93. Since computers still lack sensible experience, a person might be characterized as a sentient entity capable of programming from within. If a computer met that definition, we might have to accustom ourselves to regard such a machine (think of C3PO and R2D2) as a person, though obviously not a human being, rather than try to push the definition of a person to a new level that would again exclude the machine.

/24/   See generally Edward Hunter, *Brainwashing. The Story of Men Who Defied It* (New York: Farrar, Strauss, and Cudahy, 1965); Robert Lifton, *Thought Reform and the Psychology of Totalism. A Study of "Brainwashing" in China* (New York: W. W. Norton & Co., 1961); Edgar Schein with Inge Schneier and Curtis H. Barker, *Coercive Persuasion. A Socio-Psychological Analysis of the "Brainwashing" of America Civilian Prisoners by the Chinese Communists* (New York: W. W. Norton & Co., 1961); Note, "Brainwashing: Fact, Fiction and Criminal Defense," 44 *University of Missouri-Kansas City Law Review* 438, 441-49 (1976). The terms "brainwashing," "coercive persuasion," and "thought reform" have all been used to refer to mind-controlling processes and their results.

/25/   *In re* Shapiro, No. 471805 (Middlesex P. Ct., Mass. Nov. 3, 1976), transcript of hearings at 33.

/26/   Plato, *The Republic*, trans. P. Shorey, in *The Collected Dialogues of Plato*, ed. Edith Hamilton and Huntington Cairns (New York: Bollingen Foundation, 1961), 575, 747–72.

/27/   Frances Fitzgerald, *America Revised* (Boston: Little, Brown & Co., 1979).

/28/   Board of Education v. Pico, 102 S. Ct. 2799 (1982). Cf. Lawrence Tribe, *American Constitutional Law* (Mineola, NY: Foundation Press, 1978), Section 15-6 at 902.

/29/   Cf. Thomas Robbins, "Cults and the Therapeutic State," 10 *Social Policy* 42, 44 (1979). The test for personhood is the inverse of one proposed over 30 years ago in the field of computers and artificial intelligence to answer the question, "Can machines think?" The mathematician Alan Turing would have placed an interrogator in a separate room from two respondents, one of whom would try to deceive the interrogator as to the respondent's identity and the other of whom would try to help the interrogator. (Teletype printers would be used for both questions and answers.) A machine would then take the place of the deceiving respondent, and the original question would become whether the interrogator could tell the machine from the person. If the machine acted like a person, it would be deemed a person. Alan Turing, "Computing Machinery and intelligence," 59 *Mind* 433 (1950); see also D. Hofstadter, supra n. 23 at 595–99.

/30/ Situations involving undue influence, fraud, coerced confessions, or diminished capacity and the insanity defense, which are occasionally cited as analogues for brainwashing cases, do not in fact offer useful comparisons. When someone makes a will subject to the overbearing influence of another person, the legal response is to invalidate the instrument that benefits the influencing party. The remedy directly affects the wrongdoer, by negating a specific act. By contrast, brainwashing is supposed to be an ongoing condition, for which the proposed cure would be to change the victim's own mind. The remedy for fraud similarly negates the act that the defrauded party performed, thereby depriving the wrongdoer of fraudulently procured gain. At no time, however, is the victim's will extinguished, but simply acts on false information. Though someone may be the victim of a fraud practiced by a religion, many "core" religious claims are by their nature unverifiable (those about salvation and revelation, for example) and may not be examined or attacked by the state. In neither event do claims of fraud shed light on at least Type-II brainwashing allegations. Psychological and physical coercion will invalidate a confession in a criminal case. Rules prohibiting such behavior by police and other governmental authorities are designed to protect the individual against the state. By contrast, a deprogramming process authorized by the state would expose an individual to governmental intrusion. Even if coercive persuasion has occurred to a sect adherent, other sanctions exist to punish a coercing party, such as criminal statutes and tort relief for kidnapping and false imprisonment. Finally, some individuals are held not to be responsible for actions that would otherwise be crimes, because a mental illness or defect prevents them from forming the requisite criminal intent. Again, the defense of diminished capacity and the insanity defense are designed to protect the individual. In keeping with the presumption behind the criminal law that individuals "have" something called free will, the requirement of "voluntary" action for a person to be guilty of committing a crime respects the perceived autonomy of the individual and limits state intervention. To assert that brainwashing is a kind of mental impairment that justifies deprogramming turns the policies of the criminal rules inside out. If psychiatric treatment is to be justified in any case, mental illness must exist; even after a successful insanity defense, treatment is always predicated on independently determined grounds of mental illness and dangerousness to self and others. But parents do not want a finding of mental illness "against" their children, and in that situation conventional psychiatric treatment would not be justified even if brainwashing had occurred. Or if a brainwashing claim meant that the victim was no longer a "person," something more than conventional psychiatric treatment would be required. In either event, brainwashing cases differ from criminal cases involving the insanity defense.

/31/   Warren & Brandeis, "The Right to Privacy," 4 *Harvard Law Review* 1983, 205 (1890).

/32/   See Stanley v. Georgia, 394 U.S. 557, 565 (1969).

/33/   Stanley v. Georgia, 394 U.S, 557, 565 (1969).

/34/   Board of Education v. Pico, 102 S. Ct. 2799 (1982).

/35/   United States v. Seeger, 380 U.S. 163, 166, 176 (1965).

/36/   Welsh v. United States, 398 U.S. 333, 341–44 (1970).

/37/   Paul Tillich, *The Shaking of the Foundations* (New York: Charles Scribner's Sons, 1948); see United States v. Seeger, 380 U.S. 163, 187 (1965).

/38/   Welsh v. United States, 398 U.S. 333, 341–44 (1970).

/39/   Tillich, supra n. 37, at 10–11.

/40/   Cantwell v. Connecticut, 310 U.S. 296, 303 (1940); Reynolds v. United States, 98 U.S. 145, 166 (1878).

/41/   Sherbert v. Verner, 374 U.S. 398, 402, 406 (1963). See also Wisconsin v. Yoder, 406 U.S. 205, 215 (1972).

/42/   See, e.g., McLean v. Arkansas Bd. of Educ., 529 F. Supp. 1255 (E.D. Ark. 1982); Note, "Evolution, Creationism, and the Religion Clauses," 46 *Alabama Law Review* 897 (1982).

/43/   Heffron v. International Society for Krishna Consciousness, Inc., 452, U.S. 640 (1981). But cf. International Society for Krishna Consciousness, Inc. v. Barber, 650 F.2d 430 (2d Cir. 1981). Decision of other federal courts, coming down on both sides, are set forth in *Heffron*, 452 U.S. at 646, n. 9.

/44/   446 F.2d 65 (2d Cir.), *cert. denied*, 404 U.S. 985 (1971). Cf. *in re* Guardianship of Roe, 1981 Mass. Adv. Sh. 981, 421, N.E.2d 40.

/45/   See Robert Bellah, "Civil Religion in America" in *American Civil Religion*, ed. Russell E. Richey and Donald G. Jones (New York: Harper & Row, 1974); William C. Shepherd, "The New Religions and the Religion of the Republic," 44 *Journal of the American Academy of Religion* 509 (1978); cf. Dick Anthony and Thomas Robbins, "Spiritual Innovation and the Crisis of American Civil Religion," 111 *Daedalus* 215, 216–18 (1982).

/46/   See Note, "Religious Exemptions Under the Free Exercise Clause: A Model of Competing Authorities," 90 *Yale Law Journal* 350 (1980).

/47/   See James Madison, "A Memorial and Remonstrance on the Religious Rights of Man" (1784), quoted in *Cornerstones of Religious Freedom in America*, ed. Joseph L. Blau (New York: Harper & Row, 1964), 34; Thomas Jefferson, "Notes on Virginia," *Query* xvii (1781-82), quoted in id., at 81. For Jefferson, freedom of religion was closely tied to a more general freedom of mind; Dumas

Malone, *Jefferson and the Rights of Man* (Boston: Little, Brown & Co., 1965), 110. See generally "Conservatorships," supra n. 1 at 1256-67; cf. Gary Willis, *Inventing America* (New York: Vintage Books, 1978), 167–259.

/48/ Delgado, "Religious Totalism," supra n. 1, at 59.

/49/ Marcia R. Rudin, "The Cult Phenomenon: Fad or Fact," 9 *New York University Review of Law and Social Change* 17, 25 (1979–80).

/50/ Jeremiah Gutman, "Constitutional and Legal Aspects of Deprogramming," in *Deprogramming: Documenting the Issue* (American Civil Liberties Union, 1977), 210–11, quoted in Robbins & Anthony, supra n. 17, at 292–93; see also "Constitutional Protection," supra n. 1, at 795 and n. 210.

STATE REGULATION
OF NEW RELIGIOUS MOVEMENTS

THE "DEFORMATION" OF NEW RELIGIONS: IMPACTS OF SOCIETAL AND ORGANIZATIONAL FACTORS

James T. Richardson

There is a strong tendency when discussing social movements, including religious ones, to focus on selected internal factors to the near exclusion of external factors that might be of considerable import in explaining what happens to a social movement and its "member" organizations. Thus there is usually a great deal of attention paid to the beliefs of the movement, to the type of people who join, and particularly to the leadership of movement organizations. Concern is also sometimes expressed about how the organizations making up a movement support and maintain themselves, but even that concern is usually focused on what individuals do in this regard.

This psychologizing of the problem is well-illustrated in the area of new religions. There is a great deal of concern in our society about the rapid growth of new religious movements. Some even claim that a major crisis exists because of the development of new religions. Much of the attention in this area has been given to group leadership, and many commentators claim there is considerable authoritarian leadership in the new religions. There is much speculation about why otherwise well-to-do, well-educated youth would take such a drastic step of cutting ties with society by affiliation with a new and strange group. Thus "brainwashing" and "mind control" myths have evolved and are circulated as supposedly adequate explanatory devices to understand why people join, why they stay, and implicitly, why the movement organizations are successful (a movement cannot be successful without members).

Supposedly, under these myths, a leader who is interested in financial gain, sexual favors, or just plain power starts a new group using some extraordinary powers of hypnosis or mind control. He somehow "zaps" potential converts simply by looking them in the eye and uttering a few magical phrases, or by tricking them into participating in a high pressure group recruitment process. Thus the recruit falls completely under his command, and becomes a deployable robot, also, interestingly, imbued with this magical power to trick people into joining. These new converts go out and convert even more people through similar processes,

and the new group is off and running. This process allegedly will cause
the group to continue growing until it is huge and threatening to society.
The membership is controlled via some type of ESP, and through this
mental power all the members do the masters' bidding for eighteen
hours a day or more. The organization continues to grow because this
power of the leader, even if passed on through member evangelizers, is
so strong as to defy efforts by the converts to leave. Thus, so the myth
goes, once a Moonie (or Hare Krishna, or Divine Light Mission, or Children of God) recruiter "looks you in the eye," you are a "goner," des-
tined to live out your life as virtually a slave to the omnipotent group
leader./1/

This mythology about why and how new religions start and succeed is
very appealing, particularly to those who feel somehow threatened by the
growth of new religions. Such myths furnish ammunition for fighting the
growths of new religions. Thus deprogramming, legislative action, and
governmental bureaucratic controls of various kinds (using the brainwashing myth as a justification) may be visited upon new religions. The myth is,
as Anthony, Robbins, and McCarthy have said, a "social weapon" to use
against unpopular groups./2/ The myths abound because they serve a serious function in our society, that being social control of deviant groups with
their strange belief systems and practices. However, these myths are almost
totally useless as explanatory devices about why social movements start,
grow, and maintain themselves (or die out) over time. Carried to their
logical conclusion the myths suggest that everyone in a society would, if the
powers of the leaders and his or her agents are as claimed, be compelled to
join a given movement. The obvious fact that this is not the case with new
religions, and that most of the new groups are really quite small and growing slowly, if at all, puts the lie to the myth. The high attrition rates that
scholars have found in the new groups undercut the myth, and instead
support more "normal" explanations about why and how people join such
groups and why they also leave./3/

Some still insist that the myths of brainwashing and mind control
"work" by pointing to the small cadre of full-time and long-term members in the group, implying that "obviously" no one would remain in
such strange groups for any length of time if they were really acting out
of their own volition. Thus the high attrition rates are dismissed, on the
grounds that only a minority of people are susceptible to the brainwashing and mind control, but that brainwashing still works with that minority and thus the groups should still be controlled or even stamped out
completely. Such claims refuse to address the solid evidence accumulat-
ing from scholars administering personality assessment tests to members
of various new religions, resulting in the finding that members are fairly
normal people, and, further, that they are not mentally ill or unable to
function normally./4/

A SOCIOLOGICAL APPROACH TO NEW RELIGIONS

The conclusion that must be drawn by examining the ever-growing record of solid research by sociologists and others on the new religions is that the myth explains little (except something about social control) and that more sophisticated approaches are needed to explain what happens to new movements. This paper is an attempt to take a more reasoned look at the problem of religious social movement development and growth, treating the organizations as the unit of study. Hopefully, this will avoid psychologizing the problem, as has been the case with the brainwashing approach.

The general perspective presented herein can be subsumed under both the generic rubric of "resource mobilization" theory, which is the theoretical approach gaining a dominant position within the sociology of social movements, and the "natural history" approach./5/ The resource mobilization approach focuses on management of resources available to a social movement organization. The term resources is defined quite broadly within the tradition, and often involves "management" of things outside the organization's direct control, such as potential recruits, the media, or even governmental agencies and services. Thus the attention in this view is directed away from individual members and leaders, and instead looks at the *resource environment* both external and internal to the group. Social movements are viewed as derivative of a specific "contextual arrangement" or historical situation, instead of deriving from effects of a given individual attempting to start a new group or of certain types who join a movement. The natural history approach is supposedly atheoretical, and focused on the stages through which a social movement passes. Natural history research is mainly descriptive in its focus but can be decidedly different from the purely psychological "motivational" approach to the study of social movements, if attention is paid to societal and organization level considerations.

Assuming a more sociological approach, a number of questions arise about the development of new religions and the controversy, even crisis, that surrounds them. How did "new" sets of religious ideas and practices develop within the different societal and cultural context of American society? How did the initial mundane needs of the organizations and their members interact with the beliefs and practices within the situational context to arrive at the original organizational forms? How did the organizations change once they formed and perhaps became focused upon by the societal and cultural environment? What internal and external factors influenced the development of the group within this more "focused environment"? This paper will offer some speculative answers to these questions.

THE SOCIOLOGICAL CONTEXT

The growth of new religions must be viewed against the historical backdrop of decades of growing secularization in society that includes expansionism by governmental agencies at all levels./6/ Government is, for good or ill, impacting more of our lives than has been the case in the past. Some say that this expansionism is a result of the implementation of the "liberal agenda," which may be partially true. The development of the "strong state" has coincided with a weakening of influence of religion over our lives, and with the development of what Luckmann calls "privatized religion."/7/ Thus, it might be surmised, admittedly somewhat simplistically, that the state has been expanding and traditional religion has been retreating, in terms of the everyday impact on the lives of those in our society.

Within this context the new religions have been a significant anomaly. The new movements were not supposed to happen, according to views of many, and they were not expected to start vying with the omnipotent secular state for total control of their members' lives and for complete autonomy of an organization's actions./8/ The growing totalism of the state clashed with the totalism (perceived or real) of some of the new religions. There may even be hints of anti-religious prejudice among some who operate in the name of the state, a not too surprising development given the conflict between enlightened liberal values and the values of some of the new religions. The thrust of the development of many of the new religions seems antithetical to the liberal agenda and value system, and this colors the perceptions of many in our society, including, but by no means limited to, some agents of governmental bureaucracies. Thus controversy arises where it perhaps would not have some decades ago.

This situation is compounded considerably by the rise of the new religious right in our society (and in other societies such as Iran). Also, many in our society have been made aware of the continuing work of the "old religious right" in the political arena by virtue of the attention paid to the emotional issues of abortion and the ERA, on which such groups as Mormons and Catholics have taken strong public stands./9/ The growing perception of the involvement of the religious right in politics, and the absorption of members and sympathizers of this segment of society into governmental elective and appointed positions can be viewed as the potential coup de grace to liberalism in our society. But the battle continues to rage, and the eventual winner is unclear at this time. That notwithstanding, the rise of the religious right has made many in our society more sensitive to the development of all things religious, and this includes the newer religious groups that are attracting sizable numbers of the more affluent youth of society. Thus we see media discussions of the rise of religious influence and impact on our society that mention the Hare Krishna, Jerry Falwell, the Moonies and Religious Roundtable within the same context. And tragic anomalies such as Jonestown, the Manson Cult, or mass murderer "Son of Sam" are talked about in religious terms, sometimes, as was the case with Jonestown, to the exclusion of other more useful interpretations./10/

General economic and social unrest in our society has also contributed to the contextual background of the reaction to new religions. Some have made an argument that new religions, particularly the communal ones, offer an alternative way of self support, if only people are willing to make commitments to such groups. In simple terms, it may have appeared more logical to be a Moonie or a Jesus freak than to be unemployed, hungry, and without shelter. But, while this type of thinking may imply that the unsettled social conditions actually encouraged the growth of new religions, it should also be recognized that those same unsettled conditions may have made for a more hostile environment for new religions. Some people react to disorganization by attacking new and unknown elements within the context. This type of scapegoating response may help explain the strong negative reaction encountered by most new religions.

This impact of social and economic conditions has been amplified by two related factors. One is the sharp contrast between the beliefs and practices of certain new religions and more traditional religious beliefs and practices. To see a friend or offspring accept a strange set of beliefs is one thing, but to see them get involved in a totalistic communal living situation is worse, at least from the point of view of some members of society. And, in an economic situation in which well-paying jobs are rare, many parents are upset to see their children leave the competition for jobs and opt for life as a chanting Hare Krishna member or as a fundraiser for the Moonies. Some of the parents simply cannot believe that their children would, of their own volition, choose such a life. To admit such a choice is to admit that their son or daughter rejected them, their values, and perhaps more importantly, the hope and plans that those parents had for the offspring in terms of education and occupation. This insight about the concern of many parents over affiliation helps explain why there had developed such a strong critique of the new movements in the media, and why the so-called "anti-cult" movement has gained such impetus in our society./11/ Some relatively affluent parents of members are located strategically within society in terms of access to resources that can be used to combat the new religions. Thus there has been, as one important result, an encouragement of the expansionist state by a number of parents and anti-cult organizations. The strong demand that government (at various levels) "do something about the cults" has been aided by media attention to the new religions.

The confluence of these and other conditions have resulted in the new religions encountering a general negative response from some major institutions within society. This may seem surprising since America is renown for its propensity to select religious solutions to problems of personal or social disorganization, and past waves of revivalism have not usually met with such strong animosity. But that same American religious consciousness has revealed some remarkably intolerant episodes, such as the reaction to certain practices of Mormons. Similarly, the oddness of some of the new religions' beliefs and practices has contributed to a reaction against them, and that reaction has been compounded by the tendency for the expansionist state and other key segments of society to adopt a general negative position vis à vis the new religions. Thus the various levels and some segments of the state and of major institutions, such as organized religion and the psychiatric and "helping" professions, have joined together to defend against the encroachment of the new religions into their hard-won territory./12/

This generally negative reaction has become a fact of life for many new religions, and has helped shape them into different kinds of organizations than they might have become otherwise. Those that have attracted the most attention have become "deformed" by virtue of their having to invest considerable resources in defensive capabilities. Thus the Unification Church and Scientology have legal prowess of great talent and significance, and their organizational public relations units are much larger than otherwise might be expected. The same can be said for other groups such as the followers of Bhagwan Rajneesh. Some organizations have had to change the ways in which they support themselves because of the pressure that has been brought to bear on them by legal authorities and by public opinion./13/ Other aspects of the new groups have also sometimes been directly influenced by the impact of public opinion and society's social control agencies. Thus the Unification Church has been forced to modify its overt involvement in the political process and some communal groups have been encouraged to change their basic pattern of living because of IRS rulings on what type of groups can and cannot be tax exempt.

This last comment about the IRS bears expansion because this agency is perhaps the most influential government agency in shaping new religions. Efforts to maintain tax exempt status for new religions have resulted in dramatic changes in some groups, including modifications of both beliefs and behaviors. IRS regulations and rulings concerning "proper" uses of money, types of activities that may be done (particularly the exclusion of political action), and the types of property that can be tax exempt have all engendered considerable controversy. Some claim the IRS is acting in a discriminatory fashion vis à vis new religions. Others less sympathetic to new religions suggest that the IRS is just "doing its job" of protecting the American public from religiously justified frauds. Whatever the correct evaluation, it is clear that the IRS is a major instrument of social control of new religions and that IRS regulations dictate not only substantive considerations, but also the "rules of the game" whereby substantive rules are applied. Both the substantive and procedural rules seem to demonstrate a negative view of newer religions by the IRS./14/

In sum, the new religions have in general evolved in a negative climate. And that development within a predominantly hostile environment has dictated that the groups take certain forms, some of which seem odd indeed when one considers that, after all, these are supposed to be religious groups./15/ The exact organizational forms and practices adopted by the new groups has also been the result of the impact of certain more *internal forces*, and it is to these that we now turn.

INTERNAL PRESSURES ON ORGANIZATIONAL FORMS OF NEW RELIGIONS

When the new religions first came to the attention of the media and began receiving large amounts of publicity, they were fairly homogeneous groups. The membership was, as has been said, mainly middle- to upper-class white, and relatively well-educated. A majority were males, and most were single. They had, to varying degrees, left normal society and were used to surviving with fewer creature comforts than had been the case previously for most members.

The structures of the organizations were also relatively uncomplicated. The leadership cadre was usually small, and usually made up of people quite similar to the regular members. There were few levels of authority in the groups. The needs of the organization were meager because all that was required was enough money and resources to keep the youthful members at a minimal level of support. Thus the organizations were simple structures made up of relatively nondemanding members. Life was uncomplicated.

But, as the organizations grew and started attracting different types of members, things changed. Also, the membership within the groups changed through normal processes of maturation. For instance, members grew older and more "settled." Many of the groups encouraged marriage between members as well, partially to keep members satisfied, but also to guarantee continuation of the organization itself. Thus families were formed, and children became a significant consideration and a major drain on group resources. More females were drawn into the groups as a result of the move toward family formation in many groups. Levels of expectation about support levels changed as some of the groups developed more lucrative ways to support themselves. Some types of people not formerly associated with the groups at their beginning began to come into the group, including people who sometimes had a different idea about what was an acceptable level of sustenance for members. The organizations sometimes recruited or retained selected members to do highly skilled tasks required by the growing organization. Thus some groups recruited or trained (or paid for the training of) physicians, architects, lawyers, and other professional level people./16/

The organizations themselves sometimes changed drastically, adding layer upon layer of bureaucracy and developing specialized functions within the group in order to accomplish essential tasks, including specialized arms to deal with the media and with the legal system./17/ Thus the Children of God became an international organization with at least twelve levels of organizational authority. The Unification Church developed Mobile Fund-Raising Teams that they sent around the country and even into foreign countries and the church also became prominent in certain industries./18/ Schools were established for members and children of members within some groups such as the Unification Church, the Way International, the Hare Krishna, and many others. Capital investments were made which required large sums of money and management after the purchase or construction. Perhaps the best known of the groups, in this regard, are the Moonies and the followers of Bhagwan Rajneesh, the latter having established their international center in an area of rural Oregon by building a large community there. The Unificationists have purchased large amounts of property in several areas of the country and abroad.

Thus domestication and bureaucratization have overtaken many of the new religions, and these considerations have interacted with the demands of the greater society, including its major arms of social control of religious groups such as the IRS. Today some of them look more like large businesses or perhaps traditional denominations than they do social movement organizations. And the change has been, in some cases, extremely rapid and so thorough-going that earlier followers of certain movement groups might not even recognize the group today. The internal and external pressures have "deformed" the groups in some odd and unexpected ways.

STRUCTURAL CHANGE AND BELIEFS

The rapid changes in many new groups have been guided to some extent by the beliefs and philosophy of the specific organizations. Thus strongly held beliefs about the sanctity of the family have been implemented in part through through mass marriages that have helped make the Unification Church so famous (or infamous). Christ Communal Organizations (CCO) developed a pervasive work ethic based on their interpretation of certain Biblical texts. And the development of unique mission teams within the Children of God was motivated by their desire to witness, a desire that also led almost inadvertently to the "witnessing" that became their chief form of financial support./19/

But, even though theology often impacted organizational behavior, quite often more material considerations seemed to influence the beliefs and general culture of the groups. Johnston writes about how concern for financial gain molded the development of TM in this country. Shupe and Bromley write about how Mobile Fund-Raising teams were justified as training devices and commitment-testing mechanisms for the Unification Church. Richardson, Stewart, and Simmonds write about how desire for privacy and the growing affluence within CCO led to the move away from communal lifestyle that had served it so well in its history. The cooling of missionary zeal in both CCO and Children of God because of the requirements of financial support also illustrates the point. CCO developed many large work teams and many members were used mainly for this purpose within a few years of the group's inception. The Children of God, once they found out that people would donate money for the literature they were dispersing, began to attend more and more to the amount of money gained through literature distribution and less and less to actual witnessing and recruitment./20/

A MORE GENERAL FORMULATION

What has been presented is mainly descriptive of the general forces that have molded new religions in the past fifteen to twenty years in America since they started coming to the attention of the public. The combining of external and internal forces leads to modifications of organizational form and of beliefs and general culture as well. What is being proposed is a dynamic "feedback" model of development of such social movement organizations. This model is outlined in Figure 1 (next page), using as illustration some of the considerations discussed herein.

Note that the movement starts with a set of initial ideas, beliefs, and practices within a diffuse societal and cultural context. The original ideas must of necessity interact with the mundane material considerations of the fledgling group. Even if the requirements are minimal, there are still requirements that must be met, if the movement or group is to survive at all. Out of the interaction of the material and ideal arises the original organizational form of the groups.

Once the group forms, it can become a focus of attention from the society and its social control agents and from the guardians of cultural values, and it is within the glare of this focus that dramatic shifts in organizational form and activities take place. External factors of many types bring pressure to bear on the fledgling form and interact with the mundane internal concerns of a growing and changing organization. What arises out of this cauldron of organizational ferment may differ

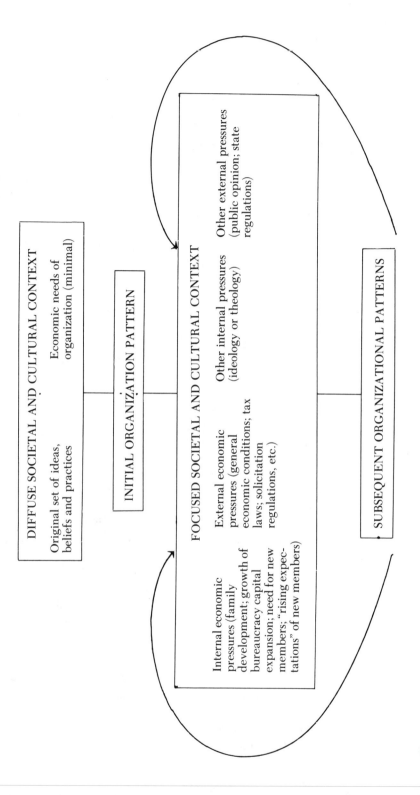

FIGURE 1. SCHEMATIC OF EXTERNAL AND INTERNAL FACTOR IMPACTS ON FORM OF RELIGIOUS MOVEMENT ORGANIZATIONS

DIFFUSE SOCIETAL AND CULTURAL CONTEXT

Original set of ideas, beliefs and practices

Economic needs of organization (minimal)

INITIAL ORGANIZATION PATTERN

FOCUSED SOCIETAL AND CULTURAL CONTEXT

Internal economic pressures (family development; growth of bureaucracy capital expansion; need for new members; "rising expectations" of new members)

External economic pressures (general economic conditions; tax laws; solicitation regulations, etc.)

Other internal pressures (ideology or theology)

Other external pressures (public opinion; state regulations)

SUBSEQUENT ORGANIZATIONAL PATTERNS

widely from the initial pattern of organization and the originating set of ideas and practices. Thus we may see meditators turning into high pressure salesmen, Hare Krishna members wearing wigs and suits and ties for fund-raising, and Eastern gurus becoming frantically evangelical—all in response to conditions of the society in which they are seeking a permanent place. The ways in which such anomalous activities begin and are eventually justified is of considerable interest and deserves careful study.

CONCLUSIONS

The thrust of this paper may seem quite mundane to some readers and plainly misguided to others. However, I think the perspective presented herein is useful, and it can lead to important research on organizational change and on the relationship of those changes to theological evolution. I have attempted to get away from "great person" theories of the history of social movements in general and new religions in particular. Instead I have attempted to take a sociological view of the naturally occurring internal pressures on new movement organizations to change. I also focused attention on external pressures that may arise specifically related to a historical environment in which the new religions began to develop. These structural and historical conditions probably have more of an impact on what eventually happens to the new movement group than do decisions of leaders in the group. This may seem an "over-socialized" view of new religious movements, and it may well be. But it is hoped that considering the point made herein will add some balance to an interpretation of the new religions that is much too ahistorical, acultural, and psychologized in its approach.

NOTES

/1/   This admittedly overdrawn mythological interpretation of new religions is illustrated in the work of Richard Delgado, a legal scholar, and of Margaret Singer and John Clark, two prominent psychiatrists associated with the Anti-Cult Movement. See Richard Delgado, "Limits to Proselytizing," 17(3) *Society* 25 (1980); John Clark, "Cults," 24(3) *Journal of the American Medical Association* 281 (1979); Margaret Singer, "Coming Out of the Cults," 12 *Psychology Today* 72 (1979).

/2/   Dick Anthony, Tom Robbins, and Jim McCarthy, "Legitimating Repression," 17(3) *Society* 39 (1980).

/3/   See Fred Bird and Bill Reimer, "Participation Rates in New Religious Movements and Para-religious Movements," 21(1) *Journal for the Scientific Study of Religion* 1 (1982); James T. Richardson, "Conversion, Brainwashing, and Deprogramming," 15(2) *The Center Magazine* 18 (1982); David Bromley and James T. Richardson (eds.), *The Brainwashing/Deprogramming Controversy* (Toronto: Edwin Mellen Press, 1983).

/4/ See Marc Galanter, "Psychological Induction Into a Larger Group: Findings from a Modern Religious Sect," 137 *American Journal of Psychiatry* 1574 (1980); Marc Galanter, R. Rabkin, J. Rabkin, and A. Deutsch, "'The Moonies': A Psychological Study," 136 *American Journal of Psychiatry* 165 (1979); Thomas Ungerleider and D. K. Wellisch, "Coercive Persuasion (Brainwashing), Religious Cults and Deprogramming," 136 *American Journal of Psychiatry* 279 (1979); J. T. Richardson, "Psychological and Psychiatric Studies of Members of New Religions," in *New Perspectives in Psychology of Religion*, ed. L. Brown (New York: Pergamon Press, 1983); Anne-Sofie Rosen and Ted Nordquist, "Ego Developmental Levels and Values in a Yogic Community," 39(b) *Journal of Personality and Social Psychology* 1152 (1980).

/5/ On resource mobilization theory see Mayer Zald and John McCarthy, *The Dynamics of Social Movements* (Cambridge, MA: Winthrop Publishers, Inc.), and John McCarthy and Mayer Zald, "Resource Mobilization and Social Movements: A Partial Theory" 82(6) *The American Journal of Sociology* 1212 (1977); on the natural history approach see Kurt Lang and Gladys Lang, *Collective Dynamics* (New York: Thomas Crowell, 1961).

/6/ See the valuable collection illustrating the growth of government particularly as it impacts religious groups, edited by Dean Kelly, *Government Intervention in Religious Affairs* (New York: Pilgrim Press, 1982).

/7/ Thomas Luckmann, *The Invisible Religion* (New York: MacMillan, 1967).

/8/ For a good example of a prominent secularization theorist who is not appreciative of the counter trend to secularization referred to as the new religions, see Bryan Wilson, *The Contemporary Transformation of Religion* (London: Oxford University Press, 1976).

/9/ See the paper by J. T. Richardson, "The Old Right: Mormon and Catholic Involvement in an ERA Referendum," in David Bromley and Anson Shupe, Jr. (eds.), *New Christian Politics* (Macon, GA: Mercer University Press, 1984).

/10/ See Shiva Naipul, *Journey to Nowhere* (New York: Simon and Schuster, 1980), and J. T. Richardson, "People's Temple and Jonestown: A Corrective Comparison and Critique," 19(3) *Journal for the Scientific Study of Religion* 239 (1980), for more thorough analyses of the Jonestown tragedy.

/11/ Anson Shupe, Jr., and David Bromley, *The New Vigilantes* (Beverly Hills, CA: Sage, 1980).

/12/ See Brock Kilbourne and J. T. Richardson, "Psychotherapy and New Religions in a Pluralistic Society," *American Psychologist* (1983) for one analysis of this conflict between institutions in our society. See also J. T. Richardson, "From Cult to Sect: Creative Eclecticism in New Religions," *Pacific Sociological Review* 139 (1979), for another discussion of general external pressures on new religions.

/13/ See J. T. Richardson, "The IRS and New Religions," paper read at the annual meeting of the Society for the Scientific Study of Religion, Providence, RI (1982).

/14/ See the discussion of problems newer communal religious groups are having with the IRS in Meade Emory and Lawrence Zelenak, "The Tax Exempt Status of Communitarian Religious Organizations: An Unnecessary Controversy?" in this volume.

/15/ This conclusionary statement suggests a certain viewpoint based on several years of research on new religions. Alternative views are possible, of course, including the extreme one that new religions are *not* religions and that the environment is reacting properly in attempting to regulate and control them.

/16/ See John Lofland and J. T. Richardson, "Religious Movement Organizations: Elemental Forms and Dynamics," in Louis Kriesberg (ed.), *Research and Social Movements, Conflicts and Change* (Greenwich, CT: Jai Press, 1984); for a general discussion of this process and for specific illustrations, see J. T. Richardson, M. W. Stewart, and R. B. Simmonds, *Organized Miracles* (New Brunswick, NJ: Transaction Books, 1979), and David Bromley and Anson Shupe, Jr., *'Moonies' in America* (Beverly Hills, CA: Sage, 1979) for some of the same processes in another new religion.

/17/ See Lofland and Richardson, ibid., for illustration and general discussion of this organizational elaboration process.

/18/ See Rex Davis and J. T. Richardson, "Organization and Functioning of the Children of God," 37(4) *Sociological Analysis* 321 (1976); John Lofland, *Doomsday Cult* (New York: Irvington Books, 1977; Revised Edition); and Bromley and Shupe's *'Moonies' in America*, ibid.

/19/ See David and Richardson, ibid.

/20/ On TM see Hank Johnston, "The Blanketed Social Movement: A Case Study of the Rapid Growth of TM," 23(3) *Pacific Sociological Review* 333 (1980); on the Moonies, see Bromley and Shupe's book; on CCO see Richardson et al., *Organized Miracles*, ibid.; and on the Children of God, see Davis and Richardson, ibid.

THE TAX EXEMPT STATUS OF COMMUNITARIAN RELIGIOUS ORGANIZATIONS: AN UNNECESSARY CONTROVERSY?

Meade Emory and Lawrence Zelenak

A church is a community of believers. Just as a church's belief may take many different forms, so too may its community. Its members may simply acknowledge that they hold shared beliefs, they may come together for weekly worship, or they may share all aspects of their lives through communal living. The fullest form of religious communion, because of its all-encompassing nature, is that in which the members share everything—not just praying, but also working, eating, playing and the other activities of daily life. It is, therefore, ironic that in two recent cases/1/ the Internal Revenue Service (the Service) has successfully taken the position that communitarian religious organizations are ineligible for tax-exempt status/2/ under section 501(c)(3) of the Internal Revenue Code (the Code)./3/

This article briefly discusses the history of communitarian religious organizations. It then examines the Service's position, as approved in recent court decisions, and discusses why that position may conflict with section 501(c)(3), fundamental principles of administrative law and the first amendment. Finally, the article suggests how the Service could respond to legitimate concerns about possible use of exempt status by some organizations, without denying exempt status to all communitarian religious organizations.

I. COMMUNITARIAN RELIGIOUS ORGANIZATIONS: AN OVERVIEW

In the Christian tradition, religious communal living can be traced back to the time of the apostles and is reflected in the Bible. During the third century A.D., the cenobitic, communal life monastery was originated by the "Desert Fathers" of Egypt. Cenobitism, which required eating, sleeping and living together, embodied the principles on which

---

For a fully footnoted version of this article, readers may refer to 50 *Fordham Law Review* 1085 (1982).

all later Christian monasticism was based. Although modern Christian communitarian life is not limited to monasticism, with its emphasis on celibacy and the renunciation of worldly goods, monasteries and convents were the most important form of Christian communal life for many centuries. While the traditional Christian monastic orders exerted their greatest influence in the Middle Ages, they continue to thrive today. Their importance to Christianity, both historically and presently, can hardly be overstated.

Non-monastic Christian communities, modeled after the type of religious community described in The Acts of the Apostles, have thrived primarily in Protestant countries. In the United States, Protestant common-life organizations have proliferated since the colonial period. The longest lasting of the American Protestant communitarian societies has been the Shakers—the United Society of Believers in Christ's Second Coming—which originated in the late eighteenth century in New England and still exists today. Their official narrative explains the impetus behind Christian communal living:

> To constitute a true faith of Christ, there must necessarily be union of faith, of motives and of interest, in all the members who compose it. There must be "one body and one bread" and nothing short of this union in all things, both spiritual and temporal, can constitute a true church, which is the body of Christ./4/

In recent years, there has been a resurgence of interest in communities of this type in the United States. Although the reasons for renewed interest may be rooted in dissent from the values of modern secular society, the adherents of many of these new communities express themselves by acknowledging and working within the larger society, rather than by withdrawing, as was done in classical monasticism.

Christian communitarianism, despite its long history and continued vitality, possesses no monopoly on religious common-life organizations. Buddhist monasticism, which was well established by the time of Christ, emphasizes the monastic life-style more than does Christianity. Also predating Christianity were the Jewish Essene communities which inhabited the Judaean desert from 110 B.C. to 68 A.D. Monasticism is also a tradition in Hinduism, Taoism, Islam and Jainism.

The historical foundations of religious communitarianism demonstrated that its practitioners are trying nothing new. Neither cultists nor faddists, they are simply trying to live by age-old religious precepts that have fallen into disuse. Whatever their theological differences, these diverse religious organizations agree on the value of communal living. Almost all would be in accord with the following passage from the Shaker's narrative:

In this united capacity, the strength of the whole body becomes the strength of each member; and being united . . . they have a greater privilege to serve God than they possibly could have in a separate capacity, and are better able to be mutual helps to each other; and they also find a greater degree of protection from the snares of a selfish and worldly nature./5/

II. THE *BETH-EL* DECISION

The statutory framework within which religious organizations enjoy tax-exempt status has developed over a number of years. The tax exemption for charitable or religious organizations was first enacted in 1894/6/ and reenacted in 1913./7/ Groups organized and operated exclusively for charitable or religious purposes were granted tax exempt status because of the benefit the public obtains from their activities./8/ The grant of exemption is qualified, however, by three requirements: (1) the organization must be organized and operated exclusively for one or more exempt purposes; (2) no part of the organization's net earnings may inure to the benefit of a private individual; and (3) the organization may not be actively involved in legislative lobbying and political campaigns./9/ In denying exempt status to communitarian religious organizations, the Service has made two basic arguments: that such organizations are not organized and operated exclusively for exempt purposes because furnishing the necessities of life to their members is a significant non-exempt purpose, and that the net earnings of such organizations inure to the private benefit of their members, through the members' receipt of food and shelter./10/

In *Beth-El Ministries* v. *United States*,/11/ the leading recent case in this area, the Service successfully defended its denial of exempt status to a communitarian religious organization./12/ *Beth-El* involved a group whose purpose was "to be a non-profit, interdenominational religious community." The organization had two types of members—staff and associates. The staff members lived together as a Christian community in the fullest sense. The community provided all staff members with the necessities of life and a parochial school education for their children. Each staff member committed all of his possessions to the community upon joining, and those members who were employed outside the community donated their entire salaries.

The district court upheld the Service's denial of tax-exempt status to the organization because "[t]he members of Beth-El receive benefits in the form of food, clothing, shelter, medical care, recreational facilities and educational services from the organization. Accordingly, private benefits inure to the members."/13/ The court also relied on the 1928 Court of Claims in *Hofer* v. *United States*/14/, and accepted the Hofer court's conclusion that "a corporation whose members devoted their time, services, and earnings to the corporation, whose property is owned for the common use and benefit of its members, is not a corporation organized and operated for religious purposes."/15/ The *Beth-El* court thus apparently concluded that communitarian religious organizations inherently fail to satisfy two of the required of section 501(c)(3). First, the court's reliance on *Hofer* indicates that such groups *cannot* be "organized and operated exclusively for religious . . . purposes."/16/ Second, in concluding that the receipt of meals and lodging constituted private benefit, the Court found that Beth-El was an organization "part of the net earnings of which inures to the benefit of [a] private shareholder or individual."/17/

It is surprising that the *Beth-El* court took such a narrow view of the issues before it. In its terse opinion, the court did not even hint at the existence of the historical and scriptural foundations for the way of life practiced by the Beth-El community, nor did it engage in the kind of close statutory analysis which proper treatment of the issues demands.

III. A STATUTORY ANALYSIS

A. *Operated Exclusively for Religious Purposes*

Communitarian religious organizations, by definition, care for the temporal, as well as the spiritual, needs of their members. Given the nature of religious communitarianism, tending to these temporal needs is an aspect of religious observance and is consistent with being organized exclusively for religious purposes within the meaning of section 501(c)(3).

It has long been recognized that, in order to decide whether an organization is operated exclusively for religious purposes, the *activities* in which the group engages must be distinguished from the *purpose* behind those activities. The statute itself states that it is the purpose, and not the activity, which must be exclusively religious./18/ The regulations promulgated 501(c)(3) also recognize this distinction: "An organization will be regarded as 'operated exclusively' *for one or more exempt purposes* only if it engages primarily in *activities which accomplish one or more of such exempt purposes* specified in section 501(c)(3)."/19/ Thus, in determining whether an organization is operated exclusively for religious purposes, the objective nature of the organization's activities is not dispositive. Activities take on their coloration by reason of the purposes for which they are undertaken. As the Tax Court noted in *B.S.W. Group, Inc.* v. *Commissioner*, "the purpose toward which an organization's activities are directed, and not the nature of the activities themselves, is ultimately dispositive of the organization's right to be classified as a section 501(c)(3) organization."/20/ Consequently, to the extent that the *Beth-El* court concluded that supplying the necessities of life was inherently non-religious, it did not properly interpret the statute. It should be focused on whether the necessities were supplied to accomplish an exempt purpose. Given the relationship between the communitarian way of life and the religious beliefs of the organization's members, the argument is sound that the "purpose" of such activities was to create a totally religious environment.

The tax administrator may not decide whether a particular religious belief or way of life is fallacious or meritorious, true or false, reasonable or ridiculous, as long as the belief is sincerely held./21/ In accordance with this principle, a wide range of activities has been held to be consistent with the operation of an organization exclusively for religious or charitable purposes. In *Golden Rule Church Association* v. *Commissioner*, for example, a church subsidiary managed several businesses—including a laundry, a hotel, a nursery, a ranch, and a sawmill—in order to demonstrate to the world that the Church's teaching applied to daily business life./22/ The Tax Court held that the mere fact that religious organizations normally do not operate such businesses did not justify a refusal to recognize that the organization at issue had engaged in its activities for exclusively religious purposes. The court ruled that the organization was tax-exempt. Most American religious organizations do not furnish room and board to their members. That is no reason, however, to refuse to recognize that organizations which do furnish room and board may do so exclusively for religious purposes.

The position of religious communities is analogous to that presented in *San Francisco Infant School, Inc.* v. *Commissioner*. The Service claimed that the Infant School was not operated exclusively for educational purposes, because the school also supplied custodial day care services to its young students. The Tax Court rejected the Service's argument, finding that "the custodial care was a necessary concomitant of the education. Without its custodial services, education could not have been furnished to its students."/23/ Similarly, the furnishing of life's necessities by a religious communitarian organization to its members can be an activity which is a concomitant part of the organization's religious purpose.

In similar situations, the Service has accepted the assertion that room and board can be furnished exclusively for religious purposes. Monasteries, convents, and religious orders routinely satisfy the temporal needs of their members. Most of these organizations are affiliated with well-established religious orders and have been routinely granted tax-exempt status by the Service. When established or long-standing communities are involved, the Service apparently has no problem with either of the issues raised in the *Beth-El* case./24/ The Service's treatment of new or unconventional communitarian religious groups is thus inconsistent with its treatment of long-acknowledged ones.

B. Serving a Public Interest

In elaboration of the statutory requirement that exempt religious organizations be operated exclusively for one or more exempt purposes, the Commissioner's regulations state that "[a]n organization is not organized or operated exclusively for [religious purposes] unless it serves a *public* rather than a *private interest.*"/25/ This regulation provides the Service with an argument that communitarian religious organizations cannot be tax-exempt, because they serve only the private interests of their members. This point was not raised in the Beth-El case. When the regulation is considered in light of the statutory language it interprets, however, it is clear that communitarian religious organizations do not violate the rule prohibiting operation for private benefit. The primary function of most, if not all, religious organizations, including communitarian groups, is to provide for the religious needs of their members. The regulation must therefore be interpreted to mean that when such needs are satisfied, a religious organization serves a public interest. To interpret the regulation in any other way would deprive the vast majority of religious organizations of their tax-exempt status.

Furthermore, if the Service interprets the statute to require an organization to do more than serve the needs of its immediate membership—by proselytizing, sponsoring social welfare programs or opening its service to the public—the Service would be violating both the free exercise clause and the establishment clause of the first amendment: first, by coercing a particular form of religious expression,/26/ and second, by discriminating between religions on the basis of whether their doctrines coincide with the Service's concept of contribution to the public interest./27/

C. Inurement of Net Earnings to Private Individuals

The *Beth-El* court accepted the Service's argument that the provision of room and board by a religious organization to its membership violates the statute against the inurement of net earnings to members of the organization. Net earnings are the amount remaining after operating expenses have been deducted from gross receipts./28/ Operating expenses, therefore, constitute no part of earnings. For communitarian religious organizations, the cost of supplying the necessities of life is a reasonable and necessary operating expense. If the religious purposes of the community are to be achieved, it is essential that the members live together. Indeed, their communal life style is an integral part of their religious expression.

It has been recognized that furnishing the necessities of life, under appropriate circumstances, can be an operating expense that does not result in private inurement./29/ Religious orders, convents, and monasteries all supply the necessities of life to their members. In such situations, the Service has not alleged that the order's net earnings inure to the individual members. The Service's position, therefore, must be that the cost of room and board is an operating expense of such organizations and that the net earnings do not inure to the benefit of the individuals members.

Because communal living is not essential to most religious organizations, the cost of supplying room, board, and other necessities to members would not be a legitimate expense for most religious organizations. Costs of this nature are, however, necessary expenses of communitarian organizations, because the religious beliefs of their members require that they live together as a community.

IV. THE CONSTITUTIONAL REQUIREMENT OF CONSISTENCY

The Service has routinely recognized the tax-exempt status of the converts, monasteries and religious orders of familiar religious groups, despite their communal lifestyles. Yet, the Service's position is that the same conduct of supplying room and board, in the context of a new and unfamiliar religious group, constitutes a significant non-exempt purpose, serves a private interest and results in private inurement of net earnings. This distinctive treatment by the Service conflicts with the due process clause of the fifth amendment, the first amendment guarantee of religious freedom, and the principle of administrative consistency.

A. Administrative Consistency

It is a well-established principle of administrative law that an agency must treat all similarly situated parties alike./30/ When a party challenging an agency's action is able to show apparent inconsistency, the reviewing court will place the burden on the agency to explain what relevant differences, if any, exist between the party challenging the action and other similarly situated parties that have been treated differently. If the agency does not explain the apparent inconsistency, or if the reasons it offers are not relevant differences within the applicable statutory framework, the reviewing court will order the agency to treat the aggrieved party in the same way that the agency has treated other parties.

The demand for administrative consistency is based upon the presumption that the policies committed to an agency by Congress will be best implemented if a settled rule is followed. "From this presumption flows the agency's duty to explain its departure from prior norms."/31/ This duty is to set forth clearly the grounds for the departure and to specify the factual differences between the cases. The "factual differences [will] serve to distinguish the cases only when some legislative policy makes the differences relevant to determining the proper scope of the prior rule."/32/ In the present context, it would thus be insufficient for the Service to point out that most of the communitarian religious organizations it has recognized as tax-exempt are associated with an old, familiar religious body. The Service must demonstrate the relevance of such a distinction in light of section 501(c)(3)./33/

One commentator has suggested that the Internal Revenue Service often acts as if it had some special dispensation from the requirement of consistency that applies to all other administrative agencies./34/ The Service's apparent belief that it need not be consistent may be based partially on the recently enacted provision relating to the disclosure of private letter rulings. Section 6110(j)(3) provides in part: "Unless the Secretary otherwise establishes by regulations, a written determination may not be used or cited as precedent. . . ."/35/

It is possible to argue that this provision exempts the Service from the otherwise universal rule that an administrative agency must be consistent in its treatment of similarly situated parties. Whatever the validity of that argument in those situations where section 6110(j)(3) applies, the argument has no application to rulings relating to tax-exempt status. Section 6110(k)(1) specifically states that section 6110 shall not apply to "any matter to which section 6104 applies."/36/ Because section 501(a) tax exemption applications are governed by section 6104, the language of section 6110(j)(3) is inapplicable./37/ Additionally, the Service's claim that it need not be consistent has been rejected by courts outside the exempt organizations area./38/ Consequently, the normal principle of administrative law, that an agency must treat similarly situated parties parties consistently, should apply to determinations of tax-exempt status under section 501(a).

This requirement of consistency is further mandated by the equal protection of the laws and the recognition that "nothing opens the door to arbitrary action so effectively as to allow . . . officials to pick and choose only a few to whom they will apply legislation and thus to escape the political retribution that might be visited upon them if larger numbers were affected."/39/

B. The First Amendment

The Supreme Court has repeatedly declared that the first amendment's prohibition of any law "respecting an establishment of religion" means that the government may not favor any one religion over another./40/ In *Walz* v. *Tax Commission*, the Court said that the primary purpose of the religion clauses of the first amendment "is to insure that no religion be sponsored or favored, none commanded, and none inhibited."/41/ Freedom of religious choice is assured by the clause's proscription of all favoritism in matters of belief. By refusing to recognize the exempt status of communitarian organizations that lack the longevity and affiliation of the convents and monasteries of older religions, the Service violates the first amendment.

Implicit in the many Supreme Court pronouncements concerning governmental neutrality among religions is an analysis similar to that employed under the equal protection clause of the fourteenth amendment. As Justice Harlen explained in his concurrence in *Walz*: "Neutrality in [the law's] application requires an equal protection mode of analysis. The Court must survey meticulously the circumstances and governmental categories to eliminate, as it were, religious gerrymanders."/42/ The use of the term "religious gerrymanders" emphasizes that all departures from governmental neutrality among religions are forbidden, whether overt, or in the form of subtle gerrymandering that subjects religions to unequal treatment. The discriminatory treatment of communitarian organizations appears to be of the subtle gerrymander type. It is not officially acknowledged by the Service—perhaps not even recognized as discrimination—but it is nevertheless discriminatory, and thus unconstitutional.

In *Gillette* v. *United States*, the Court concurred with Justice Harlan's language in *Walz*, but went on to add that "a claimant alleging 'gerrymander' must be able to show the absence of a neutral, secular basis for the lines government has drawn."/43/ In the context of communitarian religious organizations, the only apparent distinction between organizations that have been granted exempt status and those that have not is that the latter tend to be newer organizations, not formally affiliated with large and well-established churches. This difference does not constitute a "neutral, secular basis" for distinguishing among organizations. On the contrary, favoring older, larger, and more established organizations simply because they *are* older, larger, and more established is a clear example of a forbidden establishment of religion./44/

New or unfamiliar religious groups are entitled to the same treatment afforded more familiar groups; indeed by very reason of their newness and unfamiliarity, such groups are particularly in need of fair and even-handed treatment from the government. Unintentional discrimination is not immune from challenge; the Supreme Court has warned of the "danger of unintended religious discrimination—a danger that a claim's chance of success would be greater the more familiar or salient the claim's connection with conventional religiosity could be made to appear."/45/ Insofar as communitarian religious organizations are concerned, the danger has become a reality.

The result of the Service's distinction between religious groups is that the newer communitarian groups are being singled out and taxed because of their religious activities. Their communal life as mandated by their religion is the cause of the denial of their exempt status. The tax imposed on them is in reality a tax on their form of religious expression. The unlimited power to tax is the power to destroy, and withholding an otherwise available tax benefit is unmistakably a penalty. To validate the Service's action is to sanction a device that suppresses or tends to suppress the free exercise of religion as practiced by minority groups./46/

Given the Service's favorable treatment of traditional communitarian religious organizations, any communitarian religious organization should be able to obtain a favorable judicial decision based solely on the Constitution and the principle of administrative consistency, without consideration of whether the organization actually meets the requirements of section 501(c)(3). Why, then, is discussion of statutory issues meaningful? The answer is simple. The Service can solve its consistency problem in one of two ways. It can recognize the exempt status of all communitarian organizations, or it can refuse to recognize the exempt status of any communitarian organization. The Constitution and the principles of administrative law dictate that the Service adopt a consistent policy, but they do not dictate what that policy must be. The proper content of that policy can be determined only by a careful analysis of the requirements of section 501(c)(3).

V. CONSIDERATIONS INFLUENCING THE SERVICE'S POSITION

The Service's consistent exemption of communitarian organizations connected with the Roman Catholic Church and other well-established religions indicates that the Service recognizes there is nothing inherently inconsistent with an organization being both communitarian and tax-exempt. The Service correctly perceives, however, that the form of a communitarian religious organization can easily be misused by persons whose main purpose is to evade taxes. Nevertheless, its response of denying exemption to new communitarian religious groups has been overbroad. Potential abuse can be overcome without a per se denial of exempt status to communitarian organizations otherwise qualified.

A. The Specter of the "Hippie Communes"

The Service may fear that if it grants exemptions to unusual religious communities, it will have to grant exemptions to every "hippie commune" in the country. Although such communes may not be as numerous as they once were, the Service is understandably unable to view this circumstance with equanimity. The Service's concern, however, can be assuaged easily: not all communes are exempt—only those that are organized and operated for a religious or other exempt purpose are entitled to that status. In *Wisconsin v. Yoder*, the Supreme Court very narrowly defined what constitutes such a religious purpose:

> A way of life, however virtuous and admirable, may not be interposed as a barrier to reasonable state regulation of education if it

is based on purely secular considerations; to have the protection of the Religion clauses the claims must be rooted in *religious belief*. . . . Thus, if the Amish asserted their claims because of their subjective evaluation and rejection of the contemporary secular values accepted by the majority, much as Thoreau rejected the social values of his time and isolated himself at Walden Pond, their claims would not rest on a religious basis. Thoreau's choice was philosophical and personal rather than religious, and such belief does not rise to the demands of the Religion Clauses./47/

This narrow definition provides the Service with a firm basis for denying demands for tax-exempt status by countercultural groups. The majority of these groups are based on precisely the kind of philosophical belief that the Supreme Court would not qualify as religious in nature./48/ Those few communal groups that would qualify as religious communities under the *Yoder* approach should be given tax-exempt status.

One problem presented by this case-by-case approach is that both the Service and the courts must inquire into whether particular communes are religious. Such an inquiry, however, does not rise to the level of excessive entanglement of government in religious matters./49/ Section 501(c)(3) continually requires the determination of whether an organization is religious. Communes present no greater difficulties in this respect than do other organizations that claim to be religious.

B. Untaxed Benefits

The greatest potential for abuse lies in the untaxed receipt by members of a religious community of substantial non-cash benefits from the community, such as food, shelter, clothing and health care. Yet, the solution to this problem could not be more simple: tax the organization's members on the value of the benefits they receive. There is no inconsistency between treating the organization as tax-exempt and taxing persons who receive economic value from the organization./50/ Exempt organizations commonly pay salaries that are taxable to the recipients without destroying the community's exempt status./51/ In many religious communities, the benefits received would be sufficiently related to work performed for the community to justify treating the benefits as compensation for services rendered. Even in organizations where the benefits cannot be treated as compensation, they would nevertheless fall under the broad sweep of the definition of gross income in section 61 of the Code./52/

In any event, the question of whether benefits are taxable to the recipient is unrelated to the question of whether the community is exempt. Just as non-exempt entities can make distributions that are not taxable, such as gifts excludable under section 102 of the Code, exempt organizations can make distributions that are taxable, such as salaries. Denying religious communities exempt status is an ineffective and inappropriate way of dealing with the problem of untaxed benefits.

An advantage of taxing all members of religious communities on the value of benefits received is that it will tend to least affect members of legitimate religious organizations, and most affect members of sham and questionable organizations. The standard of living in most sincerely religious communes is quite low. The members of these organizations often receive insufficient benefits to generate any tax liability. On the other hand, the standard of living would be naturally higher among the members of organizations formed primarily to evade taxes. Thus, taxing individuals on the value of the benefits received would go far toward destroying the appeal of the "religious" community as a device for avoiding taxes, while having little, if any, effect on most valid religious communities.

C. The Quid Pro Quo Problem

In some religious communities, members have outside income from investments or from part-time employment outside the community, some or all of which they donate to their community. The Service may deny exempt status to insure that contributing members will be unable to claim improper charitable deductions for their contributions./53/ A full charitable deduction in this situation would be improper, because the member may have received substantial benefits from the organization "in exchange" for his contribution./54/ Solving this problem, however, does not require the denial of exempt status to the organization. All that is needed is a determination of the value of the benefits the member has received in exchange for the donation. The member is entitled to a deduction to the extent, and only to the extent, that his contribution exceeds the value of the benefit received./55/ This is precisely the approach the Service has long used in the analogous area of deductions from bargain sales to charities./56/

D. Private Churches

Perhaps the most common form of a sham religious organization is what might be termed the "private church" or "mail-order ministry." Typically, an individual forms a church and declares himself to be a minister. He donates or assigns his income to the church, claiming a charitable deduction for the amounts donated. The church's money is available to the individual to use as he sees fit in his capacity as the church's "minister," and he generally uses it to maintain the standard of living that he and his family enjoyed before his ecclesiastical transformation./57/ He may also claim that some or all of the church funds used for his benefit are excludable parsonage allowances under section 107 of the Code. There are many variations in the details—a private church may be completely independent or it may be formally, although not financially, affiliated with some national mail-order ministry, an individual may form his own church or several individuals may form a church in which all are ministers, and so on—but the basic pattern is the same.

Although these private churches are not usually communitarian organizations, they do generally pay the expenses of members and their families./58/ It may be that the Service is so wary of any new religious organization that pays the living expenses of its members that it has decided to deny exempt status to all such organizations, regardless of whether they are sham private churches or sincere communitarian religious organizations. If so, the Service paints with too broad a brush— especially because the Service has the tools to attack sham private churches without also attacking sincere religious communities.

Both the Service and the courts have readily recognized that these private churches fail to satisfy the requirements of section 501(c)(3). They are usually able to demonstrate little or no religious activity, but rather are created and operated for the primary purpose of tax avoidance./59/ In addition, by serving only the private interests of their ministers, the churches arguably fail to satisfy the regulation's requirement that they serve a public, rather than a private, interest. Finally, the private churches have no defense against challenges based upon private inurement. The benefits their ministers receive are, by the very nature of these sham churches, disproportionate to the services, if any, that the ministers render to the organizations and are often in direct proportion to the monetary contributions made./60/ The benefits cannot therefore be justified as reasonable compensation for service. Nor can they be justified as a legitimate cost of operation, because supplying the necessities of life to church members is not essential to the accomplishment of any religious purpose.

The Service has used these arguments to prevail consistently against sham private churches. None of these arguments, which have proven so effective against sham private churches, has any relevance to legitimate communitarian religious organizations./61/ The Service can continue to attack sham private churches without threatening the exempt status of religious communitarian organizations.

E. The Problem of Insincerity

Closely related to the problem of private churches is the problem of insincerity, which may be the most significant difficulty with granting exemptions to communitarian religious organizations. Because of the recent proliferation of unusual new religious organizations, and the obvious advantages of exempt status, this concern with the good faith of new organizations is understandable. A substantial minority of new religious communities may be organized and operated not for religious purposes but to avoid taxes./62/ Traditionally structured monasteries and convents, however, are generally familiar and established, and the Service does not question their sincerity. This may be one of the reasons for the difference in treatment between monasteries and convents, on the one hand, and new communitarian organizations, on the other. But the effect of this approach is necessarily to discourage new religious organizations while entrenching old ones, resulting in an establishment of religion.

The proper response of the Service to suspect claims of religious motivation is not to deny exemption requests of new or unfamiliar organizations by applying a standard to them that is not applied to traditional organizations. Rather, if the Service is concerned about sincerity, it should investigate sincerity. Although the government cannot evaluate a religious creed for its truth or falsity, orthodoxy or unorthodoxy,/63/ it is not without power to prevent the exploitation of the first amendment by religious frauds./64/ A finding that beliefs are not sincerely held would preclude exempt status because it would mean that the organization was not, in fact, organized and operated for religious purposes./65/

While an inquiry into an organization's sincerity must be conducted with care and sensitivity, it can and must be done. The Service has recognized that it has "the right and the duty to inquire into the sincerity of the beliefs professed by a church or [religious] organization seeking preferred tax treatment . . . under [section] 501(c)(3)."/66/ In addition, the Tax Court is willing to rely on the degree of sincerity of an organization's members in deciding the exemption issue./67/

Fortunately, it is usually necessary for either the Service or the courts to rely explicitly on insincerity when denying an exemption request. Because an organization with insincerely held religious beliefs is usually a mere tool for enriching those in control, such an organization will almost always be marked by prohibited inurement of its earnings. A denial based on inurement carries considerably less potential for major controversy than does a denial based on lack of sincerity.

F. Section 501(d)

Section 501(d) of the Code grants exempt status to:

> Religious or apostolic associations or corporations, if such associations or corporations have a common treasury or community treasury, even if such associations or corporations engage in business for the common benefit of the members, but only if the members thereof include (at the time of filing their returns) in their gross

> income their entire pro rata shares, . . . of the taxable income of
> the association or corporation. . . . Any amount so included . . .
> shall be treated as a dividend received.

The Service may feel it is improper to grant communitarian organizations exempt status under section 501(c)(3) because certain communitarian religious organizations are specifically exempted under 501(d). The latter exemption, however, is unsatisfactory to most communitarian organizations. First, many communitarian organizations do not have a common treasury, and so cannot qualify under section 501(d). Second, exemption under this provision does not carry with it eligibility to receive deductible charitable contributions.

Section 501(d) was added to the Code in 1936 by an amendment made on the Senate floor. Its legislative history consists solely of a short speech by Senator Walsh./68/ Prior to its enactment, several court decisions had denied exempt status to religious communities that operated commercial businesses, primarily on the theory that the operation of the business constituted a substantial non-exempt purpose./69/ Not only were these organizations non-exempt, but because their rules prevented members from holding property in an individual capacity, the organizations were also subject to what is now the tax on accumulated earnings./70/ The only purpose of the 1936 amendment was to relieve such organizations possessed of commercial operations from the burden of the accumulated earnings tax. The amendment was to apply only to religious communities without commercial operations. Before the 1936 amendment, religious communities without commercial operations, including many monasteries, convents and religous orders, had been routinely treated by the Service as exempt under the predecessor of section 501(c)(3), and nothing in the amendment indicates any congressional intent to change the tax treatment of those organizations. Accordingly, it cannot be construed as designed to penalize communitarian organizations that were already eligible for exemption.

In any event, section 501(d) may have lost most of its importance since the enactment of the unrelated business income tax./71/ The cases that held organizations with substantial commercial activity to be non-exempt and thus gave rise to the need for section 501(d) were decided prior to the enactment of the unrelated business income tax provisions. With the addition of that tax, the Service recognized that operation of a trade or business is not a bar to exempt status if the organization "is not organized or operated for the primary purpose of carrying on an unrelated trade or business, as defined in section 513."/72/ This regulatory statement suggests that as long as the primary purpose of an organization is the operation of a religious community, rather than the maintenance of a commercial business, it should be exempt despite substantial commercial activity. The organization would, of course, be subject to tax on unrelated business income from its commercial activity. Such an organization would thus appear to have a choice of being treated as a section 501(c)(3) organization with unrelated business income or as a section 501(d) organization.

There might be support, however, for an argument that sections 501(c)(3) and 501(d) are mutually exclusive positions. In the Supreme Court's recent decision in *HCSC Laundry* v. *United States,*/73/ the Court concluded that a cooperative hospital laundry service cannot qualify for an exemption under section 501(c)(3). The Court noted that hospital laundry services are conspicuously absent from section 501(e) of the Code, which provides for the exempt status of various other kinds of cooperative hospital service organizations. Although Congress had explicitly considered including laundry service organizations within section 501(e), it had decided not to do so at the urging of commercial laundry services. The Court ruled that, given this legislative history, cooperative hospital service organizations could qualify for exemption only under section 501(d), thus precluding the possibility of exemption under section 501(c)(3).

If this analysis is applied to communitarian religious organizations, it could be argued that they must qualify for exemption, if at all, under section 501(d). That argument, however, will not survive careful analysis. Section 501(d) applies only if the organization's members include in their gross income their pro rata shares of the organization's taxable income. By its terms then, section 501(d) applies only to religious and apostolic organizations that have taxable income—in fact, the legislative history of the provision makes clear that it applies only to organization with income from commercial activities. Thus, at most, section 501(d) might be the exclusive basis upon which exemption could be granted to communal organizations with commercial activities.

The legislative history of section 501(d) further demonstrates that its sole purpose was to confer a new exemption, not to limit the exemptions available to communitarian organizations under section 501(c)(3). When the addition of the unrelated business income provisions increased the extent to which an organization could engage in commercial activities without losing its exempt status under section 501(c)(3), communal organizations with substantial commercial activities were among the beneficiaries of that change. To say that they were not so benefitted, because of section 501(d), would be to turn a provision that was intended to assist communitarian organizations with commercial activities into a punitive provision. Such an approach would, of course, subvert the congressional intent. This situation is entirely different from section 501(e), wherein Congress intentionally excluded cooperative hospital services from exempt status. Nothing in section 501(d) indicates any congressional intent to exclude specific organizations from exempt status.

CONCLUSION

The discriminatory manner in which the Service grants exemptions to familiar communitarian organizations, while denying them to unfamiliar, cannot be justified or excused. There will always be some communitarian religious organizations whose qualifications for exempt status are doubtful, and drawing the line between exempt and non-exempt communitarian organizations will not always be easy. Line-drawing problems will arise most frequently in relation to the issue of whether an organization is operated exclusively for religious purposes. Organizations whose activities do not fit the mold of traditional religious activities will receive especially close scrutiny from the Service and the courts. The Service must bear in mind, however, that the crucial issue is not the objective nature of an organization's activities, but the purpose behind those activities. An inherently non-exempt activity does not exist. Nor are there any activities in which a communitarian religious organizations *must* engage in order to be exempt. No doubt, some allegedly religious organizations will be unable to demonstrate that they are operated exclusively for religious purposes. The Service and the courts will not be able to make this determination, however, simply by referring to checklists of exempt and non-exempt activities. A delicate inquiry into the purposes motivating an organization's activities is required. A case-by-case approach may place more of a burden on the Service, but it is the only approach that is consistent with the Internal Revenue Code, the principles of administrative law and the Constitution.

POSTSCRIPT

In GCM (General Counsel Memorandum) 38827, dated December 7, 1981, the Office of Chief Counsel to the Internal Revenue Service concluded that it is possible for a communal religious organization to qualify as an organization described in section 501(c)(3). Although the document does not refer to Mt. Bether Bible Center, Inc. (mentioned in note 1 of the article) by name, the organization which it describes, and which it concludes qualifies for exempt status, is clearly Mt. Bether. The issuance of this detailed, closely reasoned memorandum suggests that the Service's stipulation in the Mt. Bether case represents a basic change in policy, rather than merely a tactical decision that the case was a poor litigation vehicle for the Service.

NOTES

/1/ Martinsville Ministries, Inc. v. United States, 80–2 U.S. Tax Cas. (CCH) Pl9710, at 85, 329 (D.D.C. 1979)(mem.); Beth-El Ministries, Inc. v. United

States, 79–2 U.S. Tax Cas. (CCH) Pl9412, at 87, 517–519 (D.D.C. 1979) (mem.); see also Basic Unit Ministry of Alma Karl Schurig v. Commissioner, No. 81–1247 (D.D.C. January 15, 1982) *(per curiam)* (tax-exempt status denied to a communitarian religious group). Recently, in Mt. Bether Bible Center, Inc. v. Commissioner, No. 20363–81 "X" (T.C. filed December 28, 1981), the Service stipulated that the communitarian religious organization at issue was tax-exempt. It remains to be seen whether this represents a change in Service Policy or merely a tactical decision that the particular case was a poor litigation vehicle for the Service.

/2/   Religious organizations described in Section 501(c)(3) are tax exempt under Section 501(a). Unless otherwise indicated, all statutory references are to the Internal Revenue Code of 1954 through the date of amendment by the Economic Recovery Tax Act of 1981, Public Law no. 97–34, 95 Stat. 172 (codified in scattered sections of 26 United States Code).

/3/   I.R.C. Section 501(c)(3). This section allows an exemption only if three conjunctive requirements are met. Failure to satisfy any of these requirements results in a denial of tax-exempt status.

/4/   C. Green and S. Wells, *A Summary View of the Millennial Church or United Society of Believers (Commonly Called Shakers)* (1823) 51 (footnote omitted) (quoting I Corinthians 10:17 [King James]).

/5/   Green and Wells, supra note 4, at 51.

/6/   Act of August 27, 1894, ch. 349, 32, 28 Stat. 556. The income tax imposed by this Act was declared unconstitutional in Pollock v. Farmers Loan & Trust Co., 158 U.S. 601, 637 (1895).

/7/   Act of October 3, 1913, ch. 16 Section II G(a), 38 Stat. 172. The successor of this statute is now codified at I.R.C. Section 501.

/8/   See H.R. Rep. No. 1860, 75th Congress, 3d Session 19 (1939) ("[T]he government is compensated for the loss of revenue by its relief from financial burden which would otherwise have to be met by appropriations from public funds, and by the benefits resulting from the promotion of the general welfare.").

/9/   I.R.C. Section 501(c)(3).

/10/   See Beth-El Ministries, Inc. v. United States, 79–2 U.S. Tax Cas. (CCH) Pl9412, at 87, 517–519 (D.D.C. 1979) (mem.). The prohibition against private inurement of net earnings appears redundant because such a benefit would be inconsistent with operating exclusively for an exempt purpose. B.H.W. Anesthesia Foundation, Inc. v. Commissioner, 72 T.C. 681, 684 n.3 (1979); Lowry Hospital Association v. Commissioner, 66 T.C. 850, 857 n.8 (1976).

/11/   79–2 U.S. Tax Cas. (CCH) Pl9412 (D.D.C. 1979) (mem.). The organization involved in *Beth-El* maintained its action under Section 7428 of the Code, which permits an organization seeking initial or continuing qualification under 501(c)(3) to sue for a declaratory judgment in either the Tax Court, the Court of

Claims or the District Court for the District of Columbia, after its administrative remedies have been exhausted. I.R.C. Section 7428(a)-(b).

/12/   79-2 U.S. Tax Cas. (CCH) at 87, 518.

/13/   Id.

/14/   64 Ct. Cl. 672 (1928).

/15/   79-2 U.S. Tax Cas. (CCH) at 87, 518.

/16/   I.R.C. Section 501(c)(3).

/17/   Id. In Martinsville Ministries, Inc. v. United States, 80-2 U.S. Tax Cas. (CCH) Pl9710 (D.D.C. 1979) (mem.), Judge Richey, author of the *Beth-El* opinion, noted simply that he found the facts of the case indistinguishable from those of *Beth-El*, and therefore granted summary judgment for the government on the issue of exemption. Id. at 85,329.

/18/   I.R.C. Section 501(c)(3).

/19/   Treas. Reg. Section 1.501(c)(3)-1(c) (1981) (emphasis added).

/20/   70 T.C. 352, 356-57 (1978). The same principle had been expressed earlier in Golden Rule Ass'n v. Commissioner, 41 T.C. 719 (1964), where the Tax Court said, "the statutory language treats as a touchstone, not the organization's activity, but rather the end for which that activity is undertaken." Id. at 728; see Pulpit Resource v. Commissioner 70 T.C. 594, 603 (1978); A. A. Allen Revivals, Inc. v. Commissioner, 22 T.C.M. (CCH) Pl281, at 1443 (1963); Sharon Worthing, "'Religion' and 'Religious Institutions' Under the First Amendment," 7 *Pepperdine Law Review* 313, 325-32 (1980).

/21/   United States v. Ballard, 322 U.S. 78, 86-87 (1944); Universal Life Church, Inc. v. United States, 372 F. Supp. 770, 776 (E.D. Cal. 1974). In an analogous situation the Court held that the Military Selective Service could not evaluate the truth of falsity of beliefs espoused by applicants for conscientious objector status under the Military Training & Service Act of 1948, 50 U.S.C. app. Section 456(j) (1976). Welsh v. United States, 398 U.S. 333, 342-44 (1970); United States v. Seeger, 380 U.S. 163, 166 (1965). The Court states in *Seeger* that the appropriate test is whether the belief is "sincere and meaningful [and occupies] a place in the life of its possessor parallel to that filled by the orthodox belief in God." 380 U.S. at 166.

/22/   41 T.C. 719, 721, 723-724 (1964).

/23/   69 T.C. 957, 964 (1978); see Michigan Early Childhood Ctr., Inc. v. Commissioner, 37 T.C.M. (CCH) Pl186, at 810-11 (1978).

/24/   Many of these monasteries, convents, and religious orders are Roman Catholic and are covered by the annual group exemption letter the Service issues to the United States Catholic Conference. Thus, their exempt status is not approved individually, but simply as components of the Roman Catholic Church of the United States. In a series of private rulings, the Service confirmed the tax-exempt status of eleven Cistercian monasteries. Private Letter Rulings Nos. 7838028–7838036 (June 21, 1978). One of the rulings notes that "[a]s long as [a] monk remains in [the] monastery . . . he [will receive] food, shelter, clothing and medical care [for life]." Private Letter Ruling No. 783028 (June 21, 1978). The rulings found support of the monks to be an exempt function of the monastery. See also Rev. Rul. 76–323, 1976–2 C.B. 18 (orders supplying room and board to members deemed to be operated "exclusively for religious purposes"); Rev. Rul. 63–209, 1963–3 C.B. 469 (convents exempt under Section 501[c][3]).

/25/   Treas. Reg. Section 1.501(c)(3)–1(d)(1) (ii) (1981) (emphasis added). The regulation further states, "Thus, to meet the requirement of this subdivision, it is necessary for an organization to establish that it is not organized or operated for the benefit of private interests such as designated individuals, the creator of his family, shareholders of the organization, or persons controlled, directly or indirectly, by such private interests." This requirement of public benefit is consistent with the legislative history of the tax-exempt status of religious organizations.

/26/   See Torasco v. Watkins, 367 U.S. 488, 495 n. 11 (1961); United States v. Ballard, 322 U.S. 78, 86–87 (1944); Watson v. Jones, 80 U.S. (13 Wall.) 679, 728 (1871); United States v. Kauten, 133 F.2d 703, 708 (2d Cir. 1943).

/27/   See Malnak v. Yogi, 440 F. Supp. 1284, 1322–23 (D.N.J. 1977), aff'd per curiam, 592 F.2d 197 (3d Cir. 1979); Stevens v. Berger, 428 F. Supp. 896, 900 (E.D.N.Y. 1977); Universal Life Church, Inc. v. United States, 372 F. Supp. 770, 776 (E.D. Cal. 1974).

/28/   "The term 'net earnings' in the inurement-of-benefit clause, as stated in section 501 . . . has been construed to permit an organization to incur ordinary and necessary expenditures in the course of its operations without losing its tax-exempt status." Founding Church of Scientology v. United States, 412 F.2d 1197, 1200 (Ct. Cl. 1969) (citations omitted); accord Morey v. Riddell, 205 F. Supp. 918 (S.D. Cal. 1962); A. A. Allen Revivals, Inc. v. Commissioner, 22 T.C.M. (CCH) Pl281, at 1444 (1963).

/29/   See Golden Rule Church Association v. Commissioner, 41 T.C. 719, 731 (1964) (church subsidiary furnishing room and board to student ministers); Saint Germain Foundation v. Commissioner, 26 T.C. 648, 658–59 (1956) (organization teaching religious principles in several cities paid all teachers' living expenses).

/30/   W. Gellhorn, C. Byse, and P. Strauss, Administrative Law 393–98 (7th ed., 1979); see Secretary of Agriculture v. United States, 347 U.S. 645, 654–55 (1954); Frozen Food Express, Inc. v. United States, 535 F. 2d 877, 880 (5th Cir. 1976); International Union v. NLRB, 459 F.2d 1329, 1341 (D.C. Cir. 1972); CBS v. FCC, 454 F.2d 1018, 1026 (D.C. Cir. 1971); Greater Boston Television Corp. v. FCC, 444 F.2d 841, 852 (D.C. Cir. 1970), cert. denied, 403 U.S. 923 (1971); Burinkas v. NLRB, 357 F.2d 822, 827 (D.C. Cir. 1966); Melody Music, Inc. v. FCC, 345 F.2d 730, 732 (D.C. Cir. 1965).

/31/   Atchison, T. & S.F. Ry. v. Wichita Bd. of Trade, 412 U.S. 800, 808 (1973). Alternatively, the agency may announce a general change in policy, so that it will henceforth treat all parties in the same way it is treating the party challenging its action. Id. In the context of the present discussion, this would mean revoking the tax-exempt status of all religious organizations that furnish food and shelter to their members.

/32/   Id.

/33/   I.R.C. Section 501(c)(3); cf. Niedert Motor Serv. v. United States, 583 F.2d 954, 962 (7th Cir. 1978) (ICC must explain departure from prior practice regarding application for carrier permits); Squaw Transit Co. v. United States, 574 F.2d 492, 495–96 (10th Cir. 1978) (same); Office of Communication of the United Church of Christ v. FCC, 560 F.2d 529, 532 (2d. Cir. 1977) (FCC must explain variations in consideration of renewal applications); Greyhound Co. v. ICC, 551 F.2d 414, 416 (D.C. Cir. 1977) (per curiam) (ICC must explain departure from prior practice regarding regulations of securities transactions); Contractors Transp. Corp. v. United States 537 F.2d 1160, 1162 (4th Cir. 1976) (ICC must explain departure from prior practice regarding application for carrier permits).

/34/   See 2 K. Davis, Administrative Law Treatise Section 8:12 (2d ed. 1979). Davis states: "Of all the agencies of the government, the worst offender against sound principles in the use of precedents may be the Internal Revenue Service. . . . Its basic attitude is that because consistency is impossible, an effort to be consistent is unnecessary; therefore, it need not consider precedents, and it may depart from precedents without explaining why." Id. at 206, 208–9.

/35/   I.R.C. Section 6110(j)(3); see Emory, "Private Rulings: What May Practitioners Expect from the New Procedure," 47 *Journal of Taxation* 322 (1977).

/36/   I.R.C. Section 6110(k)(1).

/37/   There is no language in Section 6104 similar to that of Section 6110(j)(3) regarding the precedential weight of rulings.

/38/   United States v. Kaiser, 363 U.S. 299, 308 (1960) (Franfurter, J., concurring) ("The Commissioner cannot tax one and not tax another without some rational basis for the difference."); Ogiony v. Commissioner, 617 F.2d 14, 18 (2d. Cir.) ("consistency over time and uniformity of treatment among taxpayers are proper benchmarks [by which] to judge IRS actions") (Oakes, J., concurring), *cert. denied*, 449 U.S. 900 (1980); Sirbo Holdings, Inc. v. Commissioner, 476 F.2d 981, 987 (2d. Cir. 1973) ("[T]he Commissioner has a duty of consistency toward similarly situated taxpayers; he cannot properly concede capital gains treatment in one case and, without adequate explanation, dispute it in another having seemingly identical facts which is pending at the same time"); IBM Corp. v. United States, 343 F.2d 914, 923 (Ct. Cl. 1965) (like treatment important for all tax rulings), *cert. denied*, 382 U.S. 1028 (1966). Contra Davis v. Commissioner, 65 T.C. 1014, 1022 (1976) (each case should be decided on its facts).

/39/   Railway Express Agency, Inc. v. New York, 336 U.S. 106, 112–13 (1949) (Jackson, J., concurring).

/40/   Torcaso v. Watkins, 367 U.S. 488, 495 (1961); Everson v. Board of Education, 330 U.S. 1, 15 (1946); see, e.g., Committee for Public Education & Religious Liberty v. Nyquist, 413 U.S. 756, 793–94 (1973); Lemon v. Kurtzman, 403 U.S. 602, 622–23 (1971); Watson v. Jones, 80 U.S. 13 (Wall.), 679, 728 (1871).

/41/   397 U.S. 664, 669 (1970).

/42/   Id. at 696.

/43/   401 U.S. 437, 452 (1971).

/44/   See Epperson v. Arkansas, 393 U.S. 97, 103–4 (1968); United States v. Ballard, 322 U.S. 78, 87 (1944). In a similar case in which the Tax Commission of New York denied tax-exempt status to the Unification Church because of its political activities, the special Referee stated: "[I]f you could point to a structure, a church structure similar to the Catholic Church with the well-defined sphere of activities of the Catholic Church, we wouldn't be sitting here and this wouldn't be the case. You would just fall within the well-organized parameters." Brief for Petitioner-Appellant at 16–17, Holy Spirit Association for the Unification of World Christianity v. Tax Commission, 81 A.D. 2d 64, 438 N.Y.S. 2d 521 (1981), rev'd, No. 238 (N.Y. May 6, 1982).

/45/   Gillette v. United States, 401 U.S. 437, 457 (1971).

/46/   See First Unitarian Church v. County of Los Angeles, 357, U.S. 545, 548 (1958) (Douglas, J., concurring) ("There is no power in our Government to make one bend his religious scruples to the requirements of this tax law"); Cantwell v. Connecticut, 310 U.S. 296, 305 (1940) ("a censorship of religion as the means of determining its right to survive is a denial of liberty protected by the First Amendment").

/47/   406 U.S. 205, 215–16 (1972) (emphasis added).

/48/   But see United States v. Seeger, 380 U.S. 163, 165–66 (1965) (required only that sincere belief be meaningful and parallel to that filled by orthodox belief in God).

/49/   See Lemon v. Kurtzman, 403 U.S. 602, 614 (1971) (some involvement and entanglement are inevitable).

/50/   This taxation may, however, be barred by the existence of a particular exclusionary provision, such as the exclusion provided by Section 107 for the rental value of parsonages.

/51/   See Enterprise Ry. Equip. Co. v. United States, 161 F. Supp. 590, 594 (Ct. Cl. 1958); Golden Rule Church Association v. Commissioner, 41 T.C. 719, 731 (1964); Saint Germain Foundation v. Commissioner, 26 T.C. 648, 658–59 (1956).

/52/ I.R.C. Section 61. Certainly, there would be few, if any, situations in which the benefits would qualify as excludable gifts under the "detached and disinterested generosity" standard of Commissioner v. Duberstein, 363 U.S. 278, 285 (1960) (quoting Commissioner v. LoBue 351 U.S. 243, 246 (1956).

/53/ Section 170 of the Code allows a taxpayer to deduct a contribution from his personal income tax if the beneficiary of the contribution is organized exclusively for religious, education or charitable purposes. I.R.C. Section 170. A similar deduction appears in the estate tax law, I.R.C. Section 2055(a), and in the gift tax law, I.R.C. Section 2522.

/54/ See Riker v. Commissioner, 244 F.2d 220, 227–28 (9th Cir. 1957).

/55/ Of course, the member should not be, in effect, taxed twice for the benefits received from the organization. If he is taxed on the benefits as compensation, then the same benefits should also be used to decrease the amount of his charitable deduction.

/56/ See Treas. Reg. Section 1.170A–4(c)(2) (1972); cf. Rev. Rul. 72–506, 1972-2 C.B. 106 (denying a charitable deduction where the transfer is made in a quid pro quo context).

/57/ See Church of the Transfiguring Spirit, Inc. v. Commissioner, 76 T.C. 1, 4–6 (1981): Western Catholic Church v. Commissioner, 73 T.C. 196, 213–14 (1979), aff'd mem., 631 F.2d 736, (7th Cir. 1980).

/58/ See Bubbling Well Church of Universal Love v. Commissioner, 74 T.C. 39 (1980) (single family "church," all funds support home and family expenses), aff'd, No. 80–7358 (9th Cir. Nov 27, 1981); Unitary Mission Church v. Commissioner, 74 T.C. 507, 513–15 (1980) (all "church" funds supported travel and living expenses of three ministers), aff'd mem., 674 F.2d 163 (2d Cir. 1981).

/59/ Carl v. McGahen, 76 T.C. 41, 43 (1981): Southern Church of Universal Brotherhood Assembled, Inc. v. Commissioner, 74 T.C. 1223, 1226–27 (1980); Unitary Mission Church V. Commissioner, 74 T.C. 507, 513–14 (1980), aff'd mem., 647 F.2d 163 (2d Cir. 1981); J. Howard Self v. Commissioner, 41 T.C.M. (CCH) 1465, 1469 (1981); Truth Tabernacle v. Commissioner, 41 T.C.M. (CCH) 1405, 1408–9 (1981); Daryl B. Hall v. Commissioner, 41 T.C.M. 1169, 1170 (1981).

/60/ See Church of the Transfiguring Spirit, Inc. v. Commissioner, 76 T.C. 1, 3–6 (1981); Unitary Mission Church v. Commissioner, 74 T.C. 507, 513–14 (1980), aff'd mem., 647 F.2d 163 (2d Cir. 1981).

/61/ Some legitimate communitarian organizations also have characteristics that make them particularly suspect, such as an extremely small number of members or an accumulation of funds far in excess of those needed to meet operating costs. Even characteristics such as these, however, are not automatic bars to exemption. An extremely small number of members may serve as an indication to the Service that it should look for hidden inurement, but there is nothing inherently non-exempt about an organization with a small membership.

Similarly, an accumulation of funds may be an indication of the existence of a non-exempt purpose, but funds may also be accumulated for exempt purpose— such as to finance an organization's expansion. See Randall Foundation, Inc. v. Riddell 244 F.2d 803, 804-5 (9th Cir. 1957); Western Catholic Church v. Commissioner 73 T.C. 196, 212-13 (1979), aff'd mem., 631 F.2d 736 (7th Cir. 1980).

/62/ The concerns here are illustrated by the tax revolt in Hardenburgh, New York. To protest high taxes, 90% of the adult population of the town became Ministers in the Universal Life Church (ULC) and claimed property tax exemptions as members of the clergy (New York Times, July 17, 1977 at 14, col. 3). The ULC, whose only creed was "do your own thing," mailed credentials of ministry to anyone requesting them and sent a doctorate of divinity degree to anyone who made a $20 "free will offering." Id., May 29, 1977, at 26, col. 3. Many of the citizens of Hardenburgh stated their action was a direct protest against the erosion of the local tax base caused by exemptions given to other charitable and religious groups. Id., July 17, 1977, at 14, col. 4. Although the ULC has been granted exempt status, Universal Life Church, Inc. v. United States, 372 F. Supp. 700, 776 (E.D. Cal. 1974), its local "congregations" have not been as fortunate. See Kellman v. Commissioner, 42 T.C.M. (CCH) 1508, 1511 (1981); Riemers v. Commissioner, 41 T.C.M. (CCH) 838, 841 (1981); Brown v. Commissioner 41 T.C.M. (CCH) 542, 546 (1980).

/63/ United States v. Ballard, 322 U.S. 78, 86-87 (1944); Universal Life Church, Inc. v. United States, 372 F. Supp. 770, 776 (E.D. Cal. 1974); see United States v. Kahane, 396 F. Supp. 687, 698 (E.D.N.Y. 1975).

/64/ See Theriault v. Carlson, 495 F.2d 390, 394 (5th Cir.) (prisoner's sect organized to cause or encourage disruption of prison discipline), cert. denied, 419 U.S. 1003 (1974): United States v. Kuch, 288 F. Supp. 439, 445 (D.D.C. 1968) (one of the "LSD and marijuana church" cases).

/65/ I.R.C. Section 501(c)(3). In Walsh v. United States, 398 U.S. 333 (1970), the Court stated that insincere beliefs would not be protected by the first amendment, and defined insincere beliefs to be those that did "not rest at all upon moral, ethical, or religious principle but instead rested solely upon considerations of policy pragmatism, or expediency." Id. at 342-43.

/66/ Internal Revenue Service, Exempt Organizations Annual Technical Review Institutes for 1980, at 44.

/67/ Pulpit Resources v. Commissioner, 70 T.C. 594, 612 (1978).

/68/ 80 Cong. Rec. 9074 (1936) (statement of Sen. Walsh): "Mr. President, under existing law religious, education and charitable corporations are exempt from taxation under income-tax title. This amendment adds a new paragraph to section 101 of the revenue act, which exempts certain corporations from taxation under the income-tax title. It has been brought to the attention of the committee that certain religious and apostolic associations and corporations, such as the House of David and the Shakers, have been taxed as corporations, and since their rules prevent their members from being holders of property in an individual capacity the corporations would be subject to undistributed-profits tax. These organizations have a small agricultural or other business. The effect of the proposed amendment is to exempt these corporations from the normal corporation tax and the undistributed-profits tax, if their members take up their shares of the corporations' income on their own individual returns. It is believed that this provision will give them relief, and their members will be subject to a fair tax." Id.

/69/   Hofer v. United States, 64 Ct. Cl. 672, 683–84 (1928); *In re* Hutterische Bruder Gemeinde, 1 B.T.A. 1208, 1211 (1925); see Whelan, "'Church' in the Internal Revenue Code: The Definitional Problems," 45 *Fordham Law Review* 885, 905–13 (1977) (discussion of the Service's treatment of the Christian Brothers' Winery).

/70/   I.R.C. 531.

/71/   I.R.S. Section 511–15.

/72/   Treas. Reg. Section 1.501(c)(3)–1(e)(1) (1981).

/73/   45 U.S. 1 (1981) *per curiam.*

CHURCH, STATE, AND THE
CHRISTIAN NEW RIGHT

"THERE IS NO SEPARATION OF GOD AND STATE": THE CHRISTIAN NEW RIGHT PERSPECTIVE ON RELIGION AND THE FIRST AMENDMENT

James McBride

"I believe in the separation of church and state," declared Jerry Falwell in 1980, "but I don't believe in the separation of God and State."/1/ Falwell's statement reflects the widely held opinion among Christian fundamentalists and conservative Evangelicals that the Constitution unconditionally protects the free exercise of religion in all spheres of American life, both public and private, and proscribes only a State-mandated religious ideology or State church. In their view, however, republican principles derived from Scriptural sources are being jeopardized by the rise of a modern, democratic secularism which places a wall between the true faith and government while promoting the religious philosophy of secular humanism, i.e., the ideology of the modern State. Based upon what they feel is a distortion of the Jeffersonian doctrine of separation, this development conjures up a "separation illusion"—that "[America] can deny God and yet survive"—which is detrimental to both the Christian community and the nation as a whole./2/

Since the Second World War, an expanding federal bureaucracy which envisioned itself as the guarantor of individual rights has produced a Leviathan State which seeks the routinization of all aspects of the body politic. Fueled by the religious revival of the "Fourth Great Awakening," the simultaneous occurrence of the "born-again" religious phenomenon responded to the same popular needs which sparked much of the growth in what has been called the "new religious movements."/3/ The parallel expansion of both religion and the State made conflict between conservative Christianity and the government inevitable, generating what most assuredly will be the central Constitutional issue of the 1980s: the boundaries of Church-State relations. The impact of this conflict has stimulated two alternative legal postures by the conservative Christian community: the defense of the community's traditional rights and an attack on the ideology of the State. Fighting in the courts and legislatures of America, the Christian New Right rests its case on explicit Constitutional grounds by arguing, on the one hand, that recent Supreme Court decisions have altered the original intent of the

Founding Fathers' provisions protecting religious liberty, and, on the other hand, that the ideology of the State, i.e., secular humanism, violates the spirit of these same decisions and the Constitution itself by establishing a State religion.

In the eyes of the Christian New Right leadership, the republican principles of the Constitution were replaced by the alien philosophies of liberalism and modernism whose coercive influence conservative Christians have resisted in their own religious communities for decades. Construing the problem in a theological framework, these leaders mimetically appropriate the biblical mythology of the Fall as the precipitating cause for this "shift" in the nation's legal foundation./4/ Accordingly, the temptation—"Ye shall be as Gods"—which seduced Adam and and Eve underlies the philosophy of "materialism" and secular humanism which substituted the seductive promise of human autonomy for biblical absolutism, thereby resulting in the direst consequences for human society. For just as the personal, moral "degeneration" of contemporary America can be ascribed to the philosophy of Joseph Fletcher's *Situation Ethics*, so, too, can the disintegration of the social fabric be blamed on the rise of "situational law" which betrays the divine law upon which the Constitution purportedly rests./5/ The Christian New Right therefore argues for a return to a political or Constitutional fundamentalism akin to its own religious Fundamentalism, effected during the Third Great Awakening (1890-1920). As a candidate for the Presidency, Ronald Reagan perceived this intimate relationship between the nativist construction of law and faith. Speaking before the Dallas National Affairs Briefing in August of 1980, he declared that "over the last two or three decades, the federal government seems to have forgotten *both* 'that old time religion' *and* that old-time Constitution."/6/

The purpose of this paper is to discuss this "old-time Constitution," i.e., the Christian New Right's interpretation of the First Amendment religious freedoms, and to describe both philosophically and pragmatically the legal defense of conservative Christian infrastructures, e.g., ministries, schools, against State bureaucratic regulation. Although these court battles are generally regarded as the reason for conservative Christianity's "politicization," "the involvement in politics will, of course, not be motivated simply by a design to 'protect' Christians or evangelize the political world (narrowly speaking) but to address the very core issues of political/public/social life."/7/ By focusing on such "core issues," the latter part of the paper will sketch the legal front in the current conflict between secular humanism and conservative Christianity by identifying the Constitutional and philosophical questions raised by the Christian New Right which are implicit in the secular ideology of the State.

"THAT OLD-TIME CONSTITUTION"

"There is ample historical evidence to prove that the original intent of our Founding Fathers is exactly what they wrote in the First Amendment to the Constitution and not what our courts and legislators have interpreted it to mean in recent years."/8/ Applying the standards of Fundamentalist Scriptural hermeneutics to the Constitution, Falwell and other conservative Christians argue for a "literalist" or "common sense" interpretation of the establishment and free exercise clauses of the First Amendment: "Congress shall make no law respecting an establishment of religion, or prohibiting the free exercise thereof." Viewed in the context of its time, the Constitution appears to the conservative Christian community as a revolutionary Christian document which embodied the Reformation principles of freedom of conscience through guarantees against a coercive State religion.

As espoused by the Christian New Right leadership, a "straight forward" reading of the establishment clause simply proscribes an "official" religion or State church./9/ Although a State church is deemed unconstitutional, this interpretation does not suggest that the government ought to be free of religious influences or the public realm secularized. The intimation by recent Supreme Court decisions of a thoroughly secular government during the early days of the Republic seems anachronistic to conservative Christians. "The predominant Christian orientation of the American people mitigated against the absolute separation of church and state."/10/ Hence, the "wall of separation" between religion and government was not and has never been categorical despite Justice Black's invocation of that problematic Jeffersonian phrase in *Everson* v. *Board of Education* (1947). Instead of separation, argues conservative Christian attorney John Whitehead, "the Philosophical basis of the First Amendment, then, was denominational pluralism."/11/ The function of the federal government was not therefore to purge the public domain of religious influence but to ensure that no one denomination received preferential treatment or an officially sanctioned status. In this respect, what is not restrained under the establishment clause is given free reign under the free exercise provision of the First Amendment. Hence, even the government could promote what Daniel Webster once called "general, tolerant Christianity independent of sects and parties" as long as it did not foster a coercive influence favoring one denomination over another. Although the federal structure of governance proscribed Congress from interfering in matters of faith, no such boundaries originally inhibited the states from advancing religious beliefs or regulating churches. "The powers not delegated to the United States by the Constitution, nor prohibited by it to the States, are reserved to the States or to the people" (Tenth Amendment). This states' rights interpretation of the

Constitution put forth by conservative Christian lawyers (most notably John Conlan and John Whitehead) seems to be confirmed in the early history of the nation. At the time of the Revolution, eight out of thirteen colonies had State churches—a situation that continued for some time after the ratification of the Constitution in 1789. Even as late as 1833, the established religion of Massachusetts was the Congregational Church whose clergy was paid by the State government. Maryland mandated belief in the Christian religion as a prerequisite to public office until 1864, and the law requiring New Hampshire legislators to be professing Protestants remained on the books until 1877. And although the Torcaso v. Watkins decision (1961) prohibited theistic beliefs as an obligatory qualification for public office, similar laws were recently challenged in suits pending before Texas and Mississippi courts (*O'Hair* v. *Hill* and *Tirmenstein* v. *Mississippi*).

Instead of categorical separation, the Church and State during the nineteenth century enjoyed a felicitous partnership which rendered mutual support. The Protestant philosophy of "benevolence" which characterized the consciousness and behavior of evangelicalism underwrote the social welfare of the body politic while its moral teachings guaranteed the social order. In return the State recognized the privileged position of the church—a position which conservative Christian leaders nostalgically recall today. These informal ties between Church and State were formally recognized by Supreme Court rulings. Throughout the nineteenth century, the Court held that this country was a "Christian nation" (*People* v. *Ruggles*, 1811; *Church of the Holy Trinity* v. *U.S.*, 1892) and reaffirmed the view that "we are a Christian people" as late as the 1930s (*U.S.* v. *McIntosh*, 1931). To the Christian New Right, the confluence of Christian and Constitutional heritage is therefore a matter of factual history./12/

THE "SHIFT" TO CATEGORICAL SEPARATION
OF CHURCH AND STATE

In the wake of the Depression and the New Deal, both the states' rights construction of the First Amendment and the concurrent symbiotic relationship of Church and State were rejected by the Supreme Court. In rulings which applied the Fourteenth Amendment to the free exercise clause (*Cantwell* v. *Connecticut* [1940]) and establishment clause (*Everson* v. *Board of Education* [1947]), the High Court declared that the restrictions placed upon Congress were incumbent upon the states as well. For southern Democrats and later conservative Christians, the first rift in that "old-time Constitution" began to appear.

> The First Amendment declares that Congress shall make no law respecting an establishment of religion or prohibiting the free exercise thereof. The Fourteenth Amendment has rendered the

legislators of the states as incompetent as Congress to enact such laws. (Cantwell v. Connecticut, 310 U.S. 296 [1940], at 303)

In these decisions, the "due process" clause of the Fourteenth Amendment ("no state [shall] deprive any person of life, liberty or property without due process of law") was declared to incorporate the First Amendment thereby universalizing restrictions on governmental interference in matters of religion. Extending this provision to establishment as well as free exercise cases, Justice Hugo Black wrote that

> the 'establishment of religion' clause of the First Amendment means at least this: Neither the state nor the federal government can set up a church. Neither can pass laws which aid one religion, aid all religions, or prefer one religion over another. (Everson v. Board of Education, 330 U.S. 1 [1947] at 15)

The prohibition of laws which "aid all religions" would have serious ramifications.

Implicit in the *Cantwell* and *Everson* decisions was the refutation not only of the states' rights arguments still held by some conservative Christian attorneys but also of the Christian New Right interpretation of the Founding Fathers' intent: to proscribe only a State religion. Expressing the general consensus of the bench, the Court declared that "we are all agreed that the First and Fourteenth Amendments have a secular reach far more penetrating in the conduct of government than merely to forbid an established church" (McCollum v. Board of Education, 333 U.S. 203). In the face of this broad-based interpretation of the First Amendment, the foundation of that "old-time Constitution" which was predicated on the collaboration of Church and State threatened to collapse. All that was necessary would be a series of decisions which would employ the principles of absolute separation between religion and government first invoked by Justice Black in 1947 and now applicable to state and local as well as federal institutions.

These decisions appeared in a group of rulings during the early 1960s by the controversial Warren Court (1953–1969). Although Earl Warren and his fellow justices were villified for the liberalizing effect of their decisions on American society and were even charged with usurping Congressional powers of legislation, the High Court in these controversial decisions closely followed the precedent of the *Cantwell, Everson* and *McCollum* rulings. Declaring unconstitutional a Maryland law requiring theistic beliefs of all state office-holders, the justices alluded to both the *Everson* and *McCollum* decision by emphatically stating,

> We repeat and again affirm that neither the State nor the Federal government can constitutionally pass laws or impose requirements which aid all religions as against non-believers. . . . (Torcaso v. Watkins, 267 U.S. 488 [1961])

The *Torcaso* ruling indicated that the Supreme Court no longer recognized an amorphous Christianity (as it once had in the nineteenth and
early twentieth centuries) to be inherent in common law or in the
Constitution, no matter how general or tolerant that theistic belief might
be. Hence, even so-called "non-denominational" school prayer, encouraged by state public school systems, e.g., New York Board of Regents,
was clearly unconstitutional (*Engel* v. *Vitale* [1962]). To the dismay of
many conservative Christians, the doctrine of denominational pluralism
which purportedly embodied the intent of the Founding Fathers no
longer had validity in arguments before the High Court. Rejecting a
Pennsylvania law requiring the daily reading of ten Bible verses without
comment in public school classrooms, the controversial *Abington Town-
ship School District* v. *Schempp* opinion reiterated, "This court has
rejected the contention that the establishment clause forbids only governmental preference of one religion over another" (374 U.S. 203 [1963] at
206). To conservative Christians the Warren Court completed the emas-
culation of that "old-time Constitution" whose strengths had rested on its
"biblically-based" republican principles.

The shift from symbiosis to separation had been effected largely by
an appeal to Thomas Jefferson, the historical figure most influential in
defining Church–State relations. Citing Jefferson in the *Everson* ruling,
Justice Hugo Black interpreted the First Amendment as the Constitutional provision which erected "a wall of separation between church and
state." According to lawyers Edward Corwin and John Whitehead, Jefferson specifically articulated the implications of his notion of separation
only in his Second Inaugural Address in 1805 when he declared that
"religious exercises" ought to remain "as the Constitution found them,
under the direction of church or *state* authorities acknowledged by the
several religious societies."/13/ In the context of this speech, Jefferson's
notion of "Church-State" separation appears to be applicable to the federal government alone.

Conservative Christian lawyers suggest that not only does Jefferson's
phrase *not* apply to the categorical separation of Church and State but it
also confirms their own states' rights interpretation since his Second
Inaugural Address refers to the separation of governmental jurisdictions
rather than institutions. The implications of the High Court's misappro-
priation of the Jeffersonian "wall of separation" are therefore fundamental and far-reaching. "If the Court's precedent-setting case (*Everson*) is
based on an erroneous assumption," argued Robert Cord in a *National
Review* article, "then all the subsequent court decisions, federal and
state, . . . are logically questionable."/14/

The trend of post-war Supreme Court decisions suggests that religion
ought to be excluded from the governmentally-regulated public sphere.
Although to the liberal Constitutional authority Leo Pfeiffer "religion as a

private matter is a part of the American credo"/15/ and to sociologists like Bryan Wilson, Peter Berger, and others, this privatization of religion is generated by a pluralist society, conservative Christians hold that the aetiology of this crisis is neither Constitutional nor sociological but rather theological. Stripped of its inner worldly concerns during the Third Great Awakening, the worldview of American conservative Christianity fragmented into sectlike pietistic beliefs which abandoned the struggle to prevail over increasingly modernist institutions. The Swiss Evangelical Frances Schaeffer has argued that the secularization of the State originated in this pietistic inwardness which came to dominate the conservative American Protestant spirit/16/—a view shared by other Christian New Right leaders, e.g., Jerry Falwell, Tim LaHaye, Ed McAteer, Ed Rowe. This "defective view" of Christianity generated a separatism which was "in" this world but not "of" it. "[A]mong Evangelicals in the twentieth century, the pietistic pendulum has all too frequently swung to such an extreme. . . ."/17/ Consequently, the retreat by conservative elements into millenarian isolation created a vacuum in social institutions which secular values could fill.

Espousing the values of a secular society which seeks to insulate the public domain from religious institutions, the Supreme Court established the basis on which the modern bureaucratic State stands. Shifting from its former posture of collaboration, the government has moved through its executive agencies to enforce the mandate of categorical separation of Church and State at the most mundane levels. And it is this inexorable routinization process of the modern bureaucracy which galls conservative Christians the most. "I think there are vast conspiracies in government," complained Christian defense lawyer William Ball.

> I think there are of course secularists in government, ideologists, who don't like religion. But a great deal of what happens is inadvertent. Some of it's due to very sloppy drafting of statutes and regulations and a general gross overreaching by government that isn't initially at least motivated by a desire to put religion down./18/

Faced by intransigent officials who are incessantly driven toward "gross overreaching" by the impetus of government expansion, conservative Christians have felt the claustrophobic "iron cage" of modern bureaucracy.

CONFLICT WITH THE BUREAUCRATIC STATE

Whereas in the nineteenth century the law was understood as the defender of the Christian community and its values, e.g., the *Reynolds* (1879) case which denied protection to a Mormon polygamist, law no longer appears as the guarantor of that social order coined "Christian civilization" by its champions. To the Christian New Right, the law represents an alien force which is used as a tool to refashion traditional institutions into a radically different society. These institutions or "mediating structures,"/19/ such as schools, churches, and families, which bridge the gap between the individual and the State, received the full brunt of bureaucratic regulation. Through its regulatory agencies, the State scrutinizes the very institutions which constitute the backbone of the conservative Christian community—a necessary task to some but a "tidal wave of repression" to others (William Ball).

Although absolute separation applies generally in questions involving the establishment clause, religious communities are not thereby necessarily free from government inquiry and restrictions in free exercise matters. "[A]ny incidental burden on free exercise of an appellant's religion," reasoned the Supreme Court in *Sherbert* v. *Verner*, "may be justified by a 'compelling state interest in the regulation of a subject within the state's constitutional power to regulate'" (374 U.S. 398 [1963] at 403). Regarding the decision as an invitation to monitor religious communities in matters of finance, labor relations, safety and education, the federal bureaucracy has shifted the burden of proof onto churches to demonstrate their compliance with federal, state and local statutes. Sharing the sympathies of those Americans who elected Jimmy Carter in 1976 and Ronald Reagan in 1980, the conservative Christian community sought the dismantling of the federal bureaucracy and a concomitant move from regulation to deregulation.

In the wake of federally ordered desegregation and the concurrent secularization of the public schools, the United State witnessed a boom in the growth of private schools, particularly private conservative Christian schools. Leaping in number from 1,500 in 1961 to a reported 18,000 in 1982, these schools embodied the hopes of conservative Christians to maintain their communal identity and guarantee their future leadership. Yet, in spite of their attempt to circumvent federal regulation and secular influence, these conservative Christian schools were not immune from State scrutiny. In *Board of Education* v. *Allen* (1968), the Supreme Court had affirmed the rights of state bureaucracies to establish minimum hours of instruction, prescribe secular subjects and certify teachers in private religious schools. As the Court later expressed, such regulation reflected the "state's special interest in elevating the quality of education in both public and private school" (Norwood v. Harrison, 413 U.S. 455 [1973] at 463.) The legitimate paternal interests of government struck the burgeoning Christian school movement as an unwarranted assertion of State hegemony. These claims of jurisdiction conjured up fears that the State would become the arbiter of which religions would be allowed to exist, i.e., *cultis licita*.

This direct assertion of State power compelled conservative Christian pastors who administered these schools to resist State supervision as a matter of conscience, *vide* defendant brief in State v. Columbus Christian Academy, No. 78 CVS 1678 (Wahe County Superior Court, N.C., Sept. 1, 1978), *vacated as moot and dismissed* (N.C., May 4, 1979). (This North Carolina case was dropped due to the deregulation of private schools by the state legislature in May, 1979.) As one angry Baptist minister declared, "We may not allow any temporal authority to stand in Christ's stead to certify, license, approve or accredit."/20/ Although Christian lawyers have won one significant case in this area, e.g., State of Ohio v. Whisner, 351 N.E. 20 (Ohio Supr. 1976), by successfully arguing that the state regulations were "too broad," more often they have lost, e.g. Damascus Community Church v. Clackamas County, 45 Or. App. 1065, 610 p2d 173 1980, Nebraska ex. rel. Douglas v. Faith Baptist Church, No. 43029 Neb. Sup. Ct. In both of the latter cases, the Supreme Court dismissed appeals by the churches on the grounds that the government had a "compelling state interest" and the church schools' refusal to cooperate had been unreasonable and arbitrary.

To the conservative Christian community, this State intrusion into what are regarded as church business and religious matters constitutes nothing short of harassment. Although Congress passed legislation in 1969 placing "integrated auxiliaries" (schools, daycare centers, children's homes, etc.) under the umbrella of 501(c)(3) tax exemption, the IRS in January of 1977 interpreted "integrated auxiliaries" to mean "exclusively religious," i.e., they must have no secular counterpart. Since these institutions clearly had secular counterparts, they were considered under the jurisdiction of IRS regulation and subject to IRS audit. Following suit the National Labor Relations Board attempted to define Christian schools as only "religiously associated," not "completely religious." Since its regulations did not contradict any "tenet of faith," the NLRB claimed jurisdiction, demanding the participation of private Christian schools in the unemployment compensation program and asserting its right to supervise "the terms and conditions of employment."

The conservative Christian community openly resisted this bureaucratic encroachment. Refusing to accept the diminution of the community's authority by the State, their lawyers rejected the bureaucratic distinctions of "exclusively religious," "completely religious," and "religiously associated," and defied State regulatory directives. Although the federal government occasionally backed down, often the conflict ended up in court where conservative Christians had some victories. The Supreme Court, for example, recognized the integrity of religious schools, excluding them from NLRB supervision and resulting in their exemption from participation in the unemployment compensation program.

Reflecting what William Ball denounced as that "gross overreaching by government," the bureaucratic fiat of "compelling state interest" has been complemented by ancillary "public policy" considerations. The

Internal Revenue Service denied tax exempt status to virtually dozens of private religious schools, most notably Bob Jones University and the Goldsboro Christian Schools, Inc., on the grounds that these institutions practiced some form of racial discrimination in violation of 42 U.S.C. 1981. As in the *Reynolds* case involving the Mormon practice of polygamy, the free exercise clause does not countenance practices which would irreparably harm the social fabric, e.g., racial discrimination; yet, the "public policy" accretion supplementing the doctrine of "compelling state interest" makes the bureaucracy rather than the judiciary the arbiter of what is an "incidental" and what a "substantive" burden on free exercise. The emergence of "public policy" considerations as the manifestation of bureaucracy's routinization character is regarded by conservative Christians as the symbol of arbitrary government harassment. Invoking the fears of conservative Christian pastors at the National Affairs Briefing, candidate Reagan won the support of the Christian school movement through pledging to fulfill the education plank of the Republican platform (suggested to Reagan by Falwell and other Christian New Right leaders). "We will halt the unconstitutional regulatory vendetta launched by Mr. Carter's IRS Commissioner against independent schools."/21/

On January 8, 1982, Reagan made good on his pledge to get government "off the backs" of Fundamentalists and conservative Evangelicals by dropping the IRS veto on the tax exempt status of 111 private schools which included both the controversial Bob Jones University and the Goldsboro Christian Schools, Inc. The Reagan Administration's decision to overrule the IRS and vacate judgments against these and other schools was met with elation—but an elation which was short-lived. In the face of a public and mass media outrage by the accommodation of racism, Reagan asked the Supreme Court on February 25, 1982 to hear the Bob Jones University/Goldsboro Christian School case and submitted a bill to Congress which would deny 501(c)(3) standing to "organizations maintaining schools with racially discriminatory policies." In short, the Reagan Administration capitulated to pressure and forsook its conservative Christian allies. Yet the Administration has charted a new tack to win back the allegiance of its conservative Christian constituency by offering legislation to reinstate Christian values which would both resurrect that "old-time Constitution" and symbolize its bond with the "old-time religion."

LEGISLATING A BIBLICALLY-BASED SOCIETY

Today, the secular humanists with their liberal ideology have been successful in twisting the concept of the separation of church and state to mean separation of God from government. . . . It is time to reject the godless, communistic definition of separation of church and state that says there is no place for biblical moral law in public policy./22/

Although Jerry Falwell and other Christian New Right leaders joined in the chorus of protest against "big government," their nativist movement harbors neither libertarian nor isolationist sentiment. Their political expression voiced an apparent ambiguity which called, on the one hand, to get government "off our back," and, on the other hand, to "put God back into government."/23/ "While the right to read, to speak and to assemble for worship is not yet in jeopardy," wrote Julius Poppinga, President of the Christian Legal Society, "the encroachment of government controls is causing the Christian community to focus upon the free exercise clause of the First Amendment."/24/ Citing *Wisconsin* v. *Yoder* (1972) which holds free exercise values supreme, the Christian New Right interpretation recognizes two dimensions of the free exercise clause: (1) freedom from government regulation, and (2) freedom to influence the government as long as no one denomination becomes the established church. Whereas the Reagan Administration may be failing in attempts to actualize the first, the White House is cooperating with the Christian New Right to promote the second.

While it is true that conservative Christians feel obliged to support the State based on the reading of the Pauline epistles (Rom 13:1: "Let every soul be subject unto the higher powers. For there is no power but of God: the powers that be are ordained of God"), such obedience is conditional upon the State's fulfillment of its divine obligation to protect the Church and ensure an environment amenable to Christian values. Since the State therefore derives its mandate from and stands under the judgment of God, the notion of a secular State is alien to this conservative Christian worldview./25/ In the legitimation of marginal relations and the disestablishment of a "general, tolerant Christianity," the government has recognized a pluralist, secular society which, in the eyes of the conservative Christian community, manifestly violates its God-given obligations. The metamorphosis of the State under the impact of High Court decisions prompted a call to resistance which sees the present government as at best a caricature of its proper role and at worst the incarnation of evil. The political struggle which ensued embodies the attempt to restore the State to its divinely sanctioned form by orchestrating a frontal assault on pluralism. "The Christian community should denounce pluralism when it is used to justify non-Christian or inhuman acts. There is truth and non-truth. There is good and evil. Christianity is truth."/26/ In the face of the dual evils of privatization and secularization, the Christian New Right seeks to fulfill the second logically derived imperative of the free exercise clause—to "put God back into government"—by "Christianizing" the system once more;/27/ however, according to the *Lemon* v. *Kurtzman* tripartite test (1971), legislation must have a "secular purpose," neither "advance nor inhibit" religion, and must not foster "excessive entanglement" with religion. To "re-Christianize" the State within the present Constitutional constraints would therefore be impossible. Only structural changes in the self-definition of the State would make such a return to the "old-time Constitution" possible./28/

For the Christian New Right the means to resurrect the collaboration of Church and State lies in the restoration of state's rights—the philosophy overturned by the Supreme Court in its application of the Fourteenth Amendment to First Amendment rights. Right-wing politicians are attempting to circumvent the court by passing Constitutional Amendments which would overturn the Court's decisions on key questions by prohibiting it from rendering judgment on particular issues involving conservative Christian values. Gathering over 120 Evangelical and Fundamentalist leaders about him at the White House on May 8, 1982, National Prayer Day, President Reagan announced his support of a Constitutional Amendment for voluntary school prayer. This amendment would functionally exclude the federal judiciary from jurisdiction over the issue by limiting decisions concerning prayer to the states. Likewise, Senator Orrin Hatch has proposed a Constitutional Amendment which would overturn the *Roe* v. *Wade* decision (1973), recognizing a woman's right to abortion, by granting concurrent power to Congress and the states to restrict and/or prohibit abortion.

HOLY WAR

Although conservative Christians have had little luck in forestalling the hegemony of federal bureaucracy or in restoring that "old-time Constitution," they nonetheless have identified what they believe to be the cause of their predicament: secular humanism. Regarded as the semiofficial ideology of the secular, pluralist State, secular humanism is held responsible (frequently in the most cliché-ridden terms) for a plethora of the nation's economic and social ills. "Today's wave of crime and violence in our streets, promiscuity, divorce, shattered dreams and broken hearts can be laid right at the heart of secular humanism."/29/ In the future bleakly depicted by nativist leaders, divinely mandated law will be displaced by the illusion of human autonomy which rests on the degenerate hedonism (LaHaye) of "situational law" (Schaeffer) and Satanism (Rowe).

This critique of secular humanism focuses on the weaknesses of the secular state and the Constitutional "Catch-22" which Supreme Court decisions have precipitated. "Humanism is a secularized version of the Christian religion: it places the transcendent spiritual realities of the Christian faith within the confines of an immanent, historical process subject to the control of an autonomous human will."/30/ Applying the logic of the High Court itself, the Christian New Right considers the present conflict between church and State theological in nature. Citing the "parallel position" argument articulated by the Court in U.S. vs. Seeger, 38 U.S. 163 (1965), Bernard Zylstra believes that humanism fits the legal profile of movements granted religious status for non-theistic beliefs. Since humanism can be legitimately characterized as a religion, the appellation of a "holy war" to the struggle is therefore no metaphor for Christian zealotry alone but rather an accurate description of the conflict between what Fundamentalists and Conservative Evangelicals consider to be true and false religion./31/ Regarding public school teachers as "change agents" who "brainwash" American children through the use of "coercive persuasion," conservative Christians seek to purge schools of courses and books which promote "non-Christian values."/32/ In the eyes of the religious right, these values articulate the ideology of the State, i.e., secular humanism, which purportedly rests on a hedonistic and materialistic foundation.

In equating secular humanism with religion, the conservative Christian community bases its claim on a series of federal court rulings of some 20 years ago. As early as 1957, the federal courts held that humanism could be classified as a religion for tax-exemption purposes since it manifested four characteristics deemed deemed essential to religion: (1) a set of beliefs, (2) cultic practices, i.e., service, (3) moral teachings, and (4) an organizational framework (Fellowship of Humanity v. County of Alameda, 153 Cal. App., 2d 673, 315 p. 2d 394 [Ct. App. 1957]). Following a similar line of argument, the Supreme Court expressed the opinion in Torcaso v. Watkins, 367 U.S. 488 (1961), that belief in God could not be a prerequisite for office-holding since it would constitute the establishment of theistic religion and violate the free exercise rights of nontheistic religions, including humanism. In a footnote (11), the High Court recognized that

> Among religions in this country which do not teach what would generally be considered a belief in the existence of God are Buddhism, Taoism, Ethical Culture, Secular Humanism, and others.

With the disestablishment of an amorphous Christianity from its preferential position in the public school system, the redefinition of secular humanism as religion rapidly became problematic. Noting the dangers implicit in disestablishment, Justice Potter Stewart wrote in his opinion for the *Abington* v. *Schempp* decision (prohibiting Bible reading in the public schools) that "the state may not establish a 'religion of secularism'" (374 U.S. 203 [1963] at 226). Yet, to conservative Evangelicals and Fundamentalists, Justice Stewart's worst fears have been realized in the past decade since the ouster of theistic beliefs from America's schools was accompanied by the institution of the ideology of the State—secular humanism.

Opponents of the Christian New Right reject this conservative Christian interpretation as a distortion of the High Court's intent. Scholars in Constitutional law argue that since there are two clauses which affect the status of of religion, there are in effect two meanings of religion: the narrower definition applicable in establishment cases and the broader definition appropriate in free exercise rulings. According to Jacob Burkholder, the former refers only to institutional religion and the latter to matters of conscience./33/ Since secular humanism was defined as a religion for free exercise purposes, it should not be considered necessarily religious in the establishment sense. Hence, the protection of secular humanist beliefs from coercive theistic teachings in the public schools ought not to be considered the establishment of secular humanism as a State church. Likewise, Harvard's Laurence Tribe, perhaps the leading Constitutional authority in the United States today, suggests a standard by which to distinguish between the alternative emphasis embodied in the two clauses. Beliefs ought to be protected if they are "arguably religious" in free exercise cases or if they are "arguably non-religious" in establishment cases./34/ By Tribe's standard, secular humanism would receive free exercise protection since it is "arguably religious"; yet, it would not constitute an establishment of religion since it is also "arguably non-religious." "Thus, under the narrow establishment definition of religion, state-supported schools would be allowed to teach secular humanism."/35/

To conservative Christian attorneys, the very notion of two definitions of religion in the First Amendment is in itself a gross distortion. Referring to Madison's *Memorial and Remonstrance*, they argue that the two clauses are "correlative and co-extensive" and that even by virtue of the much-hated *Everson* v. *Board of Education* ruling, the clauses ought to be read simultaneously (330 U.S. 1 [1947] at 15). Pursuing the line of argument in *Everson*, William Ball in his essay "What is Religion?"/36/ cites Justice Rutledge's opinion:

> 'Religion' appears only once in the Amendment but the word governs two prohibitions and governs them alike. It does not have two meanings, narrow to forbid 'an establishment' and another, much broader, for securing 'the free exercise thereof.' 'Thereof' brings down 'religion' with its entire and exact content, no more and no less, from the first into the second guaranty, so that Congress and now the state are as broadly restricted concerning the one as they are concerning the other. (330 U.S. 1 at 47)

Thus, the fiction of two definitions is manifestly illogical and not without grave consequences. If only one meaning lies within the bounds of the establishment and free exercise clauses, then the classification of humanism as religion and the introduction of philosophical and scientific courses with humanist emphases, e.g., "values clarification," MACOS, sex education, evolutionary science, into the public schools represents the establishment of secularist "religion" to the detriment of conservative Christianity.

Yet the validity of Christian New Right conclusions turns on whether the "two definition" interpretation of the First Amendment is legitimate and whether such humanist courses could be construed as the establishment of religion. The "two definition" theory was put to the test in a case akin to the status of secular humanism, Malnak v. Maharishi Mahesh Yogi, 440 F. Supp. 1284 (D. N.J., 1977) *affirmed* Fd2 (3rd Cir. Feb. 4, 1979). In this case, the defendants contended that the Transcendental Meditation program in public schools had a secular purpose and was "arguably non-religious." Therefore, the practice of Transcendental Meditation should not be construed as a violation of the establishment clause, as argued by the plaintiff. In their ruling, the federal court rejected the defendant's suggestion that a narrower definition of religion be used in this establishment case and hence found the defendant in violation of all three parts of the *Lemon* v. *Kurtzman* tripartite establishment test. Citing the *U.S.* v. *Seeger* decision (380 U.S. 163 [1965] at 180-183) which redefined "religious training and belief" in the Universal Military Service Act in terms of "ultimate concern,"/37/ the court found a "claim to an ultimate and comprehensive 'truth'" in Transcendental Meditation. Since "religious training, teaching and observance" are proscribed in the public schools by the *Everson* ruling, instruction in Transcendental Meditation techniques was considered unconstitutional.

Although the Supreme Court has not specifically offered a definitive opinion on the breadth of the establishment clause in the area of public education, the *Malnak* decision suggests that the "arguably non-religious" defense of secular humanism would not be tenable in court. But if secular humanism was defined as a religion equally under the free exercise and establishment clauses, should such secular programs as "values clarifications," sex education, evolution, etc., be construed as "religious training, teaching and observance"? Drawing on the High Court's appropriation of the Tillichian definition of religion, conservative Christian lawyers argue that it would. "Physical or historical or psychological insights can become objects of theology," suggested Tillich,

> not from the point of view of their cognitive form, but from the point of view of their power of revealing some aspects of that which concerns us ultimately in and through their cognitive form. . . . Personality problems and developments, educational aims and methods, bodily and mental health, can become objects of theology, not from the point of view of their ethical and technical form, but from the point of view of their power of mediating some aspects of that which concerns us ultimately in and through their ethical and technical form./38/

Following the Tillichian argument, secular humanism in the guise of federal and state programs which teach ethical values and a comprehensive scientific worldview would appear to conflict with the establishment restrictions imposed by the High Court. The legitimation of secular humanism as a marginal religion illustrates the Constitutional "double-bind" of the modern state. According to *Lemon* v. *Kurtzman* tripartite test which protects against the establishment of religion, the State may legislate only those programs with a "secular purpose"; however, if that secular program articulates a comprehensive humanist worldview, then the government is functionally establishing a State religion of secular humanism as defined by the *Torcaso* and *Seeger* ruling. To the Christian New Right (which like Paul lays claims to its citizenship rights), the government rather than the Christian community has abrogated the guarantees of the First Amendment by violating a series of Supreme Court decisions including the prohibition against "religious training, teaching, or observance" (*Everson* v. *Board of Education*), "advancement" of religion (*Abington* v. *Schempp*), and "excessive entanglement" (*Lemon* v. *Kurtzman*)./39/

CONCLUSION

Although the present Constitutional controversy appears to be over the categorical separation of Church and State, the Christian New Right analysis reveals an ideological conflict between opposing worldviews or theologies. In this "post-Christian" (Zylstra) or "post-American" (Whitehead) age in which the identification of a common Christian and American heritage has been forgotten, the heterodoxy of a pluralist society has become the norm. Modern man is characterized by a "heretical imperative"/40/ which reflects pluralist society's philosophy of Mannheimian relationism./41/ Defended by the State as the ideology of democracy, the values of radical pluralism are espoused by those public school courses which offend the religious beliefs of the conservative Christian community. In contrast to the Christian New Right reliance on God's law rather than reason alone, the State regards individuals as fully capable of autonomous rational decision-making within the legal bounds of the community. Yet, this reliance on "proximal truth" invoked by autonomous individuals in a pluralist society is in itself a worldview which competes with what once was assumed to be vestigial theistic beliefs in a secular age. In the eyes of conservative Christians, this "heretical imperative" embodies the incarnation of false gods and the practice of idolatry (1 Sam 8:7-9, Jer 32:35, Exod 20:3). In such a secular society which promotes its own ideology while denying other faiths equal access to public institutions, "there can be no religious liberty."/42/

The exclusion of prayer, Bible reading and other traditionally religious activities has made the public schoolroom and other public institutions a battleground between establishment and free exercise claims. Citing *Wisconsin* v. *Yoder* (1972), Christian attorneys contend that where such conflicting claims exist, free exercise rights take precedence. "The solution I am proposing," concludes Bernard Zylstra, "is the *disestablishment of secularism* in the mediating structures on the part of every level of government and the equal protection of the free exercise of religion in these structures."/43/ Accordingly, the only way to guarantee government "neutrality" in matters of religion is to allow religious activities to flourish unhindered in public institutions, including not only humanist courses but also prayer, Bible reading, and instruction in "scientific creationism."

Regardless of whether conservative Christian aims and conclusions are considered legitimate, the Christian New Right analysis of modern, secular, pluralist society identifies a key flaw in the self-image of the American system of governance. Liberal democratic thought harbors the illusion that the State only exercises the fiduciary power granted by its constituency. Yet, this kenotic exercise belies the self-interest of the State to ensure its own continuity through the dissemination of an ideology which sanctions its own existence. The ideology of the State takes precedence over competing ideologies, religious or otherwise, in the legal doctrines of "compelling state interest" and its ancillary "public policy" considerations.

Requiring an ideology to defend its bureaucratic interests in survival and expansion, American government has rapidly metamorphosed over the past four decades into what the Christian New Right regards as a Leviathan State. The conservative Christian viewpoint suggests that the myopic vision which interprets government action as necessarily benevolent is illusory. Government programs which legitimately embody a secular purpose as defined by *Lemon* v. *Kurtzman* cannot be separated from the ideology of secular humanism which harbors anti-clerical and anti-Christian prejudice. And although the Constitutional question of Church–State separation will most certainly be settled in the chambers of the High Court, the struggle between the nativist Christian movement and the "heretical imperative" of radical pluralism will continue in the political arena for years to come.

NOTES

/1/   Zofia Smardz, "Mixing Religion and Politics," *Washington Star*, 27 April 1980.

/2/   John W. Whitehead, *The Separation Illusion. A Lawyer Examines the First Amendment*, with foreword by R. J. Rushdoony (Milford, MI: Mott Media, 1977), 63.

/3/   See William G. McLoughlin's discussion of the resurgence of Evangelical and Fundamentalist Christianity in his *Revivals, Awakenings and Reform*

(Chicago: University of Chicago Press, 1978) and see also Paul Anthony Schwartz and James McBride, "The Moral Majority in the U.S.A. as a New Religious Movement," in Eileen Barker (ed.), *Of Gods and Men. New Religious Movements in the West* (Macon, GA: Mercer University Press, 1983), pp. 127–46.

/4/   Francis A. Schaeffer, *A Christian Manifesto* (Westchester, IL: Crossway Books, 1982), 44; Whitehead, *Separation Illusion*, 65.

/5/   Joseph Fletcher, *Situation Ethics. The New Morality* (Philadelphia: The Westminster Press, 1966); Francis Schaeffer introduces the notion of "situational law" in his article "Humanism vs. Religious Freedom: A Time to Act," in *Freedom and Faith. The Impact of Law on Religious Liberty*, ed. Lynn R. Buzzard (Westchester, IL: Crossway Books, 1982), 40.

/6/   "Reagan Strongly Backs Traditional Values Based on Religious View of Morality," *Conservative Digest*, Sept. 1980, 20.

/7/   Lynn Buzzard, "America Today: Shaking the Foundations," in *Freedom and Faith*, ed. Buzzard, 23.

/8/   Jerry Falwell, *Christians in Government: What the Bible Says* (Lynchburg, VA: Liberty Publishing Company, 1981), 18.

/9/   John Conlan and John W. Whitehead, "The Establishment of the Religion of Secular Humanism and Its First Amendment Implications," *Texas Tech Law Review* 10 (1), 1981: 3; Robert L. Cord, "Understanding the First Amendment," *National Review*, 22 Jan. 1982, 26; Homer Duncan, *Humanism in Light of the Holy Scripture* (Lubbock, TX: Missionary Crusader, 1981), 121; Falwell, *Christians in Government*, 19; Verna Hall, *The Christian History of the Constitution of the United States* (San Francisco: Foundation for American Christian Education, 1966), ix; Senator Jesse Helms, *Congressional Record*, 16 Feb. 1981, 5; Senator Roger Jepsen, "Christian Citizenship," *The Roundtable Report*, Feb. 1981, 4; Tim LaHaye, *Battle for the Mind* (Old Tappan, NJ: Fleming H. Revell Company, 1980), 11; Ed McAteer, "Should Church and State Be Separate?" *The Roundtable Report*, Oct. 1980, 1; Clayton Nuttall, *The Conflict. The Separation of Church and State*, (Schaumburg, IL: Regular Baptist Press, 1980), 67; Schaeffer, *Christian Manifesto*, 39; Phyllis Schlafly, *The Power of the Positive Woman* (New York: Harcourt Brace Jovanovich, 1977), 183.

/10/   Conlan and Whitehead, "Establishment," 4.

/11/   John H. Whitehead, "How We've Lost Touch with Our Founding Fathers: The Secularization of America," *Moody Monthly*, July/August 1981, 20.

/12/   William Bentley Ball, "Secularism: Tidal Wave of Repression," in *Freedom and Faith*, ed. Buzzard, 51: Julius B. Poppinga, "On Laying Hold of Religious Liberties," *The Christian Lawyer* (Spring 1979): 5; Schaeffer, "Humanism," 37.

/13/   Edward S. Corwin, *American Constitutional History* (New York: Harper & Row, 1965), 205; Whitehead, *Separation Illusion*, 89.

/14/   Cord, "First Amendment," 29.

/15/   Leo Pfeiffer, "The Legitimation of Marginal Religions," in *Religious Movements in Contemporary America*, ed. Irving L. Zaretsky and Mark P. Leone (Princeton: Princeton University Press, 1974), 14.

/16/   Schaeffer, *Christian Manifesto*, 19, and "Humanism," 36.

/17/   Edward H. Rowe, *Save America: The Power of the Christian Citizen*, with foreword by Bill Bright (Old Tappan, NJ: Fleming H. Revell Company, 1976), 56.

/18/   William Bentley Ball, transcript of ABC Broadcast *Directions*, "'Render Unto Caesar': But What is Caesar's?" (interview with Rev. Dean Kelley, Rev. Robert Maddox, and Ball by Herbert Kaplow), 22 Feb. 1981, 13.

/19/   Peter Berger, *Facing Up to Modernity. Excursions in Society, Politics and Religion* (New York: Basic Books, 1977), 130.

/20/   Nuttall, *Conflict*, 28.

/21/   "Reagan," *Conservative Digest*, 20.

/22/   Falwell, *Christians in Government*, 19.

/23/   Cynthia Wittmer West, "The State and Sectarian Education: Regulation to Deregulation," *Duke Law Journal* 1980: 801.

/24/   Poppinga, "Religious Liberties," 5.

/25/   See James McBride and Paul Schwartz, "Theopolis Americana: The Religious New Right's Campaign to Establish a Christian Republic" (paper presented to the American Academy of Religion, Western Regional Meeting, March 26, 1982).

/26/   Whitehead, *Separation Illusion*, 21.

/27/   Gary Potter, "A Christian America," *New York Times*, 15 Oct. 1980; Rus Walton, *Letter from Plymouth Rock* (Marlborough, NH: Plymouth Rock Foundation), August 1981, 4; Whitehead, *Separation Illusion*, 176.

/28/   Although the effort to restore the "old-time" Constitution led the Christian New Right to advocate Constitutional amendments, some conservative Christians urged an alternative strategy by introducing the Fundamentalist worldview to the public school system under the guise of science, e.g., "creation-science." Sponsoring bills in 19 states to ensure "balanced treatment to creation-science and evolution-science," the Christian New Right was thwarted when the Federal District Court ruled that Arkansas Act 590 (1981 Arkansas Acts) was unconstitutional since public instruction of "scientific creationism" violated all three parts of the *Lemon* v. *Kurtzman* tripartite establishment test. For a discussion of the "scientistic"

224 James McBride

epistemology of the Christian New Right which identifies Christianity with "true science," see James McBride and Paul Schwartz, "The Moral Majority in the U.S.A. as a New Religious Movement," in *Of Gods and Men: New Religious Movements in the West*, ed. Eileen Barker (Macon, GA: Mercer University Press, 1983).

/29/   LaHaye, *Battle*, 26.

/30/   Bernard Zylstra, "Using the Constitution to Defend Religious Rights," in *Freedom and Faith*, ed. Buzzard, 102.

/31/   Duncan, *Humanism*, 128: Falwell, *Christians in Government*, 19; LaHaye, *Battle*, 125; Rowe, *Save America*, 51; Schaeffer, *Christian Manifesto*, 54; Rus Walton, *The Plymouth Rock Newsletter* (Marlborough, NH: Plymouth Rock Foundation), 17 Nov. 1981, 2.

/32/   Jerry Falwell, *Listen, America!* (Garden City, NY: Doubleday and Company, 1980), 207; James C. Hefley, *Are Textbooks Harming Your Children?* (Milford, MI: Mott Media, 1979), 30; LaHaye, *Battle*, 98; Barbara Morris, *Change Agents in the Schools* (Ellicott City, MD: Barbara Morris Report, 1979), 11.

/33/   John Richard Burkholder, "'The Law Knows No Heresy': Marginal Religious Movements and the Courts," in *Religious Movements*, ed. Zaretsky and Leone, 49.

/34/   Laurence Tribe, *American Constitutional Law* (Mineola, NY: Foundation Press, 1977), 828.

/35/   John R. Munich, "Religious Activity in Public Schools: A Proposed Standard," *St. Louis University Law Journal* 24, 1980, 389.

/36/   William Bentley Ball, "What is Religion?" *The Christian Lawyer* (Spring, 1979).

/37/   See Paul Tillich's discussion of religion as "ultimate concern" in his *Systematic Theology*, 3 vols. (Chicago: University of Chicago Press, 1951–63), 1:12–14.

/38/   Tillich, *Systematic Theology*, 1:14.

/39/   Falwell, *Christians in Government*, 19.

/40/   See Peter Berger, *The Heretical Imperative. Contemporary Possibilities of Religious Affirmation* (Garden City, NY: Doubleday and Company, 1979).

/41/   See Karl Mannheim's *Ideology and Utopia. An Introduction to the Sociology of Knowledge* (New York: Harcourt Brace and World, Inc., 1936).

/42/   Ball, "Secularism," 50.

/43/   Zylstra, "Constitution," 106.

APPENDIX

EILERS V. *COY*: A MAJOR PRECEDENT ON DEPROGRAMMING?

As this volume is about to go to press, an important civil suit involving deprogramming has just transpired in Federal District Court in Minneapolis. William Eilers, a member of the Disciples of the Lord Jesus Christ, was abducted and held prisoner for five days before escaping an attempted deprogramming arranged by his parents and wife, Sandra Eilers. Mr. Eilers sued for $5.1 million in damages. His parents settled out of court and only the professional deprogrammers remained as actual defendants. Sandra Eilers, a former member of the religious group who had been successfully deprogrammed, divorced her husband and testified for the defense.

On March 6, 1984 in a surprising development, Judge Harry MacLaughlin pre-empted the jury, directing a verdict for the plaintiff on the grounds of false imprisonment while allowing the jury to determine appropriate punitive damages and whether federal civil rights laws or the plaintiff's constitutional rights were violated.

Attorneys for the plaintiff hailed Judge MacLaughlin's decision for overriding the precedent of the Minnesota Supreme Court's ruling in *Peterson* v. *Sorlien*. In the 1980 *Peterson* decision the Court held that parents and their agents could hold adult offspring for deprogramming without being guilty of false imprisonment if they had reason to believe the individual's judgment was impaired or if at some point the individual appeared to give tacit approval to the proceedings. However, in *Eilers* v. *Coy* Judge MacLaughlin questioned the constitutionality of *Peterson* and denied its applicability to this case because the evidence, in the judge's view, indicated that Eilers at no time gave consent to the deprogramming. Moreover, MacLaughlin affirmed that "the plaintiff's apparent consent is not a defense to false imprisonment." Judge Maclaughlin argued that the failure of the defendants to utilize lawful alternatives to coercive deprogramming undermined their "defense of necessity." Even if there existed a valid reason for abducting and restraining the plaintiff, the defendants had an obligation to turn him over to the proper authorities. "The right to confine a person in order to prevent harm to that person lasts only as long as is necessary to get the person to the proper legal authorities." However, the defendants "took [Eilers] to a secluded location with boarded-up windows and proceeded to inflict their own crude methods of 'therapy' on him— methods even the defendants' own expert witness has condemned."

In Judge MacLaughlin's interpretation of the law, the defendants had to establish *three points* to justify the abduction of the plaintiff: (1) that there was imminent physical danger to Eilers or others; (2) that Eilers was only confined long enough to get him to the proper authorities, and (3) that the "least restrictive means" available were employed to restrain Eilers.

On March 9, 1984, in somewhat anticlimactic proceedings, the jury rejected Eilers' claim that his constitutional rights were violated. The jury found that the deprogrammers had not acted out of animosity to Eilers' religious beliefs but had been concerned with his mental state. During the hearings, evidence of suicidal proclivities on Eilers' part was presented by the defense. The jury further refused to award punitive damages for false imprisonment and awarded only $10,000 in compensatory damages to the plaintiff. The relatively small size of the award was hailed as a victory by the defendants who surmised that the jury was sympathetic to them and might well have decided in their favor on all counts had the judge not directed the verdict on false imprisonment. Nevertheless, according to the *St. Paul Pioneer Press-Dispatch*, which covered the trial locally, MacLaughlin's ruling "undoubtedly was the most significant legal outcome of the trial, since the amount of damages awarded by the jury is not likely in and of itself to have much effect on future activities by religious deprogrammers." MacLaughlin's ruling "will be a precedent-setting decision, if it stands on appeal." Defendants will likely appeal the decision to the 8th U.S. Circuit Court of Appeals.

Thus, the trial has ended "with both sides proclaiming moral victory in a case that broke legal ground on the difficult question of where family responsibility ends and individual freedom begins."

REFERENCES: "Sandy Eilers: Still Loves Ex-Husband Despite Changes," *Rochester Post-Bulletin*, March 6, 1984, 19; "Defense Calls Eilers Ruling a Precedent," and "Judge Rules Against 5 Deprogrammers," *Rochester Post-Bulletin*, March 7, 1984, 1 and 4; "Judge Finds Deprogrammers Guilty," *St. Paul Pioneer-Press Dispatch*, March 7, 1984, 1 and 9; "Eilers Awarded No Punitive Damages," *Rochester Post-Bulletin*, March 9, 1984, 1 and 8; and "Eilers Deprogramming Verdict Sets Precedents," *St. Paul Pioneer Press-Dispatch*, March 9, 1984, 1 and 4.

NOTES ON CONTRIBUTORS

LEE COLEMAN is a psychiatrist practicing in Berkeley, California. His longstanding interest in the problems of psychiatry and law has led to two dozen articles in professional and lay journals as well as the recently published book *The Reign of Error: Psychiatry, Authority and Law* (Boston: Beacon Press, 1984).

RICHARD DELGADO is Professor of Law at UCLA Law School where he teaches courses in Civil Procedure, Constitutional Law, and Law & Medicine. A graduate of the University of California School of Law and the former Notes & Comments Editor of its law review, he has written extensively in the areas of law and medicine and church and state.

MEADE EMORY is a partner in the law firm of LeSourd, Patten, Fleming, Hartung & Emory in Seattle, Washington. A graduate of George Washington University and Boston University, he has held appointments on the law faculties of the University of Iowa, University of California at Davis, and Georgetown University and served as Assistant to the Commissioner of the Internal Revenue Service, 1975–1977.

HERBERT FINGARETTE is Professor of Philosophy at the University of California at Santa Barbara. He is the author of books dealing with philosophical and psychological perspectives on religious issues, including *The Self in Transformation*, and has written many articles published in leading American and English law, medical and psychiatric journals.

JEREMIAH S. GUTMAN is the President of the New York Civil Liberties Union, a Director of the American Civil Liberties Union, and former Vice-President, Executive Committee Member, and Chairman of the Privacy Committee of the New York Civil Liberties Union. A graduate of City College of New York and New York University, he has practiced law in federal jurisdictions throughout the country for over thirty years.

ROBERT JAY LIFTON holds the Foundations' Fund Chair for research in Psychiatry at Yale University. He is the author of many books including *Death in Life: Survivors of Hiroshima, The Life of the Self*, (with Richard Falk) *Indefensible Weapons: The Political and Psychological Case Against Nuclearism*, and *Thought Reform and the Psychology of Totalism* in which he originated concepts now employed in the discourse on new religions.

JAMES MCBRIDE is a Research Associate of the Center for the Study of New Religious Movements in Berkeley, California. A graduate of The Johns Hopkins University and The University of Chicago Divinity School, he has authored articles on the Religious Right and new religious movements. He recently completed his Ph.D. at Graduate Theological Union with a dissertation on messianism and politics in the Weimar-era writings of Walter Benjamin and Paul Tillich.

JAMES T. RICHARDSON is Professor of Sociology at the University of Nevada Reno where he has taught since receiving his Ph.D. from Washington State University in 1968. He has authored and edited three books in the area of new religions and has written over thirty journal articles focusing mainly on conversion processes but also treating new religions from a social movements perspective.

THOMAS ROBBINS is a sociologist of religion who has written numerous articles on new religious movements for leading sociological and religious studies journals. A graduate of Harvard University and the University of North Carolina, he is the co-editor of *In Gods We Trust: Patterns of Religious Pluralism in America*.

ROLAND ROBERTSON is Professor of Sociology and Religious Studies and Senior Research Fellow in the Center for International Studies at the University of Pittsburgh. Educated at the Universities of Southampton, London and Leeds in England, he is the author or co-author of *Meaning and Change, Identity and Authority, Deviance, Crime and Sociolegal Control, The Sociological Interpretation of Religion*, and *International Systems and the Modernization of Societies*.

ROBERT SHAPIRO is an Associate in the Boston firm of Ropes & Gray. A graduate of Harvard University and Fiske Scholar of Trinity College, Cambridge University (1972-73), he is the author of several law review articles dealing with the constitutional protection of religious beliefs.

The late WILLIAM SHEPHERD was Professor of Religious Studies at the University of Montana at Missoula. Educated at Yale University, he had written articles on legal issues involving the question of religious liberty and is the author of the forthcoming volume *To Secure the Blessings of Liberty: American Constitutional Law and the New Religious Movements* (Scholars Press).

ROBERT WUTHNOW is Professor of Sociology at Princeton University. Educated at University of California at Berkeley where he received his Ph.D. in 1975, he has written extensively on new religious movements and the role of religion in American culture. Among his books are *The Consciousness Reformation, Experimentation in American Religion, The New Christian Right* (editor), and *Cultural Analysis*.

LAWRENCE ZELENAK is Professor of Law at Lewis and Clark Law School in Portland, Oregon. A graduate of the University of Santa Clara and Harvard University, he is the author of several articles on taxation and religious organizations in America and an Associate of LeSourd, Patten, Fleming, Hartung & Emory in Seattle, Washington.

INDEX

accommodation to American culture, 49, 64
as family, 12
conservatorships, 17, 126, 131
diversified character, 9
fundraising, 18–19, 170
legislative investigation, 103
United Society of Believers in Christ's Second Coming (the "Shakers"),
    178

Way International, The, 102, 111, 131, 170
Weber, Max, 33–34, 46, 54
Webster, Daniel, 207
Whitehead, John, 207, 220
Williams, Bernard, 134
Wilson, Bryan, 46, 211
Worldwide Church of God, 18, 104
Wuthnow, Robert, 35–36

Zen Buddhism, 43
Zylstra, Bernard, 217, 220–21